The Children's
Ghost Story
in America

The Children's Ghost Story in America

SEAN FERRIER-WATSON

McFarland & Company, Inc., Publishers
Jefferson, North Carolina

LIBRARY OF CONGRESS CATALOGUING-IN-PUBLICATION DATA

Names: Ferrier-Watson, Sean, 1982– author.
Title: The children's ghost story in America / Sean Ferrier-Watson.
Description: Jefferson, North Carolina : McFarland & Company, Inc., Publishers, 2017. | Includes bibliographical references and index.
Identifiers: LCCN 2017010043 | ISBN 9781476664941 (softcover : acid free paper) ∞
Subjects: LCSH: Ghost stories, American—History and criticism. | Children's literature, American—History and criticism. | Children—Books and reading—United States.
Classification: LCC PS374.G45 F47 2017 | DDC 813/.0873309—dc23
LC record available at https://lccn.loc.gov/2017010043

BRITISH LIBRARY CATALOGUING DATA ARE AVAILABLE

ISBN (print) 978-1-4766-6494-1
ISBN (ebook) 978-1-4766-2908-7

© 2017 Sean Ferrier-Watson. All rights reserved

No part of this book may be reproduced or transmitted in any form or by any means, electronic or mechanical, including photocopying or recording, or by any information storage and retrieval system, without permission in writing from the publisher.

Front cover artwork, *Story of Golden Locks*, ca. 1870 by Seymour Joseph Guy, 34" × 28" (gift of Daniel Wolf and Mathew Wolf, in memory of their sister, the Honorable Diane R. Wolf, 2013, Metropolitan Museum of Art www.metmuseum.org)

Printed in the United States of America

McFarland & Company, Inc., Publishers
  Box 611, Jefferson, North Carolina 28640
  www.mcfarlandpub.com

For Fae Dani Ferrier-Watson

Acknowledgments

I am especially grateful to Susan Stewart, Karen Roggenkamp, and Hunter Hayes for their ceaseless help and patience in advising me as I wrote my dissertation, which eventually became this book. Without their valuable assistance, my work would not have reached fruition. I would also like to thank my wife Allyson Jones and my family for their love and support throughout my research process and during the late nights and early mornings of this project. To Jacob Pichnarcik and the rest of the Texas A&M University–Commerce librarians and staff, I would like to extend special thanks for their assistance with locating resources for my book. I would also like to acknowledge the assistance provided by Susie Martin from the Public Library of Cincinnati Children's Room for helping me located source material for my first chapter. To these friends, colleagues, and mentors, I am much indebted.

Table of Contents

Acknowledgments vi
Preface 1
Introduction 8

1. "Airy nothings": The Mock Ghost Story 33
2. Spectrality and Nineteenth-Century American Girlhood 63
3. Resurrecting the Supernatural for Children 81
4. The Missing Phantom in Early African American Children's Literature 106
5. New Media, New Apparitions 123
6. The Transnarrative Ghost 153

Epilogue 174
Bibliography of Mock Ghost Stories 177
Chapter Notes 181
Works Cited 183
Index 193

Preface

I recall my first experience with circumstances like those that lead to the invention of a ghost story. I was perhaps nine or ten years old. My parents had gone to bed and my younger brother and two of our best friends were having a sleepover. It was late evening and a rare summer storm had left our yard too wet for us to explore, but from our window we could see the lights from the abandoned house beside ours flicker inexplicably, dazzling us for a few seconds with a flash here and there before going completely dark. The house was old and rundown. My parents owned the house along with another dilapidated property across from it. The little house had originally belonged to an old hermit who had passed away many years before, further adding to the sense of wonder and mystery surrounding the old home. My parents kept electricity running to the house despite its condition to power a refrigerator in the kitchen and my father's power tools in the little workshop. To this day I still wonder what act of negligence on behalf of the power company allowed us to keep the place running. The house should have been condemned. Parts of the roof were caving in and almost every room leaked during a thunderstorm, particularly during a powerful one like the night in question.

Our friends had never seen the lights flicker in the old house before and my brother and I were happy to tell them about its history, exaggerating whenever possible and expounding on our various theories for the cause of the flicker; these theories of course all circled back to the old hermit. We dared each other to go out to the house, to stumble through the unlocked door or half opened window, but none of us went farther than a few steps into the yard that night, petrified we would run into the old hermit if we got any closer. When I was a few years older, probably around thirteen or fourteen years old, I was going over to the

Preface

house in the rain to grab something from the fridge and I noticed the flickering lights. I felt a bit of the old fear but pushed through it. I went inside and got a little shock when I touched the wet doorknob leading into the kitchen. I was lucky it was only a mild jolt, probably dissipated by the current being spread out across the damp house. The light flickered in the bedroom around the same time I touched the doorknob. Aside from my being relieved that I was alive and unhurt, I felt a bit sad realizing for the first time that the old house was not really haunted after all and that the flickering lights had a perfectly reasonable explanation: exposed wires must have made random connections to the light in the bedroom when wet. With a probable explanation before me, I genuinely felt a little of my childhood slip away at that moment.

Ghost stories are deeply rooted in childhood. We can all recall some ghostly tale or fear from our youth like from my story above, but few scholars have focused on the history and transmission of children's ghost stories. Folklorists have discussed the nature and influence of spooky tales in childhood in article form or as segments in book length works, but none have written an entire book focused exclusively on children's ghost stories. Literary historians and critics have also given scant attention to the ghost story for children, producing only a handful of articles and references about nineteenth- or even twentieth-century children's ghost stories and little to nothing in book form. Only a few scholarly anthologies seem to defy this tradition of neglect. When I initially started this project as my dissertation, I expected to find numerous scholarly sources on children's ghost stories, but I instead discovered a substantial drought on the topic of ghosts in children's literature scholarship, something I found surprising given how closely connected ghost stories are to childhood. In lieu of scholars studying ghost stories in children's literature, I found some scholars obsessively trying to link all spooky tales into the gothic tradition, thereby relegating the ghost and other spooky creatures into a rather formless genre, consisting of almost anything that could be dubbed as potentially scary or supernatural. While many of these scholarly works offered both interesting and useful approaches to studying gothic literature for children, they provided little insight into the history and development of children's ghost stories, particularly in American children's literature.

While children's literature scholars struggle to separate the ghost

Preface

from the gothic tradition, scholars studying ghost stories written for adults avoid discussing children's ghost stories altogether. There is certainly no shortage of scholarly works dedicated exclusively to studying ghost stories intended for adult audiences, but these works will rarely mention anything about childhood or stories specifically designed for children. Oxford and Norton have published scholarly anthologies focusing specifically on ghost stories and nothing really appears in these larger collections about children's ghost stories and their history. Oxford did release an anthology titled *A Century of Children's Ghost Stories*, but it only really examines stories from the twentieth century and features a much shorter introduction and collection than its adult ghost-story-oriented counterparts. Also, unlike the adult anthologies, *A Century of Children's Ghost Stories* was published by the fiction author Philippa Pearce, not a literary scholar or historian as seen in the other anthologies. Regardless, Pearce, a brilliant children's ghost story author herself, writes one of a handful of short studies on the history of children's ghost stories in her introduction to the anthology. Her work is one of a small few that illuminates this gap in literary history and criticism within children's literary studies. Dale Townshend and M. O. Grenby have also made valuable contributions in a few articles published within anthologies exploring the gothic tradition in literature. Charmette Kendrick and Sabine Büssing have done wonderful work with their studies on the development of horror fiction within children's literature, but none of these studies focused exclusively on children's ghost stories, leaving a definite gap in the history of this literary genre, particularly on the development of this genre within the United States.

It is my hope that this book will provide both insight into and recognition of the complicated history of children's ghost stories in the United States, particularly in its development as a literary genre distinct from the gothic but also as a genre intimately tied to both folklore and traditions occurring in ghost stories intended only for adults. My aim is to partially fill the gap in scholarship surrounding the children's ghost story. While there are many wonderful ghost stories for children around the world, I have limited my focus to just the United States. I have done this for three main reasons: (1) my access to known archived resources was greater for American children's stories than for other

Preface

nations; (2) there were only so many ghost stories I could examine in one project and limiting my focus to one nation's ghost stories made the most sense in terms of scope; and (3) the largest scholarly gap surrounding the children's ghost story involved mostly texts published in the United States. With this being said, it is important to note that the American ghost story, like all literature, did not develop in a vacuum. Other cultures and nations definitely contributed to the development of the American ghost story for children; England, of course, was particularly influential. As such, I have drawn on other nations' ghost stories and traditions when doing so will help to contextualize the development of the American ghost story for children. It should also be noted that trends in the American ghost story for children also tended to reflect trends in children's ghost stories seen in other countries, particularly nations influenced by western thought and religion. While ghost stories are unique to every culture, there are some aspects of the genre that do transcend seemingly every border. These qualities will also be discussed within my book. Finally, I am not trying to write a detailed history on the entire development of children's literature in America. My aim is much more focused. Scholars like Beverly Lyon Clark and Roberta Seelinger Trites have already done a wonderful job of exploring the history and significance of American children's literature, but I am seeking to fill a niche in children's literature studies that has not been adequately explored.

This book's introduction examines factors that have influenced the development of the ghost story genre for children in America and includes a review of important works done on ghost stories and ghost stories for children. I also discuss at length a subgenre of children's ghost story that I like to call the mock ghost story. This genre is a predecessor to the supernatural ghost stories for children that began to appear in the twentieth century. I focus a great deal of my attention in this chapter on the reasons the mock ghost story flourished in nineteenth-century American children's periodicals. My goal here is to establish the foundation the American ghost story for children grew from to reach the popularity it enjoys in America today.

In Chapter 1, I continue to investigate the mock ghost story. The scholarship of Dale Townshend and Charmette Kendrick act as the foundation for much of my research into the nineteenth century's resistance

Preface

to the published ghost story for children, but Freud's theory of the uncanny serves as my principle theoretical lens in this chapter. While the mock ghost story seems fairly tame on the surface, many of these tales deal with controversial social issues or embody shifts occurring within American child culture. The mock ghost stories featured in this section offer insight into the children's publishing industry in the nineteenth century and investigate the ways ghosts can embody complex social issues, including discussions of race and class. Finally, the chapter will examine some of the few ghost stories from the nineteenth century that do not quite fit the mock ghost story trend in children's publishing.

In Chapter 2, I explore both gender issues and issues of female empowerment as they relate to the nineteenth-century mock ghost story for children. Drawing from such scholars as Roberta Seelinger Trites, Beverly Lyon Clark, and Vanessa D. Dickerson, I argue that the mock ghost stories dealing with girlhood offer mostly progressive views on female empowerment, endorsing more liberating perspectives of girlhood and womanhood than the Victorian model; however, I also investigate some of the rare exceptions to this progressive trend. The chapter will also deal with attacks made simultaneously against ghost stories and figures of womanhood in literature, particularly accusations about nursemaids and governesses corrupting children with frightening folklore. Finally, I set the stage for viewing the ghost story for children at the beginning of the twentieth century.

Chapter 3 argues that the growing disillusionment over technology and rationalism in the wake of the world wars, combined with increases in the marketing of children's books and of holidays, led to the emergence of the supernatural ghost in children's literature. Using the scholarship of Beverly Lyon Clark, Gregory L. Reece, and Iona and Peter Opie, my third chapter explores how children's literature and the ghost story changed during the early years of the twentieth century. I closely examine how the marketing of Halloween played a large role in the supernatural ghost's emergence in children's literature, but I also explore the folklore of children, particularly their scary stories, through the scholarship of Iona and Peter Opie. In the final pages of the chapter, I analyze the emerging friendly ghost genre for children and discuss the appearance of ghosts on television, specifically Casper the Friendly Ghost. The chapter ends roughly at the middle of the twentieth century.

Preface

Chapter 4 is slightly different from the other chapters in this book. It covers a ghost story tradition for children from the beginning to the present. This was done to better show the connections within this particular genre, which otherwise would have been more difficult to demonstrate scattered over multiple chapters. It explores the development of the ghost story for children in African American literature, particularly in *The Brownies' Book*, an African American periodical for children circulated in the 1920s and founded by W. E. B. Du Bois, Jessie Fauset, and Augustus Dill. I examine the complicated history surrounding ghost stories in the African American community, particularly in the early twentieth century. I rely heavily on research done by Gladys-Marie Fry, Geraldine Smith-Wright, Paula T. Connolly, Katharine Capshaw Smith, and Richard M. Dorson. I essentially argue that the African American children's ghost story developed more slowly because the folk tradition of telling ghost stories in the African American community has deep ties to oppression and misdirection dating all the way back to slavery in the United States. This complicated history made ghost stories a risky subject in African American literature, which likely influenced its development in early children's literature.

In Chapter 5, I discuss today's ghost story for children and the many adaptations of the children's ghost that emerge after mid century. Following up on the previous chapter, I explore changing popular perceptions of ghosts and ghostliness and examine the impact of new mediums on the genre. The scholarship of Jennifer Bann, Sabine Büssing, Simon J. Bronner, Peter N. Stearns and Timothy Haggerty, and others informs my argument that ghost stories became acceptable in children's literature due largely to changing perceptions about "safe fear" and the reevaluation of the child's storied world. I analyze both popular and literary appearances of the ghost, examining such popular series as Goosebumps, Scary Stories, and Casper, but also literary manifestations of the ghost like *Sweet Whisper, Brother Rush* and *The Dark Thirty*.

I conclude with a study of current trends within the ghost story genre for children. I discuss the emergence of transmedia or trans-narrative as a new forum for the ghost story for children in the mainstream publishing world. The emergence of trans-narrative novels such as Patrick Carman's *Skelton Creek* (2009) opens new avenues for the ghost

Preface

story to explore in children's literature. While these multiplatform novels work well for mainstream publishing, I spend a great deal of time discussing creepypastas, online scary folklore, and its potential to reenergize the children's ghost story in ways never previously experienced by the genre. American children's fascination and creative input within the development of creepypastas suggest that children will play a larger role in the development of the ghost stories they read and transmit than seen in previous centuries. I rely on recent research by such scholars as Shira Chess, Eric Newsom, Andrew Peck, and Marie Tina Boyer to shed light on the inner workings of this new online genre. While I look at a variety of creepypastas, I focus on ones featuring ghostly figures. I specifically examine the creepypastas Ben Drowned and Bloody Mary, which act as interesting case examples of the popularity and complexity of these creepypastas.

My book covers a large amount of primary and secondary scholarship, but hardly scratches the surface of the vast array of books and folklore dealing with ghosts in American childhood and children's literature. I realize that my book, like any historical work, is only a survey of this much larger history, but I hope my work will shed light on a previously unexamined segment of children's literature and culture in America and will spark insightful discussion among scholars about children's ghost stories. I am particularly excited about unearthing so many early versions of the ghost story for children. Many of the mock ghost stories examined in early chapters of this book have haunted library archives for more than a hundred years now, hidden carefully away among numerous forgotten issues of *The Youth's Companion, St. Nicholas,* and other relicts of a bygone era of American publishing for children. Their rediscovery reveals interesting trends about the nature of publishing for children in America and about the sensitivity surrounding ghostly tales designed specifically for children. I hope unearthing such texts will spark intriguing debates within the children's literature community. I am also grateful to the libraries and databases that have recently digitized and published numerous pieces from these periodicals. Without the access these sources have provided, these stories may have remained hidden for decades. I hope my research on these and other stories will provide a strong framework for establishing a thorough history of the ghost story in American children's literature.

Introduction

While the ghost story has existed in both oral and literary traditions for millennia, the ghost story specifically designed and published for children has roughly a two-century history with the first half of that period open to some suspicion. Since the beginning of the children's publishing industry in the eighteenth century, when John Newbery ushered in the new genre with the publication of *A Little Pretty Pocket-Book* (1744) and *The History of Little Goody Two-Shoes* (1764–65), the ghost story in children's literature has met with numerous obstacles, often teetering on the edge of complete obscurity during a time when children's literature began to thrive in the market. The new publishing industry for children in both the eighteenth and nineteenth centuries resisted the impulse to publish supernatural ghost stories for children because of a widespread notion—embedded in American and British culture alike—that such fantastic and terrifying tales would corrupt the child and encourage a belief in superstition, an ostensibly surprising trend in the industry considering the popularity of such supernatural fiction as *The Castle of Otranto* (1765), *Frankenstein* (1818), and numerous Victorian ghost stories by such writers as Charles Dickens and Joseph Sheridan Le Fanu. In the United States, Washington Irving thrilled American and international audiences with his spooky story "The Legend of Sleepy Hollow" (1819–20), but even he never once wrote a ghostly tale exclusively for children. Indeed, in most cases, American authors and publishers appeared more hesitant about publishing ghost stories for children than many of their counterparts on the other side of the Atlantic. Why then prohibit children from reading scary supernatural fiction designed specifically for them, especially during a period when the market for children's literature begins to boom? Why keep the ghost story at bay? Clearly something was working

Introduction

behind the scenes to turn so many authors and publishers against the idea of producing ghost stories for children. This book will tackle this mystery in American literature and will reveal when and why this publishing trend began to reverse in the twentieth century. It will also reveal a vital chain of influence that will demonstrate the ghost story's significance in children's literature as a vehicle for social change and as a genre largely distinct from the gothic.

However, before investigating the origin of the ghost story for children, it is first imperative to establish an origin and working definition for ghosts appearing in both English and American literature and folklore, particularly since a definition is fundamental to identifying the ghost in children's literature. The ghost story is often incorrectly lumped into the eighteenth- and nineteenth-century gothic tradition in literature, which is unfortunate considering the ghost story's long history in oral traditions and ancient literature. For instance, though they are not exclusively ghost stories themselves, references to Wraiths, ghosts, and other spirits appear in many canonized works. *The Odyssey*, *Hamlet*, and even the Bible[1] are prime examples of the ghost lurking within the pages of ancient and early-modern texts, often following patterns of ghostliness still visible in later literature. These examples clearly secure a foothold for the ghost story far earlier than the inception of the gothic tradition in literature, but many excellent scholars studying the ghost story for children have overlooked this crucial aspect of the genre. Ghost stories are likely among the oldest and most common tales ever told in any culture or language. As Gregory L. Reece accurately observes, "They are universal, a common theme in human life" (26). To study the ghost story as *only* a part of one genre or tradition, even a tradition as influential as the gothic, is a grave mistake. While there are many ghost stories that fall within the gothic tradition during the eighteenth and nineteenth centuries, the gothic genre is not exclusively defined by the appearance of a ghost, nor is the ghost exclusively tied to the gothic tradition, which has often become the assumption of many scholarly works on the topic of ghosts in literature, particularly for scholars studying contemporary versions of the ghost in children's literature.

Defining the ghost for the purpose of literary research is an exceedingly difficult task, largely because of the sheer overuse of the

Introduction

term "ghost" in literature and in popular culture, but the term becomes even more difficult to define in children's literature and folklore. For example, if a contemporary American child were asked to tell a ghost story, they may tell a story about an axe-wielding maniac hiding in the backseat of a teenager's convertible or a story about a werewolf concealed in a young boy's closet. While these stories do not contain a ghost of any type, we would hardly be surprised to hear a child defining a ghost story in such a way. The term "ghost story" in contemporary popular culture has been appropriated to represent any short tale that might contain terrifying or supernatural elements, regardless of the absence of anything resembling a ghost. However, if a contemporary American child were asked to define or describe a ghost, we would not be shocked to hear them define it as a spirit or dead person, often appearing as a wispy figure draped in a white sheet, perhaps one very similar to those folded neatly way in their parent's linen closet. The child may also describe it as floating or transparent. This image of the ghost is well known and popular in American children's culture, despite the almost instant association of the term "ghost story" with any short terrifying tale. How do we reconcile these opposing views? How do we parcel out the ghost in children's literature? The problem of genre and characterization are particularly difficult and readily debated among scholars studying ghosts in literature, which justifies a quick look at the way ghosts have been defined and categorized among scholars.

First, we must review some established definitions of ghosts and ghost stories, particularly those that have gained traction among scholars studying such tales. In the introduction to *The Oxford Book of English Ghost Stories* (1986), Michael Cox and R. A. Gilbert argue that a ghost story "should reveal to the reader a spectacle of the returning dead, or their agents, and their actions" and that "there must be a dramatic interaction between the living and the dead, more often than not with the intention of frightening or unsettling the reader" (xvi). They offer these criteria as the two principal components of their five part definition (the other parts are largely applicable to the English ghost story only), but they also concede ghosts might include the possibility of reanimated corpses—a loophole in their definition that invites many other supernatural contenders into the ghostly pedigree (ix). They do amend this definition slightly in *The Oxford Book of Victorian Ghost*

Introduction

Stories (1991), where they proclaim the Victorian ghost as a "distinct, anti-Gothic character" and downplay the emphasis on reanimated corpses (x). Their interest in the ghost story is largely a literary one and scant attention is paid to stories derived directly from an oral tradition—an attribute that is apparent from their selection of tales. The same is true of Brad Leithauser's *The Norton Book of Ghost Stories* (1994), where a strong emphasis on the literary tradition of ghost stories tends to supersede the folk traditions, popular appearances, and historical influences on which these stories are likely based. For Leithauser, "[g]host stories reflect a variety of aims, of course, but in its essential form the tale undertakes a careful sortie into a landscape of terrors—a cyclical journey (from the natural world to the supernatural and back again) that promises to release us, chastened but intact, at its close" (10). His definition, much like Cox and Gilbert's, emphasizes the role of fear within the pages of the story and forwards the notion that the definition of a ghost story must be strongly tied to its ability to provoke fear and suspense above all other attributes.

While Cox, Gilbert, and Leithauser offer definitions that appear to function well within the parameters of the stories they have selected for their collections, they may not accurately reflect the way the ghost story has operated in practice. Ghosts are rarely so easily contained; they naturally transcend the shackles of their genres and phase effortlessly between the bonds of all storied spaces. To better understand historical and literary representations of ghosts, particularly as they might apply to children's literature, we must cast a wide net and allow for broader interpretations to prevail, but we also want to preserve some qualities of the ghost that appear to transcend traditions, specifically those qualities that distinguish the ghost from some of its more gruesome doppelgangers, like zombies, vampires, and other supernatural entities of the sort. While Cox and Gilbert and even Leithauser offer criteria that help to define the ghost in canonized literature, their definitions do not altogether function as an adequate characterization of the ghost as it often appears in early and even later children's literature, which is why it is necessary to make a few slight alterations to their definitions to include occasions where ghosts and their actions are perceived to have acted—as in the case with the mock ghost story for children, which will be discussed in greater length later in this intro-

Introduction

duction—and to exclude occasions where reanimated corpses rise from the grave. We will also want to look at the way the ghost is functioning in popular culture and folk traditions, which form close connections to the way the ghost operates in literature. This amended definition helps to eliminate some of those nasty doppelgangers mention earlier and reveals some of the secret avenues ghosts have used to enter mainstream literature for children; the dark recess of the oral traditions of ghost telling would later provide a firm foundation for the ghost to emerge in literature for children.

Before the popularity of the printed ghost story in the nineteenth century, the ghost story chiefly thrived by word of mouth, told and retold around the fireside or tavern table, with little and rare success in text. As with most folklore, these ghostly tales generally walked the line between truth and fiction: some of the tales might be based on facts and actual occurrences while other parts might simply be pure exaggeration (Marshall 18–20). Whether the audience perceived the story as truth or fiction was entirely at the discretion of the listener. The first real transformation in the transmission of ghost stories began to occur during the English Reformation with the rise of the print industry and changing perspectives on Christianity. According to Peter Marshall in "Transformations of the Ghost Story in Post–Reformation England," while the English Reformation "neither suppressed nor effectively appropriated the apparition narrative," it nevertheless brought "about a series of dislocations—theological, social, textual—which created the conditions for a freer exercise of the imagination in relation to the supernatural" (18). This newly created imaginative space of print offered a platform for the ghost story to thrive as text. Many of these early printed ghost stories were believed to be genuine, not fictionalized, accounts, based on eyewitness reports of ghost sightings (Marshall 19).

While these accounts continued to be published well into the eighteenth century and beyond, ghost stories, fictional or otherwise, suffered scrutiny and eventually criticism. With the growth of Protestantism in England came fervent reactions to theories on the supernatural upheld by the Catholic Church. Purgatory was one such hotbed of controversy. Protestants argued that purgatory was merely a ploy to swindle riches from the unsuspecting commons, that it had little or no

Introduction

biblical foundation, and was consistently abused by the clergy. In his acclaimed *Hamlet in Purgatory*, Stephen Greenblatt argues that the appearance of ghosts according to the mediaeval Catholic Church could only occur under the following circumstances:

> The purpose of spectral visitations was most often to plead for prayers, almsgiving, pious fasts, and above all masses, in order to obtain some relief from excruciating pain. Less commonly, ghosts returned, as Donne puts it, to "instruct" the living, that is, to issue warnings, disclose hidden wrongs, or urge the restitution of ill-gotten gains [41].

Any other ghostly visitations would constitute the appearance of a demon disguised as a ghost, typically attempting to either corrupt a soul or cause an evil occurrence (Greenblatt 102–03). This account, for the most part, constituted mediaeval Europe's understanding of ghostly occurrences and continued to shape the ghost story in later centuries, but a radical shift in the telling of ghostly tales started to happen after Protestantism took hold. The ghost fell under scrutiny. Since Protestants rejected notions of Purgatory, ghosts were left in a precarious circumstance after the Reformation. The ghost's principle foundation under the Catholic Church, based largely on a belief in Purgatory, had been systematically removed from the Christian doctrine in England. As Peter Marshall so wonderfully concludes, "[n]o purgatory, no ghosts" (21). This stance, along with a philosophical and social movement toward rationalism, spelled difficult times for the ghost story in western culture. Even its old safety net, the oral tradition, was undergoing massive changes during this period. Transformations in technology and industry caused substantial shifts to the everyday lives of common people throughout England and eventually America. By the beginning of the nineteenth century, real changes in the social fabric of this community began to occur. James Fowler, picking up a point made by Katharine Briggs, argues that industrialization and print media led to the decline of the oral tradition (235–6). Due to year-round working conditions in new industry, leisure time spent around the fire recounting folktales started to diminish (Fowler 236). Without the oral tradition to circulate ghost stories, print became the alternative medium for preserving and creating these tales; hence the rise of the modern ghost story and the gothic tradition and the likely decline in access of these stories among children.

Introduction

The ghost story's critics during the eighteenth and nineteenth centuries were numerous. Rationalist and Protestant alike accused the ghost story of being merely the infatuation of women and the lower classes (Townshend 17); however, despite these accusations, the ghost story's popularity and marketability continued to grow in publications for adults. The increased availability of text, coupled with the falling cost of printed materials, allowed the ghost story to flourish on the pages of numerous periodicals at a price that the average consumer could afford. The ghost story quickly became a marketing sensation, but not as quickly as another flourishing market of periodicals, the market for children's literature. With the success of Newbery's line of children's books, stories aimed at children quickly took root in the publishing industry; however, publishers and writers for children seemed unwilling to allow their newfound fascination with the ghost story to be part of this new genre. As such, the ghost story for children remained in a dubious position for most, if not all, of the nineteenth century.

John Locke, perhaps one of the most influential empirical philosophers of the seventeenth century, played a critical role in restraining the ghost and other supernatural creatures in children's literature. Locke argued that children should be sheltered from stories of spirits and goblins. In *Some Thoughts Concerning Education*, he urges his mostly adult audience to "be sure to preserve [the youth's] tender mind from all impressions and notions of *spirits* and *goblins* or any fearful apprehensions in the dark" (original emphasis) (103). His words had a devastating impact on the development of the supernatural ghost story for children in British and American literature. Dale Townshend, a leading scholar on the development of Gothic children's literature, claims that Locke's philosophy heavily influenced John Newbery, particularly his *The History of Little Goody Two-Shoes,* and therefore allowed Locke's thoughts on child rearing to dominate the literary marketplace for children. He even argues that "Newbery published *Goody Two-Shoes* partly in order to counteract the effects of orally transmitted ghost stories for children" (21). If Townshend's assertion is correct, then Locke's impact on the development of the ghost story for children is certainly profound and should be carefully scrutinized. Townshend also concludes that Locke's philosophy sparked a widespread movement against

Introduction

the ghost in children's literature. "A distinctive pattern within eighteen-century children's literature [began] to reveal itself," he argues, "Locke urged the reading of certain morally uplifting tracts over others of a more gruesome nature" (21). This movement had a polarizing effect on the development of the ghost story in children's literature and countered any effort to publish supernatural ghost stories for children. M. O. Grenby, following Townshend's lead in his article "Gothic and the Child Reader, 1764–1850," argues that a kind of "enlightened campaign" was being waged against ghosts and other supernatural creatures in children's literature (245). Thus, supernatural ghosts vanished from the pages of children's books even before they were given the chance to haunt.

Indeed, when it came to children or child culture, the supernatural ghost had few defenders in the eighteenth and nineteenth centuries. The ghost and other supernatural horrors even met with harsh criticism from some of their staunchest supporters when it came down to childhood and education. Mary Shelley's *Frankenstein*, perhaps the most critical touchstone of supernatural fiction of the nineteenth century, could not resist the temptation to join the chorus. As Victor Frankenstein proudly recounts the studies of his youth, he goes to a considerable effort to mention that none of his studies were ever polluted with tales of ghosts and other supernatural horrors:

> In my education my father had taken the greatest precautions that my mind should be impressed with no supernatural horrors. I do not ever remember to have trembled at a tale of superstition, or to have feared the apparition of a spirit. Darkness had no effect upon my fancy; and a churchyard was to me merely the receptacle of bodies deprived of life, which, from being the seat of beauty and strength, had become food for the worm [45].

We can only hope that Shelley intended this scene to instill a sense of irony, especially since a little fear of the graveyard would have certainly saved Victor some trouble later in life, but it is equally possible that Shelley merely wished to reinforce the current trend in anti-superstition for children even within the pages of a book deeply steeped in superstition. The pedagogy expressed in this scene is hardly inconsistent with the childrearing practices of the time. The mere reference of this ideology within a novel so critical to the development of gothic and supernatural literature demonstrates the pervasiveness of the

Introduction

resistance to ghosts within children's literature and education of the nineteenth century. However, within the United States, similar reactions to teaching superstition and fear abound within children's education and literature. Bronson Alcott, an influential educator and philosopher and father of the famous children's author Louisa May Alcott, avoided exposing his children to fear of any kind. "The influence of fear," he wrote, "even in its milder forms, upon the mind of infancy, must be unfavorable to its improvement and happiness. External objects should, as far as possible, excite only ideas of beauty, truth, and happiness" (qtd. in Matteson 45). According to John Matteson in his wonderful joint biography *Eden's Outcasts: the Story of Louisa May Alcott and Her Father*, Bronson Alcott recorded this entry in his unpublished journal "Observations on the Life of My First Child" after frightening his daughter Anna with a scary face. The incident seems to have solidified his resolve to abstain from exposing his daughters to fearful content, even for the sake of entertainment, which consequently might have hardened his daughter's resolve against fear as literary entertainment for children, which will be demonstrate more clearly in a later chapter.

In the United States, ghost stories published within nineteenth-century children's periodicals rejected notions of supernatural fear as literary entertainment, advancing the belief that such tales would damage the child's psyche: better to characterize the ghosts as fraudulent and irrational than threaten the child's mental stability. The perpetrator or believer of the ghostly tale frequently experiences the greatest punishment in these narratives. Some of these tales even put the very tradition of ghost telling at the heart of the conflict. Mary Bradley's "Twelfth-Night Story," a nursery poem published in *St. Nicholas; an Illustrated Magazine for Young Folks*, captured this sentiment toward ghost telling as late as 1907, where a young nursemaid is subsequently punished for telling her young wards a scary tale. The poem concludes with the following moral:

> But she learned a lesson that was not lost;
> For never, never since then,
> With a tale of witch, or goblin, or ghost,
> Has she frightened the children again [255].

Clearly superstition has no place in the nursery. Telling or promoting superstition is vilified or strongly discouraged in many of the ghost

Introduction

stories published in children's periodicals before the twentieth century, but the tradition of telling these "mock ghost" stories goes back as far as *The History of Little Goody Two-Shoes*, where the ghost first encountered the stern voice of censorship: "my dear Children, I hope you will not believe any foolish Stories that ignorant, weak, or designing People may tell you about *Ghosts*; for the Tales of *Ghost*, *Witches*, and *Fairies*, are the Frolicks of a distempered Brain. No wise Man ever saw either of them [sic]" (112). Such morals accompany most mock ghost stories. In essence, mock ghost stories are fake children's ghost stories designed to both satisfy the child's desire for ghostly tales while simultaneously discrediting and mocking the tradition of telling ghost stories or adhering to a belief in ghosts. They are akin to Ann Radcliffe's tradition of employing the explained supernatural in her novels and stories, but they are distinct from her fiction in that their singular mission was to discredit the supernatural ghost in children's literature at all cost, leaving no room for the specter to haunt.[2] Their morals were overt and their style fairly simplistic—story, characterization, consistency, and ultimately entertainment value were often cut at the expense of satisfying this singular mission. In place of the genuine article, most children's periodicals in America offered these mock ghost stories rather than expose children to any form of the supernatural ghost; the mock ghost story always revealed supernatural ghosts as frauds and generally carried an embedded rationalist nod to the perceived illogical stance of superstition. The great irony, of course, is that the ghost story flourished despite its vilification. The very act of publishing a mock ghost story suggests a hunger for the ghost tale among young readers in the nineteenth century, a hunger the mock ghost story intended to fill among American children but actually exacerbated.

Before these mock ghost stories, nothing in the way of printed ghost stories existed exclusively for children in the United States. According to Townshend, ghost stories for children only existed informally in the oral tradition before the nineteenth century, claiming that "since the early modern period, British culture had consistently associated ghosts and children with the oral tradition in storytelling" (17). In the United States, children's stories and ghost stories shared much the same history. And when the oral tradition moved into print, the publishers of these tales swapped the supernatural ghost story for the

Introduction

mock ghost story. These pseudo-ghostly tales, published in such children's periodicals as *The Youth's Companion* and *St. Nicholas*, were typically simple, short, and contained heavy-handed morals and tended to appeal to or circulate amongst middle-class white Americans.[3] Their existence demonstrates a backlash to the superstition and fancy of previous centuries but also demonstrates a questionable aversion to supernatural fiction contrary to the adult market of the time. "In a ceaseless dialectic of action and reaction," argues Dale Townshend, "the ghost is vigorously stamped out of children's literature in the same decades that witnessed the consolidation of not only the Gothic aesthetic, but a firm sense of what constituted the middle-class child, his education, and his books too" (21). The attempt to "stamp out" the ghost story in children's literature reveals a double standard in what adults perceived as appropriate and entertaining for themselves and what they deemed as appropriate for their children. Nineteenth-century America's fear of exposing children to the supernatural has roots in the faith it placed in the religion and science of its time and its perceived superiority to the religion and science of previous centuries.

Evidence of this departure from the way previous centuries' parents reared their children appears in numerous periodicals during the nineteenth century. In 1843, one anonymous contributor to the *Maine Farmer and Mechanics Advocate*, a weekly farmer's periodical published between 1842 and 1843, had the following to say on the issue:

> Many young persons have a desire to read very marvelous stories relative to ghosts, witches, haunted houses, and leagues with the devil, most of which are contrary to reason and common sense, of decided evil tendency. The time once was when these stories would have been credited—when what could not be readily understood was attributed to supernatural agency. The light of recent science has dissipated many of these visions, and a better knowledge of the human mind has satisfactorily accounted for many of them, so that now but very few well informed persons are much troubled by any of these "airy nothings" ["A Ghost Story—for the Young" 4].

The certainty and confidence of the contributor's conclusions are juxtaposed to his dismissal of the "airy nothings,"[4] which are merely the stuff of trivial fantasy and ancient superstition. Any attempt to tolerate such notions as ghosts—whether serious or fictional—is thus seen as an endorsement of superstition. However, the nineteenth-century

Introduction

mock ghost story attempted to disembody the child's sense of the supernatural by simultaneously and literally embodying the specter; contrary to its intention, the mock ghost in children's literature actually empowered the supernatural ghost story and paved the way for its revival in the twentieth century.

While the exact period of the evolutionary jump from the mock ghost to the twentieth-century supernatural ghost is debatable, Townshend claims that evidence of such changes in children's literature began with Charles Dickens, contending Dickens' ghost stories ended the drought of supernatural ghosts in children's literature and reinvigorated the tradition (33). Townshend, however, has made a grave miscalculation in his assertion. Dickens did not frequently write for children, even though many of his works had great appeal for them, nor did he ever fancy himself as much of a children's author with only a handful of stories—none of which ghost stories—appearing exclusively for children. He chose to write and publish mostly in adult periodicals, not in the popular and abundant children's periodicals of his day, which he could have easily published a ghost story in had he so desired. In fact, contrary to Townshend's claim, the ghost story for children long endured censorship long after the popularity of Dickens' tales and was not seen as appropriate for children until nearly the turn of the century. Other ghostly stories frequently misidentified as children's literature include Washington Irving's "The Legend of Sleepy Hollow," Edger Allan Poe's "The Raven" (1845), and various spooky tales by Nathaniel Hawthorne, none of which sought the child as a target audience. This book, however, analyzes texts written for and marketed to American children or circulated exclusively within American children's culture. Following in the criteria and theoretical lens established in Beverly Lyon Clark's *Kiddie Lit*, this book will focus on "the meanings of childhood and children's literature in American culture—and hence primarily in issues of reception" within historical context and therefore more concerned with "what adult gatekeepers have thought than to what children have actually read" (xiii). This book seeks the same approach with the ghost story for children; hence, stories later assigned to children's literature will not be an active part of my study, though may occasionally be discussed to shed light on common misconceptions about ghost stories for children.

Introduction

Founding the American Children's Ghost Story

Despite the apparent removal of the ghost story from children's literature, the oral ghost telling tradition remained enough of a threat to prompt the mock ghost to appear as a counter to the popular tradition of telling ghost stories. The children's mock ghost story essentially served as a rebuttal to the ghost story on two fronts: to satisfy children's appetite for the tradition without exposing them to the supernatural ghost, and to ridicule the irrational belief in superstition through the embedded morals of the tale. However, whether intentionally or unintentionally, the mock ghost did more to preserve and establish the ghost story tradition for children than it did to derail it. Since the ghost story had little established footing in the print industry for children, the mock ghost allowed the tradition to infiltrate the children's market and spark an interest in the genre. Without the mock ghost and its heavy reliance on the tradition, the ghost story would have no substantial place in children's literature of the nineteenth century or later in the twentieth century. The nineteenth-century mock ghost story in children's periodicals essentially established a framework for the tropes, themes, settings, and archetypes of the ghost story to survive in children's literature. Haunted houses and hotel rooms, vengeful spirits guarding hidden treasures, and even mysterious noises and shapes near the bedside are preserved in these mock ghost stories and might have been lost or limited without the genre's existence in children's literature.

While children's periodicals rarely published supernatural ghost stories in the nineteenth and early twentieth century, some scholars argue that ghost story authors writing for adult targeted periodicals disguised children's ghost stories as adult literature. Jane Suzanne Carroll, in "'A Dramar in Reel Life'—Freaky Dolls, M. R. James and Modern Children's Ghost Stories," argues that one of the most prominent ghost story writers of this period wrote ghost stories for children veiled as an adult tale. Carroll attempts to reclassify M. R. James' "A Haunted Doll's House" as a groundbreaking ghost story for children, not adult readers, arguing critics and editors have mistakenly characterized it as

Introduction

adult fiction (251). She makes this case based on thematic elements of the story, which insinuate James' reliance on the child doll/toy genre rather than the adult doll/mannequin genre. She argues that adult "doll-narratives" offer life-size, human-like dolls rather than the miniature-sized, unrealistic dolls common in children's doll/toy genres (256). Carroll's most interesting claim focuses on James' reversal of the typical doll/toy genre, where instead of the doll becoming human, like in *Pinocchio* (1883), it instead remains horribly trapped as a doll, more common in modern children's narratives (258–59). Her article points to more contemporary children's ghost/doll narratives, like *The Ghost in the Attic* published in 1985 and "The Un–Door" published in 2007, which Carroll argues might have been heavily influenced by James' story. Such potential reclassifications of ghost stories secretly intended for children could lead to endless controversy surrounding some canonized literature, but these stories may also suggest that some form of underground resistance to mock ghost stories or just simply to the tradition of banning the supernatural ghost for children might have existed within some circles during the nineteenth century.

Carroll is not the only scholar interested in reclassification in the realm of children's literature. Sabine Büssing, in *Aliens in the Home: The Child in Horror Fiction* (1987) is interested in the way the child has been represented in the literary canon as well, particularly in horror and gothic fiction for children and adults. She notes that horror, in some form or another, owes much of its inception to gothic literature; however, despite the deep connection between gothic and horror fiction, she claims horror differs dramatically in its treatment of child characters, often making them more substantial and villainous than passive and mute (xiii-xiv). She indicates that these changes are the product of major cultural shifts at the time. "The Gothic romance," Büssing argues, "the first genre in which fear is the main theme of interest, is considered both a subversive answer to the doctrines of the Enlightenment and an expression of Man's being endangered in a new social and moral situation" (xv). Büssing's observation about the gothic genre reveals the tension behind a time caught between the rationalism of the Enlightenment and the liberalism and relativism of the twentieth century. Her observation provides the framework for understanding how the mock ghost in children's literature can be seen as both progressive

Introduction

and conservative in regards to the evolution of the children's ghost story.

Literary Influence: Significant Contributions to the Ghost Genre

Ghosts play a significant role in many canonized text in nineteenth-century American and British literature. Before focusing almost exclusively on the stories intended for children, a quick analysis and overview of research into more canonized ghost stories might prove incredibly useful when looking at the development of the children's ghost story. Andrew Smith in *The Ghost Story, 1840–1920: A Cultural History* (2010) identifies the significance of the ghost story to the nineteenth and twentieth century by examining the social issues that may have inspired and directed these ghosts. While Smith and his contemporaries do not primarily deal with children's ghost stories, his works do contribute to an important framework about the social significance of ghosts during this time period. Smith argues that at the heart of many "true" and literary accounts of ghosts are allusions to financial and economic transactions. For instance, the transition from precious materials, like gold, as currency to paper money represents a sort of ghostly shift; paper money is a ghostly representation of the real wealth behind it (5). Abusers of wealth, he argues, are evident in such famous ghost stories as Dickens' *A Christmas Carol* (5). While Smith claims that making this argument about all ghostly accounts during this period would be extremely limiting, he feels this link to economy and finance is crucial to understanding the role ghosts played during this period.

Similar to Smith, Karen J. Jacobsen's "Economic Hauntings: Wealth and Class in Edith Wharton's Ghost Stories" and Bruce Robbins' "'They don't much count, do they?' The Unfinished History of *The Turn of the Screw*" demonstrate a definite class and economic theme in some very prominent nineteenth-century ghost stories. For instance, Robbins uses a Marxist historical perspective to analyze Henry James' *The Turn of the Screw* (1898) and concludes that the novel is actually a social commentary, almost allegory, of the nineteenth-century class system. He argues that the ghosts in the novel, two former servants, are made

Introduction

ghostly even before their deaths (378). Their status as servants makes them unimportant or irrelevant in comparison to the upper class, who they are forced to care for due to their social circumstances. Robbins shows the upper class's indifference toward the lower classes through analyzing dialogue and references to servants, where he indicates that they are hardly ever referred to by name or shown pity or remorse even in death (379). He also explains that the novel's ending is made even more horrifying when Miles, the master's nephew, dies—or is killed depending on the reading—upon having an egalitarian (almost democratic) epiphany. Miles' death eradicates the possibility in the novel for upward mobility and class reconciliation (386).

Jacobsen, on the other hand, identifies Edith Wharton's ghost stories' contribution to a commentary on the disparity in wealth distribution occurring in the early twentieth century. While Jacobsen notes Wharton's upper-class status, she contends Wharton's position as a woman and artist gives her a unique inside perspective of the wealth distribution disparity. Jacobsen and other scholars identify "Wharton as both an insider and outsider of upper-class society, a position that resulted in her own complex brand of social criticism" (101). Wharton's occupation of a liminal space between privilege and disenfranchisement allows her to use her ghost stories as a means to reveal striking disparities between wealth and poverty in the United States. In the story "Afterward," for instance, Jacobsen explains how the character Ned is literally haunted by his "former unethical business practices" at his new home in England (104).

The roles of economy and class emerge in mock ghost stories printed for children as well. "The Barber's Ghost," a story published by an anonymous author in the *Youth's Companion* in 1865, depicts the experiences of a savvy gentleman lodging in a supposedly haunted tavern somewhere in the eastern United States. The landlord tells the gentleman that the only room available in his tavern is haunted by the ghost of a murdered barber and that every lodger who stays in the room hears the ghost ask them for a shave. The gentleman, not believing in ghosts, demands the room despite the landlord's warning, boasting that "if he comes he may shave me" (142). Once settled in his bed, the gentleman starts hearing the voice of a man asking if he wants a shave. When the gentleman investigates the sound, he quickly discovers

Introduction

that the voice is being created by a tree branch rubbing against the house. To punish the superstitious landlord and patrons of the tavern, he disguises himself as a ghost and scares the gambling patrons out of the tavern.

"The Barber's Ghost," while a very simple story, carries a number of embedded nuances about class and financial sensibility. The gentleman's impeccable rationalism proves superior to the superstitions of the lowly locals. This theme is contrary to most adult ghost stories, where the superstitious wisdom of the locals' trumps the rationalism of the visitor, apparent in such ghostly tales as Bram Stoker's "The Judge's House" (1891), Ralph A. Cram's "In Kropfsberg Keep" (1895), and more recently Susan Hill's *The Woman in Black* (1983). The gentleman in "The Barber's Ghost," confident enough in his rationale to see through the ghost story, is also sensible enough to best the gamblers, whose superstitions are only matched by their poor financial sensibility. The gentleman in this story is elevated above the local riffraff—superior in class, intelligence, and finance. The moral of the story reveals that superstition is the mark of the lower classes and the illogical and that overcoming superstition will always lead to success and sensibility. Of course, the irony of this rationale can be seen in the very unveiling of the fraudulent ghost. The story's overt rationalist theme never contends with the unlikelihood that a tree branch can utter complete sentences by merely scratching the side of the tavern in a light breeze. The swapping of an illogical phenomenon for another illogical phenomenon is one startling characteristics of the children's mock ghost tradition, reminiscent of the children's cartoon show *Scooby-Doo, Where Are You!* (1969), where the cast of characters is constantly unveiling ghosts and monsters as frauds despite their pervious supernatural feats.

Interestingly, "The Barber's Ghost" is a version of two predecessors printed in periodicals principally targeted toward adults—*The New-England Galaxy and United States Literary Advertiser* in 1825 and *Saturday Evening Post* in 1862. The tale only varies slightly in each version of "The Barber's Ghost," *The Youth's Companion* version demonstrates the most dramatic departure from these earlier renderings. While these differences might seem small and insignificant, their impact on the reading of the tale shows the moral editing engine at work behind the

Introduction

scenes in children's publishing of the nineteenth century. The alterations of a few choice lines in the adult story versions render major ideological differences in comparison to the version printed in *The Youth's Companion*. In the scene where the protagonist pretends to be the ghost and frightens the taverns patrons, a few fairly significant adaptations occur in *The Youth's Companion* version. These major differences are observable in the following excerpts:

> From *The New-England Galaxy and United States Literary Advertiser*,
> "He [the protagonist] then deliberately put his basin under the table and gathered an immense sum of money into it, which had been left thereupon, secured it" [4].
>
> From the *Saturday Evening Post*,
> "Our ghost [the protagonist], taking advantage of a clear room, deliberately swept a large amount of the money from the table into the basin, and retired unseen to his own room" [3].
>
> From *The Youth's Companion*,
> "Our ghost [the protagonist] beat a hurried retreat to his room and was troubled no more that night with gamblers or mysterious noises" [143].

The protagonists of the two previous versions of "The Barber's Ghost" trick and rob the superstitious patrons of the tavern, but the protagonist of *The Youth's Companion* version only tricks the patrons of the establishment. While many possible reasons for these revisions might exist, the likely reason the children's version was altered rests with the protagonist's endorsement of theft. By robbing and tricking the patrons of the tavern, the protagonists in the previous versions endorse thievery, which counters the moral principals many children's periodicals like *The Youth's Companion* were trying to instill through their publications. However, through some clever editing, the problem is sufficiently resolved and the protagonist's moral standing is subsequently improved. While "The Barber's Ghost" presents a rarity in its ability to demonstrate this editing process, the possibility of other ghost stories in children's periodicals of the century being altered in this way exists.

"The Barber's Ghost" also reveals another important characteristic about the mock ghost story for children: it demonstrates the impeccable diligence paid to the tradition of its counterpart, the adult ghost story, with the exception of the supernatural element. "The Barber's

Introduction

Ghost" follows the narrative tradition of the supernatural ghost story until the moment the ghost is confronted, and it is only then that the story departs from the traditional genre. This very act of conforming to the tradition in some aspects while deviating in others demonstrates the mock ghost stories ability to preserve elements of the supernatural ghost in children's publishing. "The Barber's Ghost" is also quite a rarity for the time. While many of the ghost stories appearing in children's periodicals of the nineteenth century were knockoffs of their supernatural, adult oriented counterparts, "The Barber's Ghost" differs in that it features a mock ghost in both the adult and child versions, making it one of a small minority of such tales in the adult ghost story genre. Its survival is both fortunate and incredible. That such an obscure tale endured in at least three different versions over almost two centuries is nothing short of remarkable, but a fourth potential version also managed to survive into the twenty-first century as well. "The Barber's Ghost: A Legend of Bremen" was published in *Brother Jonathan: A Weekly Compend Belles Letters and the Fine Arts, Standard Literature, and General Intelligence* in 1842. This tale departs radically from the others: the setting is European, the traveler lodges in a castle, and there is a supernatural ghost. While the similarity in the title suggests connections between this tale and the others, the textual and contextual evidence are scarce; however, what the fourth tale might suggest is the possibility of a lost ur-text for all of these tales or the possibility of an obscure folk tradition of telling Barber's Ghost tales that is now almost entirely forgotten. Regardless, the textual history of the Barber's Ghost still provides great insight into the connection between the mock ghost story for children and their adult counterparts.

Empowering the Ghosts

Before the supernatural ghost story could thrive in children's literature, the traditional ghost story for adults would have to undergo some changes itself. Jennifer Bann, a scholar studying supernatural ghost stories of the nineteenth century, examines evolutionary trends of the ghost story in "Ghostly Hands and Ghostly Agency: The Changing Figure of the Nineteenth-Century Specter." She argues that the figure of the literary

Introduction

ghost began to change in the late nineteenth century. It shifted from an ethereal entity with little agency—outside of pleading with the living to a spirit with physical agency—essentially a movement away from the ghost's dependency on the living to cause events (664). She argues that the rise of Spiritualism accounts for the changing agency of ghosts in the later part of the century (664–65). This religious movement, while not readily apparent in most ghost stories of the time, had a tremendous influence on changing perceptions of ghosts, particularly on their ability to manipulate corporal things and hypnotize individuals. She specifically cites the recurrent appearance of hands in both ghost stories and séances, particularly in the works of late nineteenth-century authors. These hands, she argues, indicate the newfound agency of ghosts in late nineteenth-century literature and culture and their individual perseverance once free of their physical limitations (669–70).

Other scholars focus much more closely on the roles women play in ghostly short stories and novels. Vanessa D. Dickerson, Jarlath Killeen, and Adrienne E. Gavin all note how women and feminism played an important role in the evolution of the genre. Dickerson's book *Victorian Ghosts in the Noontide: Women Writers and the Supernatural* is the most comprehensive of the three. She links the frequent appearance of ghosts to the philosophical and literary pursuits of women in the nineteenth century, particularly their deep interest in Spiritualism, mesmerism, and supernatural fiction. She investigates the popularity of ghosts in women's fiction and finds connections through these movements and genres for many female Victorian authors. This leads Dickerson to conclude that ghosts and Spiritualism acted as a kind of conduit for women's intellectual activity, especially since patriarchal ideologies of the age were so repressive of women socially, intellectually, and politically. Dickerson, whose research focuses on literary, historic, and spiritual examples, argues that ghosts and ghostliness in women's writing typically represents the woman's liminal place in society, between the social stratospheres of the home and community (4–5). She brilliantly asserts that women used ghostliness as a metaphor for this position and as a means of challenging this space (8–9). In a sense, the ghost allowed female authors a certain amount of autonomy.

In "Victorian Women and The Challenge of The Phantom," Killeen, following in Dickerson's footsteps, investigates the long history of

Introduction

women writing in the ghost story genre, arguing that "[t]here has been a long cultural association between women and the ghostly" (81). Most of her analysis amends claims made by Vanessa D. Dickerson's *Victorian Ghosts in the Noontide: Women Writers and the Supernatural*, where Dickerson asserts that women's interests in ghost stories and spiritualism are tied to their status as "ethereal figures" within the nineteenth-century patriarchal society (Killeen 84). Killeen, contrary to Dickerson, argues that women are not often depicted as ethereal in most ghost stories; in fact, they are more often the victims of male ghosts. She explains that women's attraction to writing the ghost story had more to do with demonstrating the crimes of men against women than showing women's ethereal status. She also points to older ghost stories, like *Hamlet* and *The Castle of Otranto*, as examples of male power assuming center stage in the ghost story's plot.

Adrienne E. Gavin, adding a mixture of more contemporary (post 1950s) women ghost story writers with nineteenth-century writers, argues that female protagonists in *Jane Eyre* (1847), *Wuthering Heights* (1847), and Margaret Mahy's novels possess supernatural abilities that are tied to their womanhood, almost as manifestations of the power of their womanhood (131). To demonstrate, Gavin shows how young female protagonists in *Jane Eyre* and *Wuthering Heights* gain a sort of supernatural transcendence as they cross the threshold between childhood and womanhood. In the case of these novels, such transitions are more secretive and are tied more directly to their relationships with men. In both these novels, the female protagonist sees or mistakenly sees a ghostly version of their selves that signifies the beginning of this transition (132). In Mahy's novels, the ghosts are generally more real but still serve as tests or markers of a girl's transition into womanhood and their empowerment through this transition; however, in these cases, the power of womanhood is typically more openly expressed and not necessarily dependent on romantic relationships.

The scholarship of Dickerson, Gavin, and Killeen plays an important role in understanding mock ghost stories for children that feature female characters, particularly the nursemaid and her female charges. However, the mock ghost for children also complicates some of their findings and suggests that the female role in the adult ghost story is much different than it is in the ghost story for children. Dickerson's argument about the ethereal status of women in ghost stories is much less convincing in the mock ghost story for children, where the nursemaid plays a very active role in educating the children and the ghosts are undoubtedly more solid. The passivity usually associated with women in the nineteenth and early twentieth century is not as evident in the ghost story for children as it is in the ghost story for adults, largely because the nursemaid and the children play such dominant roles in the outcome of the story. Men are also frequently absent from mock ghost stories that prominently feature female characters, which removes them as a dominating and victimizing character as Killeen suggests. Instead men and the patriarchal society of the time float around the periphery of these stories. Their influence is felt but not directly heard or seen within the story. Most of the mock ghost stories for children featuring females in prominent roles strongly emphasize female bonding, not the impact of male domination.

While the depth and quality of these female-centered ghost stories for children vary, it is clear that almost all of them lack male characters and underscore female relationships and bonding. As such, Gavin's idea of seeing the ghost in the story—or in this case the mock ghost—as a mechanism for sparking a transition into womanhood is much more apt a conclusion than those Dickerson or Killeen draw. In fact, the theme Gavin identifies likely has its start in these mock ghost stories for children, where entering womanhood and taking over the role of caretaker are central experiences in most of these stories; however, these mock ghost stories for girls rarely see women or girls as empowering as Gavin discusses. These mock ghost stories for children depict womanhood and childhood as liminal space similar to the space occupied by ghosts. In essence, the ghost, supernatural or otherwise, serves as a perfect metaphor for the child's liminal space between infancy and adulthood and the nineteenth- and early twentieth-century woman's liminal space between social liberation and the home.

Resurrecting the Ghost

The close of the nineteenth century marks the end of the dominance of the mock ghost story in the children's publishing industry,

Introduction

and the supernatural ghost story quickly fills its vacancy. Several factors sparked this transformation in children's literature at the turn of the century: increased rights and agency for women and minorities; the growth of the middle class; advances in technology and industry, particularly in factories and warehouses; and the expansion and advancement of fields of studying human and child psychology, which began to quickly move away from the previous century's notions of the development and nature of the human psyche (which also leads to an acknowledgment of children's possible need for fear in their lives); shifts from periodicals to books for children due to advances in printing and changes in marketing trends; and increases in mass marketing to children, particularly the marketing of holidays. Perceptions regarding the use of fear in children's literature also move through a number of noticeable changes: "safe fear" or fear for entertainment purposes emerges as a new dominate feature in popular children's literature. However, with little doubt, the world wars played significantly in changing perceptions regarding ghosts and the supernatural in children's literature in America, particularly following growing public disillusionment with rationalism, technology, and science. The objectivity and security such faith in these concepts had offered in previous century quickly dwindled by comparison to the terrifying consequences the twentieth century's devastating weaponry posed. It seemed no longer possible for technology and rationalism to solve all of humanity's problems—rather, advancements in technology ushered in a whole new era of uncertainty and fear, a fear which reached its climax in the creation and use of the atomic bomb. The sheer destructive power of this weapon alone seemed to constitute a literal occurrence of the supernatural: the immediate vaporization of whole cities by the power of an unseen force seems almost magic by the standards of previous centuries. In the latter half of the twentieth century, fictional literary and film accounts of the fallout of this weapon would also draw from the supernatural. Mutants, zombies, and alien encounters would all be tied to the power behind this weapon. Thus, diminished faith in rationalism and technology, coupled with a new appreciation of a lost folkloric tradition, sparked the beginning of the supernatural ghost story genre for children's emergence, a literary phenomenon which continues to flourish even today and would not have flourished so quickly without the foundation established by the mock ghost story.

Introduction

The twentieth century ushered in a new beginning for the ghost story for children. The fear that ghost stories and supernatural tales corrupted and damaged young minds receded. Children's literature began to gravitate more and more toward entertaining rather than instructing the child. As such, the ghost story for children—a distinct genre—evolved to align itself with the more progressive trends of the twentieth century and the changing landscape of the publishing industry. The fear that once caused so many authors and publishers of children's writing to reject the ghost story faded and was quickly replaced with the widespread embrace of the terrifying, the horrific, and the ghostly. The mass marketing of holidays like Halloween also played significantly in this equation. With the introduction of Halloween readers and postcards, some of the first versions of the supernatural ghost would appear for children in the initial decades of the twentieth century, providing a foundation for future adaptations of the supernatural ghost for children. Eventually, the ghost story for children would move more firmly into popular culture and would become a highly successful marketing sensation, establishing the ghost story as one of the most significant genre's in children's literature.

1

"Airy nothings"
The Mock Ghost Story

In the final act of *A Midsummer Night's Dream*, Duke Theseus muses about the nature of fantastic story, on its ingenuity and strangeness, and concludes that such tales must only arise from the minds of lovers, lunatics, and poets (5.1.4–22). He dismisses them as "aery nothing[s]" or the product of some form of derangement.[1] Shakespeare enjoyed thoughtful wordplay and his choice of words here reflects something significant about the nature and history of ghostliness. For Shakespeare and his contemporaries, ghosts literally and figuratively occupied the same sphere as other fantastic creatures. His fairies, devils, and spirits are all composed from the same airy magic and dissolve into the netherworld before first light. In one sense, he means these spirits are literally air (like the ghosts of our popular fiction) and in a figurative sense he means they are lacking in seriousness—airy like the stuff of our abstract thoughts. He uses the uniqueness of this wording to depict the creative and eccentric nature of writing and to play on the dubious nature of the fantastic. The force of his observation was not lost on future generations. An anonymous writer in *Maine Farmer and Mechanics Advocate* appropriates his language and uses it to dismiss the ghost in children's folklore as remnants of superstitious nonsense, which "few well informed persons are much troubled by" ("A Ghost Story—for the Young" 4). To resolve these "airy nothings" and simultaneously quench the child's "desire to read very marvelous stories relative to ghosts, witches, haunted houses, and leagues with the devil" (4), American publishers for children established the mock ghost story to dismiss superstitions about ghosts by making the insubstantial substantial: the figure at the foot of the bed transforms into a coat mistakenly

The Children's Ghost Story in America

left on the corner of a chair; footsteps in the night are mice in the attic; and voices in the dark are caused by gusts of wind or creaky floorboards. In many of these cases, the extent to which authors of these children's tales would go to disprove the ghost almost results in a conclusion as illogical as the ghost itself—mice hardly sound like footsteps and gusts of wind rarely speak in complete sentences. The mock ghost story for children often defied the very logical moral it sought to uphold: that supernatural ghost stories are harmful to children because they foster irrational fears. While these stories may have been intended to undermine supernatural ghost stories, the irony is that the mock ghost story, whether intentional or not, did more to establish the ghost story tradition in children's literature than any other agent. It allowed the ghost telling tradition to materialize on the scene for children, to appear in print on the pages of their favorite or *their* parent's favorite periodicals.

While children's periodicals and other youth publications proved profitable during the nineteenth century, authors of children's literature often felt anxiety about their work in the genre, which increasingly met with criticism in the United States and elsewhere as the century progressed. In *Kiddie Lit: The Cultural Construction of Children's Literature*, Beverly Lyon Clark argues that academic and literary elites largely shunned the genre as the turn of the century neared, typically refusing to include such authors in the newly emerging academic canon (76). In *Twain, Alcott, and the Birth of the Adolescent Reform Novel*, Roberta Seelinger Trites notices authorial anxiety about children's literature happening earlier in nineteenth-century American literature. She indicates Louisa May Alcott and Mark Twain feared the children's author label might damage their literary image and even the sales of their more adult oriented works (130–36). Anxiety over the merit of children's literature might explain the frequency of anonymous works or works printed under aliases in popular children's periodicals as well. Many of the mock ghost stories for children appeared under aliases—Aunt Sue, The Exile, L, and so on—or without the authors named identified, which might indicate a fear of being associated with children's writing or possibly even the ghost story genre. Such unidentified tales appeared in even the most popular of children's periodicals.

In the United States, *The Youth's Companion* and *St. Nicholas; An Illustrated Magazine for Young Folks* easily dominated the children's

1. The Mock Ghost Story

publishing market of the nineteenth century. The success and influence of these children's periodicals has been noted by children's literature scholars. Martin Gardner, in "John Martin's Book: An Almost Forgotten Children's Magazine," acknowledges the significance of these periodicals in publishing for children in the nineteenth and twentieth centuries, particularly *St. Nicholas*, which he argues is "[b]y far the most influential" (145–46). These two periodicals had a powerful influence over the children's publishing industry, and their influence helped shape future incarnations of the ghost story for children. The mock ghost story occurred somewhat regularly in *The Youth's Companion, St. Nicholas*, and other popular periodicals for children, often emerging two or three times every few years in each periodical and generally under simple, generic titles—"A Ghost Story" or "A Haunted House." While the adult ghost-story-telling tradition might have flourished over Christmas,[2] the mock ghost story for children seems to have known no seasonal regularity. It appeared all year round with little concentration during any particular holiday or time of year. The quality of writing in these stories varies considerably. Some of the stories, particularly the anonymous ones, tend to lack strong narrative form and occasionally contain inconsistencies, frequently relying on heavy-handed morals or comic endings to round off the story. These tales typically draw from real-life experiences or oral traditions and intermittently take the form of letters to the editor; however, almost all of these mock ghost stories for children—at least all but an odd few, which I will explore later—maintain one very common trait: all will conclude their narrative with the specter revealed as a fraud.

Making the Ghost Tangible

"When you hear a ghost, children," proclaims the author Aunt Sue at the end of her tale, "be sure there is a 'loop-hole' *somewhere*" (171; original emphasis). The advice Aunt Sue provides in her story "The Haunted House"—published in *Merry's Museum, Parley's Magazine, Woodworth's Cabinet, and the Schoolfellow*, 1861—is echoed throughout the ghost-story publishing tradition for children in nineteenth-century America. In many of these tales, as in the one above, it is not merely sufficient to simply disprove the ghost by the end, but it is also necessary to confirm the specter's removal with a direct moral denouncing even the possibility of believing in ghosts. Aunt Sue even goes to the trouble of emphasizing the important words in her moral: "a 'loophole' *somewhere*" (171). She quickly follows this summation with an even more direct pronouncement, reminding the reader that Susan, the young protagonist in her tale, learned not "to attribute *supposed supernatural effects* to *natural causes*" (171; original emphasis). Thus, the intangible ghost is made tangible and the reader, presumably a child, is taught the absurdity of believing in spirits and haunted places.

A similar occurrence takes place at the beginning of "Ghost Stories" (1855) by The Exile in *The Youth's Companion*, where the author frames her narrative with a rationalist moral before even beginning her tale:

> I wonder if there are any young people, readers of the pleasant "companion" [*The Youth's Companion*], who really believe in ghosts. There are few believers, I think, in such things, in the present enlightened age; but many children are told silly stories by nurses and others, and they creep close to each other when they hear unusual noises, and run and scream if they are left accidentally in the dark, and do a great many foolish things, that would seem to themselves ridiculous if they would exercise reason, and quietly reflect instead of running and screaming [182].

The rationalist thread at the beginning of this tale is unmistakable. The author annihilates any chance of the supernatural ghost before the story begins. These hefty morals often preface or conclude the ghost stories printed in many children's periodicals of nineteenth-century America. While not all the stories went to the extremes as the examples above, most rely on such direct and overt morals to make sure the child does not confuse the point of the story.

"A Ghost Story," a tale published anonymously in *The Youth's Companion* in February of 1865, is another prime example of the typical ghost story found in these children's periodicals. It recounts the ghostly tale of a New England family from the days of the Salem witch trials. This family believes their home is haunted when a mysterious and noisy clanking begins on the second floor of their home. Fearing for their safety, the family calls upon the help of Mr. Snooks, the school master, who arrives at the home to exorcise the ghost from the premise. When he opens the door to the supposedly haunted room, a hog—which had snuck upstairs to eat their corn supplies—runs him over (26). While

1. The Mock Ghost Story

this particular story lacks the overt moral common to many of these tales, it does attempt to reinforce the ridiculousness of ghost belief through the comic ending. The family and Mr. Snooks are made fools by their superstition. It is also important to note the significance of this story taking place during the Salem witch trials, arguably the most tragic consequence of a literal belief in superstition in American history and might indicate why American children's literature adamantly attempted to divert any possibility in ghost belief.

The Influence of the Salem Witch Trials on American Literature

The literary influence of the Salem witch trials in nineteenth-century America appear prominently in crucial works by Nathaniel Hawthorne, where the superstitious history of Salem and its tragic consequences echo with a sense of eerie nearness. "Young Goodman Brown" (1835), one of Hawthorne's best remembered short stories, exploits the symbolic loss of faith through his characters Goodman and Faith, who themselves are ironic symbols for the precepts they personify. Goodman, out on a walk through the woods, is tempted by a coven of powerful witches, who almost manage to convince Goodman to participate in a satanic ritual, which is narrowly prevented by the appearance of his wife Faith being tempted as well (744). When at the end of the story Goodman discovers Faith as susceptible to evil and corruption as himself, he awakens to a world of doubt and self-loathing and dies in "gloom" (744). *The House of the Seven Gables* (1851), which Edward Bever calls Hawthorne's "Salem book" (465), is arguably in part a ghost story as well as a possible tale of witchcraft. While the story never specifically indicates it is set in Salem, Massachusetts, many hints to this conclusion are embedded in the novel's narrative, particularly in the character of Matthew Maule, who curses the Pyncheon family upon his execution for witchcraft and whose name happens to match a person actually in Salem during the witch trials (Hawthorne 7; Felt 232–33). The curse placed on the Pyncheon family and the fulfillment of that curse as Hawthorne's novel unfolds yields both supernatural and ghostly elements, particularly in the mysterious murder of Colonel

The Children's Ghost Story in America

Pyncheon (which hints at a spectral murderer) and the subsequent hardships of his descendants (Hawthorne 13).

While many of Hawthorne's works of fiction make ready use of the supernatural, they also carry within them many negative critiques of the supernatural's influence on the lives of his characters. In "Young Goodman Brown" and *The House of the Seven Gables*, the supernatural seems directly tied to wickedness: only terrible occurrences seem to arise from meddling in superstition and magic. Furthermore, the association of corruption and greed in these works to the Salem witch trials also suggests powerful warnings about belief or interest in the supernatural and the ability of those in power to abuse that interest. This sentiment is perhaps best expressed in one of Hawthorne's most memorable segments from *The House of the Seven Gables*:

> Old Mathew Maule, in a word, was executed for the crime of witchcraft. He was one of the martyrs to that terrible delusion which should teach us, among its other morals, that the influential classes, and those who take upon themselves to be leaders of the people, are fully liable to all the passionate error that has ever characterized the maddest mob [7].

Hawthorne makes clear the potential for power and the possibility of the powerful to use superstition for evil purposes. His references to the abuse of passion and mob frenzy link witchcraft—the supernatural—to madness and evil. It is not surprising then that "Young Goodman Brown" and *The House of the Seven Gables* remain ambiguous about the possibility of the supernatural in their narratives: Goodman Brown may have dreamed the incident with the coven (744) and the murder of Colonel Pyncheon may have been caused by a shadowy figure seen fleeing before the body's discovery (13). Hawthorne leaves in these narratives the definite possibility of logical explanations for all that occurs, which means that the same rationalist thread which can be found in ghost stories for American children at the time could also be found in Hawthorne's works. Marion Gibson argues Hawthorne, among other writers, searched for the "nostalgic gothic or rationalist lessons for American modernity" in writing about Salem, making this possibility of a rationalist thread running through these works very possible (88).

Mrs. Eliza A. Harriman's "A Ghost Story," published in 1870 in the pages of *The Little Corporal: An Illustrated Magazine for Boys and Girls*, roughly two decades after the publication of *The House of the Seven*

1. The Mock Ghost Story

Gables, offers another account of a false apparition that appears in the region of Salem during the time of the witch trials. The tale recounts the unplanned heroic efforts of a young man to unravel a ghost mystery. Shortly after the death of "old Mr. Smithers," an elderly man of the town, a mysterious specter is seen haunting his grave. Amos, the story's young protagonist, is much too infatuated with a girl he is courting to be deterred by rumors of the ghost. He passes the graveyard on his return and encounters a terrifying sight, which fills him with dread:

> [W]hen morning hours grew small, out all alone amid the darkness, he found himself plump up beside the graveyard, and there, in full view, on the haunted tomb, stretched at full length, beneath the glimmering stars, he plainly saw the silent, shrouded ghost. At once his gentle visions fled, his teeth chattered just a little, his heart beat a little faster, but he did not run, nor shriek, nor faint, but scaling, silently, the intervening fence, he walked in to reconnoiter [5].

When Amos reaches the tomb, he quickly discovers that the ghost is nothing more than a white turkey nesting in the soft soil of the recently covered grave (5). Despite the ghost's comic unveiling, the fear incited by the appearance of the ghost produces a very authentic effect. The story being set around the town of Salem also suggests a level of discomfort or nostalgia over the potential for superstitions to go awry, which might account for the setting's appearance in both Hawthorne's fiction and the two children's stories identified above. It is likely that the references to Salem in these narratives are not coincidental, but rather the result of a well-placed device to further deter belief in superstition by citing one of the most deplorable occurrences of superstition in American history. The reference to Salem in children's fiction of the time, combined with these tales' chiding of ghost believers, sends a very powerful message about the status of ghosts in American fiction for children during the nineteenth century.

Repressing the Ghost with Uncanny Results

Some scholars and writers studying the history of children's ghost stories have noticed this tendency to block the supernatural ghost and the gothic in children's literature of the nineteenth century. In "Gothic and the Child Reader, 1764–1850," M. O. Grenby argues that "[c]hildren's

The Children's Ghost Story in America

literature and Gothic literature were 'two contrary states,' to use William Blake's subtitle from *Songs of Innocence and of Experience* (1789–94): opposites that were nevertheless necessary to one another, each representing precisely what the other was not" (243). Dale Townshend, perhaps the most accomplished scholars thus far on the issue, firmly asserts this trend of "barring" the ghost in the eighteenth and nineteenth from the child reader (21). Charmette Kendrick, in her article "The Goblins Will Get You! Horror in Children's Literature from the Nineteenth Century," reaches a similar conclusion: "In nineteenth-century England and America, most scary stories written and published for the young had two purposes—to indoctrinate youngsters with the morals of the day and to expose superstition as a false belief system perpetuated by the foolish and the wicked" (20). Philippa Pearce, an accomplished contemporary children's author, remarks on this trend as well in her introduction to *A Century of Children's Ghost Stories*, where she admits her frustration at being unable to find a supernatural ghost story before the twentieth century (xix). Pearce, unlike Kendrick and Townshend, suspects that publishers and authors withheld the ghost for more reasons than a fear of frightening or corrupting the child with superstition. She contends that "[t]here was a continuing unwillingness of adults to admit that most children wanted—perhaps *needed*—the experience of safe fear and of a certain kind of awe" (xvi). She seems to suggest that eighteenth- and nineteenth-century England and America maintained a kind of denial about the obvious developmental needs of the child. However, despite this need for supernatural fear, children's authors "censored themselves" (xvi), which left the supernatural ghost with little haunting ground in probably one of the most pivotal centuries for children's literature in America and England.

To take Pearce's argument a step further, nineteenth-century American children likely needed a healthy sense of the uncanny in their stories, and perhaps the mock ghost story for children attempted to provide a premature outlet for the uncanny in these periodicals. Sigmund Freud offers perhaps the most famous theoretical account of the uncanny. In his work "The Uncanny," Freud investigates the origin and meaning of the word *unheimlich* (uncanny) by comparing it to its opposite *heimlich* (canny) and notes the uncanny's relation "to the realm of the frightening, of what evokes fear and dread" (123). His investigation leads him

1. The Mock Ghost Story

to explore a number of possible definitions for the uncanny[3]; however, the most useful and succinct definition he offers for the purpose of analyzing ghost stories is likely the following: "the uncanny is that species of the frightening that goes back to what was once well known and had long been familiar" (124). In *The Location of Culture*, Homi K. Bhabha offers a useful understanding of this complex dichotomy, where he calls "the uncanny sameness-in-difference," which further distinguishes Freud's definition (54). Ghosts, of course, fit within "that species of the frightening" and "sameness-in-difference" rather precisely; ghosts are the very shadows of the human form once known and familiar. The ghost's ability to negotiate the border between the known and the unknown conjures the greatest feelings of dread from their appearance to the living: it is that quality of the familiar—the comfortable, the safe—that makes the ghost so eerie.

Ghosts, whether well intentioned or malevolent, seemingly have the ability to terrify and torment by their mere existence. They shake the foundation of some of the human psyche's safest precepts, the fixed border between life and death, which is why their appearance has both a shocking effect on the characters witnessing the ghost as well as the audience observing the event; thus, the ghost's terrifying nature seems to hail from the act of appearance and the effect of that appearance. In "Uncanny Hauntings, Canny Children," Anna Jackson suggests that uncanniness is linked to the situation and effect produced from a situation:

> since the quality of uncanniness seems to belong to a situation or event, as an *effect* the situation or event produces, whereas canniness is a quality that properly belongs to a person. It might make sense, however, to understand the uncanny as that which cannot be understood cannily; as those events, situations or phenomena that do not allow for a knowing, sagacious, shrewd, and astute reading of them [158; original emphasis].

For Jackson, it seems the uncanny occurs as the consequence of an event rather than as a trait of the event itself, which means the uncanny rises from within the psyche of the canny observer. Ghosts, then, are not uncanny but rather spur the uncanny within canny characters and audiences. It is likely that this quality of uncanniness drives both the supernatural and mock ghost story and perhaps links the two to the same tradition. While mock ghost stories for children may have sought to reject superstition and out the ghost, these stories still allowed the

The Children's Ghost Story in America

elements of the ghost story tradition's uncanniness to shine through: the same uncanny thoughts are provoked in mock ghost story as are produced in a supernatural ghost story. The only difference is that the supernatural ghost story appears to fully embrace the uncanny, where the mock ghost story cultivates the uncanny only to discard it later.

A prime example of this phenomenon in the mock ghost story for children occurs in N.Y. Presbyterian's "A Ghost Story," published in *The Youth's Companion* in 1864, which depicts the uncanny experience of a well-to-do American family. The tale begins by drawing heavily from the ghost-story-telling tradition. Three travelers—a man and two women—stop for an evening's hospitality and lodging at the home of a respected acquaintance, Mr. and Mrs. Judge Blank.[4] Mr. Blank tells the ghost story by the fireside before everyone retires for the night; Judge Blank relates the story of his young child's untimely death and the child's perceived return from the dead the night of "its" funeral. To capture the full effect of the story, it is necessary to quote at length from the text. Mr. Blank describes the encounter with the ghost thusly:

> Raising my head, my blood froze within me, and the hair upon my head stood up as I saw the little thing in grave clothes, with open, but manifestly sightless eyes, and pale as when we gave it the last kiss, walking slowly towards us! Had I been alone—had not the extreme terror of my wife compelled me to play the man, I should have leaped from the window and bed without casting a look behind. But, not daring to leave her in such terror, I arose, sat down in a chair and took the little creature between my knees—a cold sweat covering my body—and gazed with feelings unutterable upon the object before me. The eyes were open in a vacant stare; the flesh colorless, cold and clammy; nor did the child seem to have the power either of speech or hearing, as it made no attempt to answer any of our questions. The horror of our minds was the more intense as we had watched our child through its sickness and death, and had been but a few hours before eyewitnesses of its interment.
>
> While gazing upon it, and asking in my thoughts, "what can this extraordinary providence mean? For what can it be sent?" the servant girl: having crept to the door, after a time suggested, "It looks like Mr.—'s child." Now, our next neighbor had a child of nearly the same age as ours, and its constant companion. But what could bring it to our house at that hour, and in such plight? Still the suggestion had operated as a powerful sedative upon our excited feelings, and rendered us more capable of calm reflection. And, after a time, we discovered in truth that the grave clothes were night clothes, and the corpse a somnambulist! And it became manifest that it was the excitement attending the loss and burial of its playmate, working upon the child's mind in sleep, to which we were indebted for his untimely and startling visit [sic] [90].

1. The Mock Ghost Story

The arrival of the ghost and Mr. and Mrs. Blank's reaction to the ghost suggest many fascinating readings, but perhaps the most interesting is the couple's inability to identify their own child, who has only been absent from their lives for a short time. It is hard to believe that any parent could fail to recognize their child in such close quarters or that their first reaction at seeing their departed child would be dread rather than joy. Mr. Blank also manages to depersonalize his story even further by leaving his child and the neighbor child both nameless and genderless until nearly the end of his tale, essentially stripping them of any qualities of personhood. The effect is quite uncanny. The thing or "it" that walks in on them is both familiar and strange. The child possesses the familiar qualities of their recently deceased son and the otherworldly attributes of a lifeless corpse. When the "thing" is revealed to be the neighbor's boy, the effect of this uncanny incident does not diminish. These characters experience the uncanny long before the ending will demystify the apparition. The uncanny is thus pure effect, remaining unaltered regardless of the absence of a genuine supernatural ghost. The experience of the frightening then, as Jackson has indicated, is the crux of the uncanny in the ghost story (158).

The false apparition in this story also operates well within the parameters of Freud's famous "double" or *doppelgänger*. The double is an essential component to Freud's theory of the uncanny: the appearance of a person or entity that is practically identical psychologically or physically to another, often eerily assuming any number of its counterpart's characteristics, behaviors, and thoughts. Freud argues that the immortal soul is the first iteration of the double, created as "an insurance against the extinction of the self" or rather "as a defence against annihilation" (142). The double therefore is a "primitive" function of the psyche, an archaic remnant of a forgotten coping mechanism. Terry Castle describes its connection to the uncanny brilliantly in *The Female Thermometer: Eighteenth-Century Culture and the Invention of the Uncanny*:

> What makes the *doppelgänger* now seem uncanny (a "ghastly harbinger of death") is precisely the fact that we have grown out of that "very early mental stage" when the double functioned as a figure of existential reassurance—just as human culture as a whole has moved beyond the animistic beliefs characteristic of "primitive" or magic-based societies like that of the ancient Egyptians [9].

The Children's Ghost Story in America

This repressed desire to double provides the foundation for the Blanks' uncanny experience. They project the familiar characteristics of their child onto the childlike figure that enters their room, but the knowledge of their child's death is unshakable, thus creating the uncanny effect: the familiar aspects of their child are overshadowed by the horrific realization of his death. This reaction prevents them from realizing the truth—that the child entering the room could not logically be their son—or possibly even from seeing the differences in the specter and their deceased child. This experience of the uncanny is relatively the same in mock ghost stories as it is in almost all forms of the supernatural ghost story—the unsettling recognition of an illogical occurrence that leads to a deep sense of dread. As such, the uncanny is an essential element to almost any kind of ghost story.

There are other aspects of the Blanks' reaction to the ghost/son/neighbor that are also quite uncanny but for far different reasons. Their reaction to seeing what they believe is a ghost falls quite in line with the horror any average person would experience under the same circumstances, yet their dehumanizing depictions of their son and neighbor are uncanny for far different reasons. Judge Blank never gives the children (presumably boys) names or refers to them with gendered pronouns at any point in the story—with the exception of one sentence, where the word "his" in reference to the neighbor's child unconsciously seems to slip out amongst a sentence filled with *it*s (Presbyterian 90). Judge Blank refuses to gender or characterize his child as a person even in the passages preceding his child's death, which would likely strike most readers, particularly contemporary readers, as very odd and impersonal. He almost seems a stranger to his own child, which in itself seems uncanny. Parents should know and recognize their children; that he does not suggests a violation of the familiar, the canny, but such characterizations of children were not uncommon for the Victorian age and earlier. "[T]oday's readers may be shocked if an author refers to the child with the pronoun 'it,'" argues Margarita Georgieva in *The Gothic Child*, "[b]ut it was not unusual in the eighteenth century and there are numerous reasons for the practice" (1). While Georgieva's assertion is correct, the narrative's continued objectification of the boy in other areas of the tale produces an unsettling effect, one likely even detectable within the nineteenth century.

1. The Mock Ghost Story

The lack of affection and familiarity Mr. Blank shows with his own child might reflect his social status as a presumably wealthy gentleman. As an upper class family, Judge Blank and his wife may have left the rearing of their child solely to servants, perhaps the very same servant who correctly identifies the ghost as their neighbor's child near the end of the story. This commentary on the upper class is not wholly absent in the ghostly tales of the time. N.Y. Presbyterian's "A Ghost Story" shares many thematic qualities with Henry James' 1898 ghostly novel *The Turn of the Screw*. While *The Turn of the Screw* is published much later and is not aimed at children, the famous novel does offer a commentary on the dynamics between masters and servants, the upper and lower class, particularly the relationship between servants and their young wards (or rather their young masters), which gives it a striking similarity to Presbyterian's ghost story for children.

In *The Turn of the Screw*, the servants and governess seem solely responsible for raising the children. Their uncle, their only living parental figure and guardian, does not even reside in the same home as the children but rather remains away for the entire story; such circumstances of childrearing for the upper class in the novel are made to seem fairly common, but such practices of parenting have an uncanny effect on the reading of the story, which perhaps suggests a critique of upper class childrearing. *The Turn of the Screw*, like Presbyterian's "A Ghost Story," seems to expose division amongst the classes and inadvertently or purposely criticize the practices of the upper class, particularly in regards to child rearing. The uncle who abandons his niece and nephew in his country home in *The Turn of the Screw* and the Blank's inability to recognize or personify their child are striking commentaries on the nineteenth century's upper class culture's perceived failure to form loving relationships with their children. Each of these stories also suggests that the children establish these loving relationships with the servants caring for them: the dead servants Peter Quint and Miss Jessel in *The Turn of the Screw* and the servant who correctly identifies the child in "A Ghost Story" seem far likelier to have established close relations with the children than the parents.

Aside from the issue of child rearing, the issue of social mobility and class strife lurks beneath the lines of many ghost stories of the late nineteenth and early twentieth centuries. In "Economic Hauntings:

The Children's Ghost Story in America

Wealth and Class in Edith Wharton's Ghost Stories," Karen J. Jacobsen observes the consistent themes of class in many of Edith Wharton's ghost stories, insisting that they "exhibit anxiety over money and class" (100). In "'They don't much count, do they?' The Unfinished History of *The Turn of the Screw*," Bruce Robbins comments on the novel's obsession with the distinctions between the classes. "In order to be a horror," Robbins observes,

> it appears, there is no need of supernatural props or special effects, no need to be a ghost at all. It is enough to occupy a gentleman's place, or wear his clothes, without being a gentleman. Here the governess as much as admits that in her mind, supernatural evil cannot be readily distinguished from the "unnaturalness" of servants stepping out of their designated place [381].

Robbins' observations about *The Turn of the Screw* suggest another possible reading of the uncanny entering into the story. The very act of servants pushing beyond their class expectations stirs feelings of "unnaturalness," which can easily be seen as a segue into the uncanny. His assertions about the uncanniness of this border between the classes are corroborated by Guy Davidson, who notes the uncanny effect of the governess assuming the liminal position between master of the house and servant (460–61). Robbins explores this idea further in the following: "The story's willingness to consider the ghosts less as supernatural phenomena than as social phenomena, and more particularly as a servant and a governess who refuse to be bound by their station, can also be deduced from the circumstances in which the ghosts are made to appear" (381). Here, Robbins seems to tie ghostliness and possibly the uncanny to the effects the ghosts produce, whether real or not. His reading strengthens the likelihood that the uncanny can form a solid connection between the supernatural and mock ghost story because both stories rely on the uncanny to create the feeling of shock and horror needed to propel the narrative forward.

Other instances of uncanny ghosts—even if not supernatural—abound in children's periodicals of the nineteenth century. George Cooper's "A Ghost Story," a poem published in *The Little Corporal: An Illustrated Magazine for Boys and Girls* in 1871, shows another occasion where parents mistake the identity of their child in a ghostly situation. The poem begins with the child begging his father to tell his ghost story. The father complies with his son's request, saying, "Then climb

1. The Mock Ghost Story

on my knee, little darling, / And mind you are still as a mouse, / While I tell of a ghost I encountered / One evening in this very house" (Cooper 43). The father then describes his harrowing trek one night through a snowstorm to reach home. When he enters his house, he is met by an uncanny sight:

> A silent form looking upon me,
> Pure white from the head to the feet!
> With fair hair drooped over its shoulders—
> A ghost! every item complete!

Not only do the specter's features offer a glimpse into the uncanny, but so does its method of travel for "This airy form glided before; / Then scampered away in the darkness, / And fled thro' an opening door" (43). The "airy form," however, is nothing more than his son in his "white cap and night gown" (43). While the father in this story confuses his son momentarily with a specter, his account of the tale produces only a brief uncanny effect. The father is initially frightened by the appearance of the ghost, but his fear quickly vanishes when he recognizes the specter's true nature—that of his beloved son. Unlike N.Y. Presbyterian's "A Ghost Story," Cooper's "A Ghost Story" does not stir feelings of alienation or terror. The poem—providing a tight structure and easy rhythm—also detracts from the uncanny, trapping it within a short line. The appearance of the uncanny is simply too brief. The ghost is unmasked much too quickly to produce the full uncanny effect, yet the presence of the uncanny still remains a principle feature of the narrative. Without the possibility of a specter, the poem lacks its primary narrative drive.

Cooper's tale, contrary to Presbyterian's, also carries much more of an endearing quality. The relationship between child and parent seems stronger at the end of the story. The father's failure to recognize his son becomes an opportunity for bonding through the telling of the story in Cooper's tale, which is exactly the opposite of what seems to occur in Presbyterian's tale, where the parents' alienation only seems to widen when the servant reveals their mistake. While it is difficult to discern social class in Cooper's tale, there are some indications that Cooper's characters are more likely to occupy a lower class position. The informality of language, such as the uses of idioms like "momma" and "papa" (43), and that the father walks through the snowy wilds without the aid of a horse or buggy in the late evening are possible indications of lower class status. If Cooper's characters are indeed of the lower class, the dichotomy the two stories produce demonstrates an interesting commentary on the relationships between parents and children within the different social strata in nineteenth-century America. While this analysis is mostly speculative, it is worth pondering this comparison considering how many ghost stories of this era tended to focus on issues of class.

Ghosts as Social Agents

Some of the ghost stories published for children in nineteenth-century America also explore other significant social issues of the time. Uncle James' "The Haunted Cabin: A Georgia Ghost Story," published in *The Youth's Companion* in 1865, touches on the subject of slavery, the most pressing issue of the nineteenth century for Americans. The tale begins at a boardinghouse in Augusta, Georgia, where the narrator of the tale and his family are staying. One night, as the boarders assemble around the fireplace, the landlord tells the tale of a haunted cabin (178). He recalls how a local drunkard worked up the nerve one night after drinking to capture the ghost. As he approaches the cabin on horseback, he spots the form of the ghost in the path before him; the ghost appears to be a white corpse with no detectable limbs or head. The horse is frightened and refuses to budge, but the drunkard feels no fear and strikes the specter with his whip. When the whip makes contact with the supposed ghost, the drunkard feels emboldened and pursues the specter on foot. When he finally tackles the ghost, he quickly discovers the specter is actually an escaped slave who had been pretending to be a ghost to scare away the locals (178).

While the landlord chuckles as he recalls this tale, the story contains elements that appall most contemporary readers and possibly many readers even at the time of publication. The language and descriptions in the story are quite racially charged, enough so that even the author attempts to offer an explanation for the crude nature of the language used. Uncle James or the editor has inserted an asterisk over the word "buck-nigger" to clarify his distaste for the word. Here is how

1. The Mock Ghost Story

the footnote for the asterisk reads: "As this story is given just as it was told at the time, I do not feel at liberty to suppress this coarse Georgia phrase" (178). The footnote signifies the apprehension circulating around issues of slavery and racism. Given the tale's November 9, 1865, publication, the final year of the Civil War, it is not surprising, then, to see elements in the tale that would create tensions, especially given the tale's harsh language and indifferent stance to the plight of fugitive slaves. The delight the landlord takes in the ghost's unmasking pales before the tragic circumstance of the fugitive slave—the slave who had so cleverly evaded the authorities for four years just to be captured by a drunkard and returned to slavery or worse. Even the circumstance and manner of his capture alludes to the brutality of his fate: the drunkard uses a whip to subdue him and reveal his ruse, which disturbingly echoes the fate of the slave after his capture. The details of the fugitive slave's ghostly ruse also display embedded racist descriptions. His ghostly costume is rather a lack of a costume. The reason why the fugitive slave appears as a torso with neither head nor limbs is because of his blackness. "He was as black as coal," recounts the landlord. "Every night he used to walk about with nothin' but his shirt on, and he frightened the folks round there out of their five sense!" (178). The emphasis on his blackness here reveals the landlord's complete indifference to the fugitive slave's plight. The slave's blackness not only identifies him as a slave, but it also renders him literally and figuratively invisible in the story.

While "The Haunted Cabin" is not a progressive story for the time, it does share some elements with more canonical pieces of nineteenth-century American literature that did offer a progressive, abolitionist tone. The title "The Haunted Cabin" bears resemblance to Harriet Beecher Stowe's *Uncle Tom's Cabin*, which, as the bestselling American novel of the nineteenth century, would have been almost instantly associated with the title (Ammons ix). The Civil War also had a significant influence on ghost stories of other canonized writers of the nineteenth century. Ambrose Bierce, arguably one of the most prominent of these writers, wrote a number of ghost stories that deal with the effects of the Civil War; however, Bierce's ghost stories rarely contend with issues of racism and slavery, but rather with the immorality, degradation, and malevolence the war produced. E. F. Bleiler argues that Bierce selected

Civil War stories because they "serve as horror-bearers" and foster "incest; the murder of a parent, with erotic overtones; the feeling of aloneness; the physical resurrection of the soulless and often malevolent dead; the power of a diseased mind to destroy itself; and the worthlessness of most human virtues" (xv). These themes and characterizations arise in a number of Bierce's ghost stories. "An Occurrence at Owl Creek Bridge," one of Bierce's more anthologized ghost stories, features many of the ideas Bleiler lists; however, it is also a rarity among these stories in that it also features a slaveholding protagonist and deals with issues of race. Peyton Farquhar, the protagonist, is "a well-to-do planter, of an old and highly-respected Alabama family" and more importantly a slave owner, who is captured attempting to destroy a bridge the Union Army plans to cross (115). He is sentenced to death by hanging on the very bridge he planned to destroy and escapes—or fails to escape—in a rather extraordinary way. Whether the result of convulsions from his neck being snapped or an out-of-body-experience, Peyton embarks on a daring escape through the stream and forest, only to vanish as he crosses the threshold of his home. The story ends thusly: "Peyton Farquhar was dead; his body, with a broken neck, swung gently from side to side beneath the timbers of the Owl Creek bridge" (120). His tale, whether supernatural or otherwise, demonstrates the persistence of social brutalities—Civil War and slavery—lurking behind the scenes of the nineteenth-century ghost story, which might explain its appearance in children's stories like "The Haunted Cabin," but his tale also reveals that ghost stories—even mock ghost stories for children—can engage some of the most complex social brutalities of their day.

Anomalous Specters

The mock children's ghost stories covered thus far have all followed a conventional unmasking formula while otherwise sharing many settings, themes, and effects in common with the nineteenth-century supernatural ghost story marketed or written for adults; however, it is also prudent to address some of the ghost stories that defy the formula or actively occupy the border between the adult and child audiences. Through these non-formulaic or rather unconventional

1. The Mock Ghost Story

children's ghost stories of the nineteenth century, the motivations and concerns of adults writing and publishing for children in this genre can be more easily understood and investigated. For instance, some mock ghost stories, or rather a small few, defy the conventions and decentralize the heavy-handed rationalist morals attached to many mock ghost stories found in American children's periodicals of 1800s. In "A Ghost Story," a tale published in *The Youth's Companion* in 1870, Lucius Goss offers a mock ghost story that avoids overtly mocking the protagonist despite his fear when confronting the mock ghost. Willie is a studious young boy on his way home from an evening spelling bee when he encounters what looks like the specter of a crazy woman floating in the cemetery near his home. After collapsing in fear trying to flee the ghostly fiend, he discovers that the specter is nothing more than an optical illusion created by a mixture of snow and light shining through the trees. Mock ghost stories typically portray the ghost believer as a false role model to better serve the moral of the story (i.e., they are miscreant children, folksy nannies, sleepwalkers, or drunkards), but this mock ghost story defies the formula by featuring an obedient and studious child falling prey to a mock ghost. The story further breaks with convention by next asking the reader to see events through Willie's eyes: "And you, too, reader, may see it, if you will examine the picture closely" (43–44?). While the confrontation with the mock ghost does produce a comic effect, the story directly asks the reader to imagine being in the protagonists shoes and understanding his predicament. This attempt to sympathize with the protagonist both undermines and distracts from the typical moral of a mock ghost story for children, but this story is not the only mock ghost story to defy convention.

These early attempts to deviate from the standard possibly represent the first foray into exploring the supernatural ghost for children, albeit a very benign version of the supernatural ghost. This deviation typically happened in four ways: leaving the intended audience for the story rather ambiguous, often through the use of clever narration or publication through a non-children's periodical or book; using the ghost as metaphor or in some other non-literal capacity; using anthropomorphic characters in place of human characters; and, in the case of one story, seemingly allowing the possibility of a ghost to remain by an act of omission. Since the latter tale falls more firmly within the

The Children's Ghost Story in America

The illustration shows Willie encountering the false specter in "A Ghost Story" (*The Youth's Companion*, 1870) by Lucius Goss. The outline of a very tall woman appears between the trees and temporarily tricks Willie into seeing a ghost. The image captures the essence of the mock ghost story—where the impractical and unlikely are used to explain away the supernatural ghost—and shows the genre's incorporation of classic ghostly settings and tropes even with the absence of a supernatural ghost.

conventions than the rest, it seems the best place to begin exploring the anomalous appearance of the supernatural ghost in fiction for nineteenth-century American children.

In 1895, just before the turn of the century, Hezekiah Butterworth, a prominent children's author and editor, published "Elder Leland's Ghost" in his collection *Elder Leland's Ghost and Other Stories for Boys*.[5] "Elder Leland's Ghost," the only ghost story in the anthology, is

1. *The Mock Ghost Story*

a rarity among children's ghost stories for its time of publication for one minor but significant deviation in the conclusion of its narrative: the possibility of a ghost is not completely eradicated—although the plausibility of its existence may be strongly doubted. The possibility of the ghost survives principally in the final lines of the story, where ironically ghosts in other mock ghost stories are decidedly ousted: "Two mysteries were explained, but Elder Leland's ghost story remains a mystery still" (31). The possible authenticity of Elder Leland's ghost lays the foundation for the child to perceive a supernatural ghost in the story, but the possibility of a specter might be negated by the story's harsh lesson about the potential of being duped.

Sweet Billy, the story's protagonist, is a town prankster. He and other Cheshire boys manage to deceive many in the town, including Elder Leland, regarding the possibility of legitimate ghost sightings. The first prank involves Sweet Billy and a few of the other Cheshire boys, who decide one night, seemingly on a whim, to pretend to be the spirit of God appearing before a local boarder, Peter Gates. The boys feel Gates has outstayed his welcome. Gates believes the ruse and quickly spreads the rumor around town (10–12). Emboldened by his success, and Elder Leland's story about a haunted spinner wheel, Sweet Billy fabricates yet another story, where he claims to have seen one of the horses of the American Revolution appear before him (12). The townsfolk readily believe these stories and accept them as further evidence in the existence of ghosts and profits. When on Thanksgiving many years later one of Sweet Billy's ruses fails, he reveals his deceptions and begs for forgiveness, expecting also to hear Elder Leland claim his spinner wheel ghost to be a fabrication as well; however, to Sweet Billy's astonishment, Elder Leland claims the sounds of a spinner wheel pursing him and his wife—on separate occasions—truly occurred (28–30).

Whether Butterworth intends children to see Elder Leland's tale as too ridiculous to be true is difficult to ascertain from the narrative itself, but Elder Leland's sketchy evidence and his almost comic description of the sound as a "whir-r, whir-r, whir-r-r-r-r" does lend some credence to this notion (28). Elder Leland does adopt some of the absurd qualities common to the mock ghost story for children. His fleeing this "whir-r, whir-r, whir-r-r-r-r" produces a clear comic tone, not a fearful

The Children's Ghost Story in America

one. It also seems many adult readers of the time may have reached this conclusion as well. In "'The Children Love Them': Paper No. III.—Hezekiah Butterworth," published in *The Interior* 1895, Harriette Knight Smith, offering a brief review of "Elder Leland's Ghost," remarks that "now even the smallest children know better [than to believe in the supernatural]" (435). Such an assertion here would suggest that Butterworth might have believed his audience—children, principally—would know better than to believe Leland's account; it is also possible that his failure to oust the ghost might have simply been the result of an omission, an oversight on the part of Butterworth to resolve the loose end. Regardless of his intent, the story still allows for the possibility of a ghost, which makes the tale a remarkable exception to the unwritten rule about ghosts for children of the time.

What makes *Elder Leland's Ghost and Other Stories for Boys* an even more interesting case is the position its author, Hezekiah Butterworth, occupied in children's writing and publishing. Butterworth held rather influential positions in the children's publishing market of his day. According to Duthie's entry in *The Oxford Encyclopedia of Children's Literature*, Butterworth was one of the editors of *The Youth's Companion* from 1870 to 1894 and contributed to both *The Youth's Companion* and *St. Nicholas*, the two most influential children's periodicals of the nineteenth century and frequent publishers of the mock ghost story for children (240). While "Elder Leland's Ghost" does not seem to have ever been published within either of these two periodicals, the fact that Butterworth carried such a strong influence with both publications might suggest that his reversals of the typical formula for children's ghost stories, no matter how slight, foreshadow the changing landscape of the children's ghost story for the twentieth century.

Hezekiah Butterworth's "Elder Leland's Ghost" may have also set the stage for another author of children's literature to sneak a ghost story into the pages of *The Youth's Companion*. In the very same year "Elder Leland's Ghost" was published, Mark Twain published an essay on storytelling in *The Youth's Companion* containing within it a complete supernatural ghost story, perhaps the first unquestionable supernatural ghost to appear in the *Companion*. "How to Tell a Story: The Humorous Story an American Development—Its Difference from Comic and Witty Stories" provides strategies from the famous Mark

1. The Mock Ghost Story

Twain on how to tell a captivating story to a live audience. He uses two stories—"The Wounded Soldier" and "The Golden Arm"—as examples within his essay, and he provides comments and suggestions for what the storyteller should be doing as the tales are told. Twain does this by offering little asides within the text of each story, generally stating something like "make a considerable pause here" and "you must begin to shiver violently now" (464).

"The Golden Arm" is his final example and an authentic supernatural ghost story. While the target audience of Twain's essay might have been parents, no mention of parents or adults is specifically made in his essay, which opens up the essay and its stories as reading material for children. It is also possible the editors at *The Youth's Companion* allowed the essay to slide on the convention for other reason. Mark Twain was one of the most popular writers of his day. However, the explanation for the lapse in convention might also have to do with the context. Twain presents "The Golden Arm" as an example within an essay on topics other than ghosts, which means the editors may have simply considered it a non-ghost story by default, but even this conclusion is problematic in terms of the convention. While Twain may be using the ghost story as a tool in his essay, he nevertheless instructs adults on how to tell a ghost story in a children's periodical, which would insinuate that he or the editor intended the story to be performed for children, a clear indication of a transition occurring in the trend of blocking ghost stories for children.

Twain's "The Golden Arm," like Butterworth's "Elder Leland's Ghost," represents another example of a transition from the mock ghost story for children around the turn of the twentieth century, but other possible exceptions to the convention, which happen to appear much earlier in the century, are Louisa May Alcott's "Our Little Ghost" and M. M. C.'s "Learning: A Ghost Story of Modern Times." While their titles seem very promising in terms of producing a legitimate ghost story, the tales contain little in the way of the supernatural or "authentic" ghost; however, they do toy with the notion of the supernatural ghost in ways that set them apart from many of the other mock ghost stories of their time. These two stories allow the specter to act as metaphor or allegory in the story, a trait not typically tolerated or popular in other children's ghost stories of the time. Alcott's "Our Little

The Children's Ghost Story in America

Ghost," published in *Merry's Museum for Boys and Girls* in 1868 and reprinted in *The Phrenological Journal and Science of Health* in 1874, uses the metaphor of a ghost to personify the child. The first two stanzas of the poem establish this metaphor fairly clearly. The speaker establishes an eerie setting, "in the silence of the night / When the lonely moon rides high, / When wintry winds are whistling" (456). The speaker then identifies "a spirit all in white" and decides "a winsome little ghost it is" (456). It has "yellow curls" and a "small cap pushed awry" and climbs among the pillows (456). The above lines show the child as ghostlike in nature but beaming with life in almost all other capacities. The metaphor accurately implies that childhood is a liminal space between infancy and adulthood; Alcott seems to recognize that the child haunts the borders of adulthood in nineteenth-century America in this way. In later stanzas, her metaphor eerily equates the vibrancy of youth with images of death. In the third stanza, she writes of "no regrets" and speaks of the child as "a sun that never sets" (456). Her language here calls forth images of unexpected loss, which might point to the ghostly presence of a child just lost, a notion perhaps confirmed by the final stanza, where Alcott has the parents praying over the "folded flower" as it sleeps (456). The piece can also be read literally: that is, the child is really sleeping. Regardless of the approach, the language still strikes a somber cord eerily mixed with vibrant nature images, which might act as a reference to the high infancy mortality rates of the time (Hacker 58), which might explain the mixing of allusions to new life and death in the same lines.

M. M. C.'s "Learning," printed in *The Youth's Companion* in 1845, focuses on much older children, likely teenagers and young adults. In this story, the spirit of learning is literally personified as a ghost that haunts children. "The White Rose," the young female protagonist, attends a ball instead of studying one evening. The spirit of learning, calling itself "the ghost of the coming Examination," subsequently haunts her and pursues her until she has studied rigorously enough to pass her examination (159). The tale is a clear allegory. The ghost can only be seen by White Rose and vanishes as the result of studying. It seems to contain no power but to inspire Rose and never truly stirs feelings of physical fear in her. While the author dubs the entity a ghost, its effect is hardly supernatural or frightening but rather appears to

1. The Mock Ghost Story

personify her inner guilt about her unscholarly habits—the likely reason the tale did not receive censor. The ghostly elements of the tale are simply too thoroughly neutralized by the force of the moral to elicit scrutiny. "Learning," like "Our Little Ghost," is the exception to the convention seemingly because the ghost's appearance is both benign and allegorical. It is likely that both the authors and editors saw these tales as non-ghost stories, which is possibly why they were allowed to be printed as children's literature. Furthermore, each of these pieces apparently lacks the terrifying uncanny effect common to both the mock ghost story for children and ghost stories for adults, further separating these tales from the mock ghost story tradition for children in nineteenth-century America. However, at least one ghostly tale printed before the turn of the century exists that might truly violate the convention.

In early October of 1875, the *Saturday Evening Post* published a short story by Margery Laird titled "A Bird Ghost," which tells the tale of a haunted birdcage. The story appeared in the youth's section of the periodical, titled "Our Boys and Girls," and depicts the tragic life of a canary and his mates. Dick or Speckled Breast, the story's protagonist, is the beloved pet of a young girl, often referred to in the story as "little mistress" (Laird 5). The tale begins with Dick's mother frantically searching for him within the downstairs aviary; however, unbeknownst to Mother Featherlegs, Dick has been given to the little girl of the house as a gift from her mother. Heartsick over the loss of his family and friends, Dick simply perches and sulks all day in his cage. Finally, his "little mistress" provides a mate, a beautiful little female canary, to keep him company. The two birds become instant lovers and quickly start a family, but Dick's happiness rapidly ends when he finds his wife dead perched upon her nest of eggs one morning. Shortly after her death, Dick's "little mistress" continuously brings him new mates but always finds them in a frightened stupor or dead by morning. What the little girl does not know—but the birds are well aware of—is that the ghost of Dick's first wife appears to his new mates every evening perched upon her ghostly nest. Eventually, Dick is forced to live alone and dies one day of overeating. The girl, over her infatuation with canaries, decides to take up gardening instead of asking for a new bird (Laird 5).

While the story has odd elements and occasional lapses in narration, it still manages to portray a very authentic supernatural ghost story. The birds in the story are anthropomorphic, but the humans, of course, cannot hear or see their sentient qualities and thus ignore the unusualness of Dick's situation without a second thought. The narration of the story also seems to further blur the lines between humans and birds through a series of lapses in proper character identification and appropriate descriptions of the birds' actions. For instance, the birds occasionally seem to have unexplained access to or familiarity with the use of lamps and keys, and there are a few occasions where the narrator describes the birds through human habits of movement such as one scene where one of Dick's mates assumes he is on a "midnight stroll" rather than a midnight flight (5). These lapses are made more striking by some of the descriptions of the human's rooms, particularly the little girl's room, which is described as "a tiny room like a bird-cage, all hung with pictures and curtained in snowy muslin" (5). This description of the little girl's room makes her sound as caged and trapped as the birds, which is perhaps very accurate considering the child's sheltered status in her upper class surroundings.

However, these slips in characterization might also indicate places in the narrative where the author attempts to force the story to adhere to more traditional hallmarks of the ghost story; nineteenth-century ghost stories commonly feature midnight strolls and unexplained lamplight. Unlike "Learning" and "Our Little Ghost," "A Bird Ghost" contains definite elements of the uncanny. When the second bird wife meets its predecessor, the uncanny effect is unmistakable:

> The odd sound she had heard at first was repeated; it was a faint grating chirp like nothing exactly, and there on a spectral nest sat a ghostly canary, with a yellow night cap on her yellow head, and four little eggs gleaming under her breast! There she sat and stared with eyes like black flames, until the poor little bird-bride fell off her perch in a swoon [5].

The bird-bride is jolted by the appearance of the ghost in her very familiar surroundings. The uncanny effect is undoubtedly clear in this scene, but perhaps is made a little silly by the character's animalistic appearance—a likely reason the editors allowed this supernatural ghost story to pass for children's literature. It might have been assumed by the author or the editor that a bird ghost was simply too ridiculous to be taken seriously, thereby excusing it of the typical censor of supernatural ghost stories for children, but this is only conjecture.

1. The Mock Ghost Story

While Margery Laird's "A Bird Ghost" presents an odd exception to the unwritten rule about children's ghost stories in nineteenth-century America, Elia W. Peattie's "Their Dear Little Ghost" (1898) raises deeper questions about audience and reception regarding ghost stories for children. "Their Dear Little Ghost," printed as part of a book promotion for her anthology in *Outlook*, features a tender story about the deceased child Elsbeth and her family's recovery after her death. Elsbeth's godmother, who always loved Elsbeth and considered her the light of her life, narrates the story (530). On the first Christmas after Elsbeth death, her brothers' spot her ghost crying because her stocking has been taken down. They try to console her but she vanishes before they can help her. On Christmas Eve the following year, the boys' godmother puts out Elsbeth's stocking, carefully placing the autoharp she so desired before her death within the stocking as her principle gift. When Christmas morning finally arrives, the stocking is found empty and later the godmother can hear the soft sounds of an autoharp playing from somewhere in the room (530). The tale is unquestionably a supernatural ghost story, although not one intended to elicit fear, but the true question is whether the story is intended for children or adults.

Appearing as one of many ghost stories in Elia W. Peattie's *The Shape of Fear and other Ghostly Tales* (1898), "Their Dear Little Ghost" stands apart from the rest of the collection in that its focus concerns children and mimics both a style and tone common to children's periodicals of the nineteenth century. This is hardly surprising considering its author's success as a writer for children. Peattie wrote prolifically for children and adults in her lifetime, publishing in such well known periodicals as *The Youth's Companion, St. Nicolas, Atlantic Monthly, Chicago Tribune, Collier's,* and *Harper's Bazaar*, but her children's publications are numerous enough to establish her reputation as a children's author. Susanne George Bloomfield, likely her most dedicated scholar, bibliographer, and biographer, has attributed thirty-one pieces of her fiction to major children's periodicals, namely *The Youth's Companion* and *St. Nicolas* (299–300), but also notes a number of children's books and collections, including *Ickery Ann and Other Boys and Girls* (1899); *Edda and the Oak* (1911); and *Our Chosen Land: A Romantic Story of America from the Time of Its Discovery and Conquest to the Present Day: An Interesting Account of the Progress and Development*

The Children's Ghost Story in America

of Our Country, Written Especially for Young Folks (1896) (Bloomfield 261; 295–96, 9). However, "Their Dear Little Ghost" is not one of the stories she categories as for children. Regardless, these publications testify to Peattie's success as a children's author, but they are hardly definitive enough to label "Their Dear Little Ghost" as a story published for children. The tale never seems to have appeared in a publication or anthology for children in the nineteenth century, nor does there seem to be any evidence that Peattie tried to place the story with a children's periodical; however, the tale seems to contain elements that would make it of interest to children, which few other ghost stories for adults of the nineteenth century do.

As with Mark Twain's "How to Tell a Story," questions about intended audience in children's literature can be hard to discern. Some children's literature scholars have contended that borders between adult and children's fiction in the nineteenth century were far more permeable than in the twentieth century. Beverly Lyon Clark, one of the most authoritative scholars on this issue, confirms the fluidity in readership in her book *Kiddie Lit*:

> The positioning of children and childhood in the American imagination has changed over the last two centuries. Children and childhood were less segregated from adults and adulthood in the nineteenth century, before the split between high culture and low, before literary authority shifted from genteel editors to the professoriate [16].

Her assertion suggests that literature was less defined in terms of audience in nineteenth-century America. In others words, authors writing for children in the nineteenth century might have just as easily been writing for adults. Using Twain as an example, Clark extends this assertion by revealing Twain's ambivalence about the target audience for his book *Tom Sawyer*:

> Although my book is intended mainly for the entertainment of boys and girls, I hope it will not be shunned by men and women on that account, for part of my plan has been to try to pleasantly remind adults of what they once were themselves, and of how they felt and thought and talked, and what queer enterprises they sometimes engaged in [qtd. in Clark 80].

While Clark may have a point about the fluidity around the borders of childhood fiction in the nineteenth century, she forgets to account for the periodicals for children in her theory about children's fiction

1. The Mock Ghost Story

in 1800s. The very existence of periodicals designed for children—such as *The Youth's Companion, St. Nicolas,* and *Merry's Museum for Boys and Girls*—show that at least some sectors of the publishing industry believed in stories specifically for children—even if the occasional adult might be interested. The trend of withholding the supernatural ghost in children's stories of the nineteenth century demonstrates the existence of genre separation in literature for children and adults, one that has different expectations based on audience appropriateness.

The Sum of a Ghost

While some anomalies in the typical children's ghost story formula for nineteenth-century America do occur, not enough evidence exists to suggest a true deviation from the mock ghost story for children. Of the sixty-nine nineteenth-century American ghost stories reviewed for this study, only these seven stories represent any real departure from the formula, suggesting that this trend dominated the industry for practically all of the nineteenth century. Furthermore, all the anomalies contained some aspect that made their status as stories to be consumed by children questionable. Whether distancing the plausibility of supernatural ghosts by using anthropomorphic characters or the ambivalence with intended audience, these anomalous ghost stories are simply too different from the rest of the tradition to upset the publishing phenomenon; in fact, these anomalies offer further evidence to the influence of the mock ghost story tradition. The fact that these ghost stories had to change other elements of their story to make them publishable for children confirms the significance of the ideology behind the mock ghost story for nineteenth-century America.

The mock ghost story for children signifies a dominant ideology about ghosts and superstitions in terms of childhood appropriateness for nineteenth-century America. There is little doubt that publishers tacitly withheld supernatural ghosts stories from children through a unified and widespread unofficial—or rather undeclared—campaign that only started to give toward the end of the twentieth century. However, despite this well-unified attempt to quash the supernatural ghost, the mock ghost story for children preserved many of the qualities of the supernatural ghost that would later emerge in children's literature and that might otherwise have been lost. And while the supernatural ghost story might seem very distant from the mock ghost story, the tales are similar in their use of the uncanny, which consistently appears throughout the mock ghost stories for children and later supernatural ghost stories for children in some form or another. Subsequently, the mock ghost story for children resembles the supernatural ghost story for children of twentieth-century America in many regards, which will be explored more thoroughly in the next few chapters.

2

Spectrality and Nineteenth-Century American Girlhood

The Mock Ghost Stories for Girls in American Periodicals

The nineteenth century marks a crucial evolution in both the ghost story and perceptions of womanhood in the United States. The women's suffrage movement has its roots in the nineteenth century. Such figures as Susan B. Anthony and Elizabeth Cady Stanton established themselves as leaders in this new movement, but women authors—including Louisa May Alcott and Edith Wharton—also contributed to changing perspectives on womanhood during the nineteenth and early twentieth centuries through their fictions and subsequently through their ghostly stories. Scholars studying girlhood and women's ghost stories published during the nineteenth century have noted their connections to the evolving role of women in United Sates. "The ghost stories written after the 1850s," argues Vanessa D. Dickerson,

> but especially in the last decades of the century, would be written in a climate of change and reform marked by such developments as the agitation for women's rights to education, employment, and suffrage; the passage of the married women's property bills; and the rise of the New Woman [133].

Dickerson contends ghost stories written by women during the nineteenth century share a fundamental connection to social reforms for women and more progressive views of womanhood for the time period. Her book *Victorian Ghosts in the Noontide: Women Writers and the*

The Children's Ghost Story in America

Supernatural investigates this phenomenon and contends that women occupied a precarious place between the home and the wider culture, which often made them appear spectral or "visib[le] and invisib[le]" (5). They quite literally seemed to occupy a liminal space. Tracking the liminal space of nineteenth-century girlhood in relation to the mock ghost story provides fertile ground to investigate the way the children's ghost story evolved and reflected the social dilemmas of a transformative age. With the help of scholars studying nineteenth-century womanhood and girlhood, the ghost story, and class strife, I argue that the mock ghost story offers a progressive depiction of nineteenth-century girlhood, one which fosters the emerging image of women's and girls' liberation and advancement in the social tapestry of the United States.

In *Twain, Alcott, and the Birth of the Adolescent Reform Novel*, Roberta Seelinger Trites draws distinctions between models of womanhood present during the later part of nineteenth-century America:

> Emerging as a result of the suffrage movement, the New Woman was the antithesis of the woman immersed in the Cult of True Womanhood—that early nineteenth-century embodiment of romanticism that conflated domesticity and piety. The True Woman was pure, pious, and homebound; she wanted nothing more than to serve those she loved. The New Woman was strong, politically convicted, and independent of thought [92].

Trites, a prominent adolescent and children's literature scholar, accurately pinpoints the struggle between diverging definitions of womanhood emerging in nineteenth-century American culture; she, like Dickerson, sees this evolution playing a critical role in women's writing of the time, particularly in writing for children. She argues that Alcott—being aware of this tension between the True Woman and New Woman—desired to walk the border in her fiction for girls, particularly *Little Women*, taking care to have her "New Women articulate their respect for family and the sanctity of marriage" (92).

While Alcott might have made some concession in her writing about womanhood and girlhood, her fiction still offers powerful models of liberation and advancement for women and girls, which figure prominently even in her lesser known fiction, particularly her ghostly tales for girls published in such periodicals as *St. Nicholas*, which will be addressed in greater detail later in this chapter. These progressive

2. Spectrality and Nineteenth-Century American Girlhood

models of womanhood and girlhood speak to cultural changes occurring in the United States, but they also show connections emerging between the ghost story genre and children's literature, which have largely been overlooked by most literary scholars. However, Roald Dahl, likely one of the most well-known and beloved children's authors of the twentieth century, has not missed this connection and explores it rather directly in his introduction to *Roald Dahl's Book of Ghost Stories*, where he laments the lack of critical attention paid to women writers, children's literature, and the ghost story. "When it comes to writing classic children's books," he contends, "women triumph over the men. They are pretty good at novels, they are better still at ghost stories, but they are best of all at children's books" (15–16). Dahl correctly identifies women's literature, children's literature, and the ghost story's exclusion from critical attention during the first half and even the bulk of the second half of the twentieth century. He realizes these genres, while often immensely popular, rarely garnered the praise they deserved from the literary elite, often relegated to the lowest circle of the literary hierarchy. "After the turn of the century," argues Beverly Lyon Clark, in *Kiddie Lit*, "elite American critics were even less likely to treat children's literature and literature by women—and hence Alcott's work—seriously" (116). Therefore, the mock ghost stories for girls—being for children, written mostly by women, and pulling from the ghost-telling tradition—likely occupied the least prestigious place in the lowest circle of literary consideration. It is no wonder, then, that these tales have fallen into almost complete obscurity, even the ones written by famous authors such as Alcott.

While not all the mock ghost stories written for girls demonstrate the highest marks of literary quality, several show at least some literary merit, particularly in what they convey about girlhood in the nineteenth century, and should at least be valued for their contribution to understanding the complicated history of girlhood in America. Mock ghost stories for girls are frequently empowering and contain progressive views about womanhood alongside more traditional—Victorian—ideas about womanhood, but perhaps more importantly, these ghost stories also resonate with later ghost stories for children and continue to show the mock ghost story's influence over the future of children's ghost stories. As such, these stories and others like them should not remain in obscurity but should be analyzed at the very least in terms of their historical, if not their literary, significance.

Progressive Women, the Victorian Woman and the Nursemaid

Scholars studying American girlhood of the nineteenth century have feverishly wrestled with questions about the influence of progressive models of womanhood versus traditional (more Victorian) models of womanhood. Both models of womanhood played powerful roles in nineteenth-century America; however, regardless of which model was more influential, American girls of the nineteenth century were definitely more educated than girls of previous centuries, especially girls from more affluent families, who would have been the target audience of many children's periodicals of the nineteenth century. Jane H. Hunter concisely summarizes the increase in literacy practices of affluent girls in nineteenth-century America:

> Even more than their parents, upper- and upper-middle-class Victorian girls lived through the written word. We know Victorian girls in the United States as avid readers of romances, biographies, histories, and serials. A rich scholarly literature now debates the significance of their reading to their own aspirations, the publishing industry, and turn-of-the-century culture. Victorian girls were also avid writers. They spent long hours at writing desks producing pages of letters, composing poetry, copying passages from literature, keeping all manner of diaries and journals [52].

Hunter attributes the growth of these practices to the emergence of greater leisure time due largely to the ability of parents to hire servants, which presumably allowed both parents and children the time to dabble in education (52). However, the addition of servants to the household, particularly nurses, also suggests places where the ghost story might have crept into the nursery without the parents' knowledge. As has been shown in previous chapters, suspicion over the nursemaid's story-telling habits worried many parents of nineteenth-century America. Charles Dickens, perhaps one of the finest writers of the nineteenth-century ghost story on the other side of the Atlantic, had mixed feelings about his nursemaid—Mary Weller—telling him ghost

2. Spectrality and Nineteenth-Century American Girlhood

stories as a child, saying at one point in *The Uncommercial Traveller*: "I suspect we should find our nurses responsible for most of the dark corners we are forced to go back to, against our wills" (102). Dickens' comment suggests his nursemaid's stories left a terrible blemish on his youthful imagination, causing him to be a more timid and superstitious adult. Similar sentiments about the effect of the ghost story on young minds circulated in the States as well. In 1889, an editor for an American periodical *Babyhood: Devoted Exclusively to the Care of Infants and Young Children* wrote the following in response to a parent's query:

> The effect of a fright which to adults might seem trivial in the extreme may make a terrible impression upon the mind of a sensitive or imaginative child. We can recall women (and men, too, for that matter) of extraordinary physical courage who confessed to a dread of passing an open door. The impression left in childhood by some ghost story or the like doubtless lay at the root of this dread [A 121].

Dickens was not alone in his suspicions about the ghost story's negative impact on young minds, but his and others' focus on nursemaids as the arbiters of this ghostly tradition raises interesting questions about womanhood and girlhood in the nineteenth century.

While parents of the nineteenth century undoubtedly suspected other avenues existed for the ghost story to reach their children, the focus on the nursemaid seems quite central to their concerns. "[M]any children are told silly stories by *nurses* and others," writes The Exile, "and they creep close to each other when they hear unusual noises, and run and scream if they are left accidentally in the dark" (182; my emphasis). The Exile, the anonymous writer of "Ghost Stories" in *The Youth's Companion*, and quoted more fully in a previous chapter, singles out the nursemaid for accusation. The nursemaid, whether rightly or wrongly criticized, seems to receive more blame for circulating the supernatural ghost story to children than any other figure of the nineteenth century, and as a female and pseudo-mother figure, the nursemaid invariably ties the ghost-story-telling tradition back to womanhood. This argument, of course, is nothing new to scholars. "At least since the early modern period," argues Dale Townshend, "British culture had consistently associated ghosts and children with the oral tradition in storytelling, and this primarily through the most maligned and misunderstood of cultural personae: the Old Wife" (17). In "Gendering the Ghost Story? Victorian Women and the Challenge of the Phantom," Jarlath Killeen reaches a similar conclusion as Townshend:

> There has been a long cultural association between women and the ghostly. At least since the sixteenth century, not only have ghost stories been dismissed as "old wives' tales," but also many intellectual luminaries have configured them as emanating from backward communities of superstitious and time-warped peasants gendered female in contrast to the masculine, progressive, rational and cosmopolitan moderns whose job it has been to demythologize, deconstruct, and, in general, explain such stories as the product of the week-minded, the fanciful or the plain old deluded [81].

While the figure of the "Old Wife" is not quite the nineteenth-century figure of the nursemaid, it is still very close and perhaps synonymous in some cases. The nursemaid, like the Old Wife, is a figure of womanhood that is strongly associated with childrearing, the lower classes, and the oral tradition, which is likely why the nursemaid seems to have inherited many of the stereotypes associated with the Old Wife. The governess, on the other hand, seems to narrowly escape stereotypes associated with the Old Wife. As a more educated and middle-class female figure, the governess seems to have only just avoided the harshest criticism; however, the governess does occasionally appear as an object of scrutiny in some ghostly tales, perhaps most notably *The Turn of the Screw*, which was explored more thoroughly in the previous chapter.

These female servants might also represent inherent instances of the uncanny. In "Not at Home: Servants, Scholars, and the Uncanny," Brian McCuskey observes that "Freud provisionally links the uncanny to servants, whose nursery stories introduce middle-class children to those primitive beliefs in the supernatural that should be surmounted in adulthood; the residue of those beliefs constitutes one major source of the uncanny" (425). While McCuskey recognizes that Freud uses this uncanny characteristic provisionally, he still establishes the possibility of reading the servant, particularly female servants, as inherently capable of transmitting or instigating the uncanny through their storytelling practices, which further link the ghost story and the uncanny to womanhood during the nineteenth century and possibly before.

2. Spectrality and Nineteenth-Century American Girlhood

What these figures and concepts of womanhood all seem to have in common is a deep connection to childrearing and service to the upper classes, which might explain why so much scrutiny was placed on their position. They essentially occupy a space where they have the ability to influence classes above their station, particularly through the rearing of their young charges. It is not surprising then that their positions were regarded with scrutiny. Subsequently, it is also possible to see the supernatural ghost story as one of many casualties in the attempt to suppress the rising influence of nineteenth-century woman, particularly women like nursemaids and governesses, who held unique positions of influence within the new generations of Americans. Scholars have noticed connections to the nineteenth-century ghost story and female empowerment. As Vanessa D. Dickerson argues, "ghost stories could provide a fitting medium for eruptions of female libidinal energy, of thwarted ambitions, of cramped egos" (8). If the ghost story acted as a tool for female empowerment in the nineteenth century, as Dickerson suggests, then it seems probable that the supernatural ghost story for children—along with the oral ghost story—might have been unconsciously or even consciously singled out for censor just as part of another attempt to stifle the rising agency of the nineteenth-century woman.

While such a claim is difficult to prove conclusively, the proximity of the ghost story to tales attempting to forward progressive views of womanhood is relatively close. Louisa May Alcott's short story "Jerseys or the Girls' Ghost," published in *St. Nicholas* in 1884 as the seventh part of her Spinning-Wheel series, offers a story that seems to use the ghost story genre to advance progressive views of womanhood. Set at a boarding-school exclusively for girls, the story follows the adventures of six girls at the school—Sally, Maud, Nelly, Kitty, Julia, and Cordy—who inadvertently stumble across a ghostly mystery. The girls begin as models of Victorian girlhood, which Alcott bluntly mocks in her narrative as physically and mentally unhealthy, captured best in a paragraph near the beginning of her story:

> Madame Stein's select boarding-school had for many years received six girls at a time and "finished them off" in the old style. Plenty of French, German, music, painting, dancing, and deportment turned out well-bred, accomplished, and amiable young ladies, ready for fashionable society, easy lives, and entire

> dependence on other people. Dainty and delicate creatures usually, for, as in most schools of this sort, minds and manners were much cultivated, but bodies rather neglected. Heads and backs ached, dyspepsia was common ailment, and "poorlies" of all sorts afflicted the dear girls who ought not to have known what "nerves" meant, and who should have had no bottles in their closets holding wine and iron, cough-mixtures, and cod-liver oil for weak lungs [680].

Alcott's criticisms are easily discernible, and this passage tends to set the tone for the rest of the story. Her emphasis on the girls' poor health and general uselessness draws the Victorian model or "old style" into contention immediately. Shortly after this passage, the girls meet their new governess, who possesses far different ideas about womanhood and who consequently agitates their perception about health and beauty, but particularly their understanding of what it means to be a woman.

"She certainly looked capable as she came into the school-room ready for her day's work," states the narrator about the new governess, "with her lungs full of fresh air, her brain stimulated by sound sleep, wholesome exercise, and a simple breakfast, and her mind much interested in the task before her" (Alcott 680). Career oriented, athletic, and bright, Miss Orne represents a more progressive, liberating model of womanhood and offers a stark contrast to Madame Stein, bedridden and literally and figuratively displaced by the arrival of Miss Orne and her new ways. "There she is, now," cries Kitty, describing Miss Orne's approach, "Girls, she's running! actually trotting up the avenue—not like a hen, but like a boy—with her elbows down and her head up" (681). Miss Orne's very arrival seems to communicate the gender challenges embodied by these more progressive women in nineteenth-century America, and her impact on the young girls is immediate. Her healthy look and bold ways are soon the desire of every one of her pupils, but the girls have been warned about such women, captured succinctly in a statement made by Maud shortly before Miss Orne's arrival: "I do hope Miss Orne is n't [sic] full of the new notions about clothes, and food, and exercise and rights and rubbish of that sort. Mamma hates such ideas, and so do I" (681). Maud's statement indicates her parents' disapproval of the more progressive and liberating changes in womanhood, but her commitment to her parents' advice proves flimsy at best. Despite Maud's initial apprehension about Miss

2. Spectrality and Nineteenth-Century American Girlhood

Orne's new ideas, she, along with the rest of the girls, is quickly converted.

Judging by Alcott's story, nineteenth-century American parents had reason to suspect the nursemaid and governess of influencing their children, but Alcott's choice to use the ghost story tradition as her means for informing her readers of progressive trends in womanhood and girlhood is even more interesting. While the ghost in "Jerseys or the Girls' Ghost" is proven false, merely the antics of a sleepwalking Cordy, the specter's association with progressive views of womanhood in nineteenth-century America is unmistakable. When one of the girls asks Miss Orne if she believes in ghosts, Miss Orne provides an intriguing answer to her question. "Not the old-fashioned sort," answers Miss Orne, "but there is a modern kind that we are all afraid of, more or less" (687). When pressed a little further, Miss Orne offers a clarification:

> There is one which I am very anxious to keep you from fearing. Women and young girls are especially haunted by it. "What—will—people—say?" is the name of this formidable ghost, and it does much harm; for few of us have the courage to live up to what we know to be right in all things. You are soon to go away to begin your lives in earnest, and I do hope that whatever I have been able to teach you about the care of minds and bodies will not be forgotten or neglected because it may not be the fashion outside our little world here [687].

Miss Orne erases the subtle line between women and ghostliness. Alcott brings the specter of women's agency in nineteenth-century America to the forefront. While the ghost the children bravely confront materializes into their sleepwalking friend, the metaphor of the specter of oppression they will face in their adult lives is all too real, but Alcott's governess has prepared the girls well. The message seems to have gotten through to her young wards. They eagerly promise to remain strong in response to scrutiny about their new ways, which perhaps justly confirms the apprehension nineteenth-century American parents might have had regarding nurses, governesses, and the ghost story. The parents of these fictional girls would have good reason to suspect their governess of using the ghost story to teach their children progressive views of womanhood.

Alcott's story easily sets the stage for this kind of analysis, but other writers also embedded progressive concepts about womanhood and girlhood in children's ghost stories in much the same way as Alcott. For example, "Learning: A Ghost Story of Modern Times," written by M. M. C. for *The Youth's Companion* and discussed in the previous chapter, also uses the ghost metaphor as a means to challenge the Victorian model of womanhood. Rose Martin or "The White Rose" neglects her studies for a night of dancing at a local social, a common nineteenth-century affair and hallmark of Victorian high culture. When the dancing comes to an end and the party starts to disperse, White Rose encounters an intriguing specter. "As all around her grew still," states the narrator, "a feeling of bitterness stole over her, and she remembered with sorrow, that much which she should have done that night had been forgotten. As she rose to go to her rest, a dim form of unearthly aspect stood by her side, and the poor Rose trembled as she looked on the fearful shape" (159). The spirit of learning or the ghost of the "Examination" materializes from White Rose's guilt and unscholarly activities. Much like Alcott's "Jerseys or the Girls' Ghost," overt with allusions to progressive changes in womanhood and girlhood, "Learning" offers progressive views of womanhood that seem to directly counter the old model of the Victorian woman. Studiousness and simplicity rise above the elegance of the ball and vanity of dress. The story tends to reward qualities of girlhood and womanhood that favor more progressive, liberating views and critique the Victorian standard, placing the tale firmly in alliance with Alcott's progressive themes.

Defying Conventions: Brave Girls, Ghostly Tales

Other mock ghost stories from children's periodicals feature different approaches about contending perspectives on nineteenth-century American girlhood. While not all the stories are as blunt as "Jerseys or the Girls Ghost" and "Learning," most use the ghost story as a vehicle to provide subtle views of female agency and empowerment through the ghost story for children. In *Constructing Girlhood through the Periodical Press, 1850–1915*, Kristine Moruzi accurately notes that "[t]he nature and ideology of girlhood in the periodical press is subject

2. Spectrality and Nineteenth-Century American Girlhood

to constant negotiation and redefinition" (14). While Moruzi focuses mostly on British periodicals, her observation rings true for American periodicals as well. Notions of girlhood seemed to experience quite a metamorphosis in the nineteenth century's periodical presses, particularly evident in works by Louisa May Alcott but in the works of lesser known writers for children as well. In "The Ghost That Lucy Saw," a short story published in *The Youth's Companion* in 1874, Maria W. Jones produces characters that display female agency through subtler means than seen in M. M. C. and Alcott, but the author still forwards progressive views of womanhood to a notable degree. Her young protagonist, Martha, unwilling to let her fears rule her, boldly confronts a specter her sister Lucy sees at the foot of their bed. This act has a profound effect on Lucy, who witnesses the dramatic display of Martha's bravery. Martha's "voice was so hearty," states the narrator, "and her manner so fearless, that Lucy herself began to feel differently and less afraid of the terrible *something*, which she somehow still thought must be there, and which it seemed very strange to her that Martha could not see" (Jones 52; my emphasis). Her older sister's boldness quickly becomes contagious and infects Lucy with the courage to confront the ghost and reveal it as "her own little white sailor-waist hanging upon the high back of an arm-chair" (52).

Martha's and Lucy's shared experience places female characters in empowering roles, where their triumph over fear counters the social expectations of nineteenth-century American girlhood. The girls react as if they have defied the behavioral expectation to be "girly," helpless, and ineffectual. Evidence of this reaction appears in Lucy's "new fear" and appeal to Martha not to "tell 'the boys'" of her pervious fearful behavior (52). Lucy's plea here seems to suggest that neither of the girls wish to appear weak and "girly" to the males in their household, evidence of their desire to embody traits of a more liberated, progressive view of womanhood and prove themselves equal to the males in terms of their bravery. While the tale lacks the clear moral presented in Alcott's story, it still appears that "The Ghost That Lucy Saw" entails a definite message of female empowerment, a trait common to numerous mock ghost stories printed for girls in nineteenth-century America.

Following in the same tradition, Mrs. Hall, the penname of an

The Children's Ghost Story in America

anonymous author publishing in *Woodworth's Youth's Cabinet* in 1850, includes two mock ghost stories in her work "Adventures with Ghosts." The second of these stories displays a unique extension to the kind of female agency demonstrated by Jones in "The Ghost That Lucy Saw." The story recounts the ingenuity and courageousness of a little girl named Lilian, referred to throughout the story as Lily, who boldly defends her parents' home from the parties of a neglectful house-sitter and babysitter named Jeanette. The story begins when Lily's parents decide to take a trip "to a distant part of the State, to be absent several weeks," and leave Lily and their eldest son behind (228). Jeanette, while promising to be quiet and respectful, begins hosting rowdy parties, attended by "wild girls, with rude curiosity," and "rough young men," clearly unsuited to be in the family home of a respected clergyman (228).

Astonished by the inconsiderate behavior of Jeanette and her party guests, Lily devises a plan to end the parties and protect her parents' home. During one of the wildest parties, soon after Lily has been sent to bed, Jeanette and her guests hear crashing noises from the room above their heads. Startled and frightened by the unexpected sounds, the partiers are for a time petrified and unable to explore the cause of the disturbance, but the bravest of the men finally ascends the stairs and investigates the noise. They first check Lily's room and find her seemingly sound asleep, with no sign of disturbance in her room. Finally, without finding a cause for the noise, the guests assume a ghost must haunt the house and quickly disperse, leaving Jeanette frightened and alone. News of the ghost quickly spreads, and soon few strangers will venture to the house to socialize with Jeanette. While the noise leaves Jeanette and her friends bewildered, Lily knows the true cause of the disturbance. As the party roared below her bedroom, Lily spun her mother's spinning wheel and removed the pin holding it together as the wheel reached its highest velocity. The resulting crash of the wheel caused the noise that disturbed the partiers. And as Jeanette and her guests remained petrified downstairs, Lily quickly concealed all evidence of what she had done and pretended to sleep as the men investigated.

Her older brother's absence is a mystery in the story. Whether he is staying at the home or at another caretaker's home is never quite made clear, though likely the latter is the case, but her brother's absence allows for Lily's boldness to flourish. She unmistakably possesses agency in this tale: she breaks the convention of the helpless Victorian girl by defending her home from potential vandals, deliberately misleading the tactless partiers with a hoax and sending them off in fear. Her reasons for perpetrating the hoax are ethical—to protect her home from miscreants—rather than mischievous, giving her actions a noble quality. However, while Lily's actions are defiant and noble, Jeanette's actions are irresponsible and disrespectful, demonstrating total disregard for her trusted position. In essence, Jeanette seems to embody the suspicion of lower class women in the nineteenth century referred to by Townshend and Killeen. She shirks her job as caretaker of the house and succumbs to superstation, thus proving her status as a member of the "backward communities of superstitious and time-warped peasants gendered female" (Killeen 81).

Class Boundaries and the Social Expansion of Girlhood

Class and economic divides are apparent in many of these mock ghost stories for girls, which might indicate something about these periodicals' readership. As Jane H. Hunter has already indicated, Victorian girls—white middle to upper class girls—in nineteenth-century America had a greater surplus of leisure time than previous generations, allowing for more time to read (52). Alcott and M. M. C.'s stories offer white affluent girls as primary characters, which lends credence to the idea of largely a white affluent young readership. In *Consumerism and American Girls' Literature, 1860–1940*, Peter Stoneley provides a succinct depiction of trends in American children's publishing figures during the second half of the nineteenth century, which tends to confirm some of the above suspicions:

> It has been estimated that there was a growth in the children's periodical product as a whole of over 400 percent in the twenty years from 1865 to 1885, from 700 titles to 3300. This huge expansion after the Civil War was largely due to improvement in printing technology, and in transportation, though the improved literacy rates that came with increased school enrolments were also

The Children's Ghost Story in America

significant. The most popular periodical for children was *Youth's Companion* (1827–1929), which had a circulation of 500,000 in 1885. Many others, though, had a readership of over 100,000, and even the most select, the *St. Nicholas* (1873–1940), had over 75,000 subscribers. There was a mirroring of social hierarchies in that there were cheaper magazines which favored sensational stories, and which embraced working-class characters and scenes. There was also a gendered hierarchy, in that the violent, underworld excitements of cheaper magazines were assumed to be designed for, and enjoyed by, boys rather than girls. Girls had higher cultural destinies and obligations than boys, and so were expected to find themselves more at home in the approved literature [37–38].

Stoneley portrays a rather stratified market in children's publishing during the late nineteenth century, showing varying levels of interests and sales depending on gender and class structures. Girls seemingly fit within the top bracket of this stratified market, supposedly because they "had higher cultural destinies and obligations than boys" (38). Interestingly, Stoneley complicates the gender-and class-based model even further by demonstrating that sales and interests in children's periodicals depended upon reception rather than price. While he notes that *The Youth's Companion* cost less than *Frank Leslie's* or *Boys of New York*, with a subscription rate between $1.00 and $1.50 compared to the nearly $2.00 and $2.50 of the other periodicals, its status as a higher-brow periodical far exceeded many of its competitors, thus situating it as a more prestigious magazine (38).

While mock ghost stories featuring affluent children might be more common in periodicals and stories aimed at girls, other stories occasionally seem to deal with girls of lower-middle class positions. "Cootie's Ghost Story," written by May Haines and published in *The Youth's Companion* in 1874, seems just such a story. The tale features a little girl by the name of Cootie, who while on her way to bed one night, becomes frightened by the possibility of a ghost. Miss Cootie, like the other girls discussed so far, has a very active imagination, which is best captured in her musings on ghosts before reaching her bedroom:

> I spected they [ghosts] were white, and had big moufs! so I fought I'd sit still a little while longer. I s'posed they had big eyes an' awful claws. 'Twas real nice on the stairs, and I fought I'd sit still a little while longer. I merembered picking a little hole in mamma's cake just for one taste—and another—and a little more. Somehow, I didn't feel like going yet, an' fought I would sit still a little while longer [339].

2. Spectrality and Nineteenth-Century American Girlhood

While the story is accompanied by an illustration of a white, middle-class girl and mother, dressed in Victorian looking attire, the language and names in the story, as shown above, appear to share similarities with African American dialects of the time; however, such a claim cannot be stated with certainty. Cootie's poor English and questionable manners definitely suggest her lower class position and distinguish her from the girls in the stories mentioned previously. She also possesses

The illustration shows Cootie being consoled by her mother in "Cootie's Ghost Story" (*The Youth's Companion*, 1874) by May Haines. The image features an interesting contrast to the text. Ethelinda Maria is missing and the character depictions are inconsistent with the African-American dialect spoken by the main characters.

far less agency in her story than the girls in stories previously discussed. Shortly after Cootie's sugar binge and fretting episode about ghosts on the stairs, Cootie's active imagination takes over and causes her to cower under her covers until her mother arrives to reveal nothing creeping in the darkness.

Unlike Lucy and her sister, Cootie needs someone else to help her overcome her fear, thus giving her far less agency in her own story and making her less involved in the resolution of the ghost than the girls of the previous stories. However, it would be a mistake to say that the story lacks any reference to progressive views of womanhood and girlhood. While Cootie displays less agency than the girls from the other stories, she and other characters from her story consider her quite progressive, even joking about her attitude at one point. When Cootie's mother tells her to go to bed and Cootie refuses, their house guests consider her quite contrary to typical models of womanhood for the time:

> Then the folks laughed, and called me a "women's righther," which means, chil'ren, a woman what can talk faster than all the men and the President of these United States, an' Jack and Gill, and the Queen who sat in her parlor, and what aint afraid of ghosts, or black men, nor cows with horns [339].

While the reference to her being a "women's righter" seems hardly positive, it does reveal the story's active engagement on issues of changing standards of womanhood and women's suffrage, not to mention other social issues and stigmas of the time, like the reference in the passage to a fear of "black men," which may carry two meanings: a fear of black men or a fear of devils. In many respects, Cootie's story seems to counter the progressive views expressed in the previous mock ghost stories for children dealing with girlhood. The sexism and possible racism revealed in the above passage demonstrates this regressive stance and certifies the existence of opposing viewpoints on womanhood and girlhood within children's periodicals of nineteenth-century America.

Unmasking the Ghost: Gender, Power and Transition

While "Cootie's Ghost Story" clashes with the progressive model of womanhood and girlhood more than any other story covered thus

2. Spectrality and Nineteenth-Century American Girlhood

far, another mock ghost story from near the turn of the century reveals further complications about the changing face of femininity in the nineteenth century. "Mask Against Mask," published anonymously in *The Youth's Companion* in 1897, offers a story—possibly a true story—that appears to unintentionally depict a rather perfect metaphor for the complicated nature of nineteenth-century American womanhood and girlhood. The narrator of the tale is staying with her friend Frances for a few days, but Frances' parents have left town and have placed her in the care of their maid. When the maid becomes suddenly sick and returns to her home to rest, the girls are left entirely alone to wait the return of Frances' parents. Since the girls received mild sunburns while picnicking earlier in the day, they decide to apply buttermilk and white linen masks to their faces to rejuvenate their complexions. As the girls wait for the parents to return home, they fall asleep still wearing their cosmetic wraps until a commotion downstairs unexpectedly awakens them. Thinking Frances' parents must have just come home, the girls light candles and outfit themselves in white wrappers before heading downstairs. When the girls reach the dining room, they see men in black masks robbing Frances' home. The girls are in shock, too frightened to move or scream, but the robbers are absolutely petrified. They believe the girls are ghosts and run from the house, leaving all their spoils behind.

While the story is very short and relatively simple, it carries with it—intentional or not—powerful metaphors about womanhood during turn-of-the-century America. The narrative pits two innocent girls against the shadowy figures of two faceless men, literally stealing the wares from their abode. The situation is perilous; help is far away and the men are criminal. The possibility of rape and physical harm are real risks in this situation, risks that would likely be just as much on the minds of nineteenth-century audiences as on the minds of contemporary audiences, but circumstances quickly change as a result of a very feminine feature—their ghostly cosmetic masks. These cosmetic masks, both feminine and modern, easily depict aspects of femininity that will be recognizable in the twentieth century; however, the masks are also ghostly or phantomlike, similar to the state of womanhood in the nineteenth century Killeen and Dickerson have mentioned (81; 133). The cosmetic masks in this story can easily be seen as metaphors for women's rising agency about to emerge in the twentieth century against the faceless and shadowy masks of patriarchal oppression marked by previous centuries. These young women represent a new generation of females actively seeking empowerment and capable of securing suffrage and other rights in the changing social and political landscape of twentieth-century America.

    The mock ghost stories for girls discussed in this chapter reveal interesting commentaries about the changing nature of womanhood and girlhood in the nineteenth and early twentieth centuries, offering unique perspectives on the way nineteenth-century Americans perceived the evolving concept of gender and rights for disenfranchised groups. Ironically, the ghost story acted as both a powerful and relatively safe place to explore progressive issues of womanhood in nineteenth-century America. As Dickerson and Killeen have discussed, the figure of the specter fits perfectly within the liminal spaces women felt they occupied in the nineteenth century in terms of social agency; therefore, it is not surprising that ghost stories featuring themes of girlhood often carried very progressive notions regarding gender and the place of women in modern America. In essence, the children's ghost story for girls in the American periodical presses of the nineteenth century became active locations for social and political reform, which very possibly influenced a new generation of women. While these stories have since fallen into obscurity, they nevertheless served as one of many powerful agents of change during the nineteenth century—an event that offers significant insights into girlhood, womanhood, and the fluid or liminal spaces they occupied. These stories of girlhood, along with other mock ghost stories for children of nineteenth-century America, occupy an important role in the history of children's literature in the United States, a history and influence I will demonstrate more thoroughly in subsequent chapters.

3

Resurrecting the Supernatural for Children

The Turn of the Century and the Children's Ghost Story

The beginning of the twentieth century heralded the start of a new technological and modern age, when many previously disenfranchised groups in United States would find greater social, political, and economic opportunity than in previous centuries, but the twentieth century would also witness transformations in the ways businesses and communities functioned throughout the country. Advances in technology literally transformed the way Americans thought and interacted with each other and the world around them. But despite these areas of positive growth and change, the twentieth century also saw monumental episodes of crisis and atrocity that were unparalleled by previous standards. World War I and II alone had a shocking impact on the national psyche of the country and forever morphed the way Americans perceived technology, faith, and fear. The ghost story was no exception to the powerful forces of transformation occurring during the twentieth century, though many of the most dramatic changes in ghost stories for children would not be apparent until nearly the middle of the twentieth century.

In the United States and other western nations at the turn of the century, modernism prevailed as the dominant movement in literature and art, easily dissociating itself with Victorianism and Romanticism with its radical departures in style and narrative. "The one thing that

The Children's Ghost Story in America

all modernists had indisputably in common," argues Peter Gay in *Modernism: The Lure of Heresy*, "was the conviction that the untried is markedly superior to the familiar, the rare to the ordinary, the experimental to the routine" (2). Modernism mirrored the radical technological and social changes taking place in the late nineteenth and the early to mid twentieth centuries. As Gay further states,

> Like a chord, modernism was more than a casual cluster of avant-garde protests; it added up to more than the sum of its parts. It produced a fresh way of seeing society and the artist's role in it, a fresh way of valuing works of culture and their makers. In short, what I am calling the modernist style was a climate of thought, feeling, and opinion [3].

Gay's assertions here accurately describe the changing artistic landscape of the twentieth century, but they do not communicate much about the evolving state of children's literature or the ghost story, though that is not particularly his aim. As Beverly Lyon Clark has admitted, "the end of the nineteenth century and beginning of the twentieth witnessed an increasing tendency to separate children's literature from literature for adults," which might explain the absence of such works in Gay's analysis (89). However, children's literature experienced a metamorphosis as well which reflected trends set by modernists. Literature for children started to abandon the Victorian values and expectations witnessed in the previous century and experimentation became commonplace.

In 1900, L. Frank Baum's *The Wonderful Wizard of Oz* became an immediate touchstone for such transformations in children's literature. Published at the onset of the twentieth century, *The Wonderful Wizard of Oz*, a now iconic American fairytale about a little girl named Dorothy and her adventures in the fairyland of Oz, depicted real changes in the kinds of stories that could be written and circulated to children in America. Illustrated by W. W. Denslow, the book was both a visual and literary success. Katharine Rogers reveals that within a year and a half it sold over 37,672 copies (88). *The Wonderful Wizard of Oz* represented marked transformations in terms of content and tone from previous children's publications, signifying a firm departure from the more moralistic and Victorian themed literature for children in the United States, though some popular exceptions do exist.[1] *The Wonderful Wizard of Oz* also demonstrated that stories dealing with elements derived from oral traditions, like fairytales and stories of magic, could produce successful children's books in the U.S. In many respects, Oz helped open the floodgates for texts dealing with magical or supernatural phenomenon in popular publishing for children of twentieth-century America, which would later prove fruitful for the supernatural ghost story for children.

The Ghost in Children's Folklore

While the supernatural ghost story for children remained scarce or nearly undetectable for at least the first decade of the twentieth century in the United States, its existence in children's culture is likely. Given that such folk traditions are spread by word of mouth, it is both difficult to confirm their existence and to determine their influence, especially when said traditions are not particularly encouraged, which previous chapters have shown is the case for the nineteenth-century supernatural ghost story for children in the United States; however, as shown in the first chapter, the ghost story has a history of rebounding and weathering the odds. "Ghosts, I suppose we could say," argues Gregory L. Reece, "are survivors. They refuse to go away, refuse to give up their place in the world, despite ghastly deaths, deep burials, and the relentless flow of time. They hang around and beat the odds. They survive" (29). In *Creatures of the Night: in Search of Ghosts, Vampires, Werewolves and Demons*, Reece explains some of the complicated cultural infatuations all societies share regarding ghosts, but one of his best arguments hinges on the ghost story's ability to survive relentless attempts to stamp it out. "Despite the dawn of the natural sciences," argues Reece, "despite the growing understanding of the world around us, despite the development of better theories, ghosts [have] survived.... Nor did it [the ghost story] go away with the forward march of science and technology, surviving still today at the start of the twenty-first century" (30).

If ghosts are indeed "survivors," imperishable elements of every storied culture, then supernatural ghost stories must lurk somewhere in the dark recesses of child culture in nineteenth- and early twentieth-century America. While the mock ghost story for children might have

The Children's Ghost Story in America

sufficed in the periodical presses, the oral tradition must have supported at least a few ghostly yarns that would have been overheard or communicated to children, thus explaining the fear authors like Dickens and The Exile demonstrated in previous chapters, but it is also probable that children applied their own efforts in preserving the supernatural ghost story as well. In *The Lore and Language of Schoolchildren*, likely one of the most influential books on the oral traditions of children published in the late twentieth century, Iona and Peter Opie explain the difference between stories told by adults to children and those circulated by children:

> While a nursery rhyme passes from a mother or other adult to the small child on her knee, the school rhyme circulates simply from child to child, usually outside the home, and beyond the influence of the family circle. By its nature a nursery rhyme is a jingle preserved and propagated not by children but by adults, and in this sense it is an "adult" rhyme. It is a rhyme which is adult approved. The schoolchild's verses are not intended for adult ears. In fact part of their fun is the thought, usually correct, that adults know nothing about them [1].

Opie and Opie suggest that children are effectively able to transmit oral stories within their own sphere of social influence, allowing for their stories to survive over generations regardless of approval from adults. Furthermore, Opie and Opie assert that these stories are far more powerful given their secretive status: "The scraps of lore which children learn from each other are at once more real, more immediately serviceable, and more vastly entertaining to them than anything which they learn from grown-ups" (1).

For the supernatural ghost story, child lore provided an important sanctuary. While the mock ghost story for children might have preserved some of the tradition's elements in print culture, children likely preserved the rest of the tradition themselves by communicating ghostly tales whenever the occasion would allow it. Under the covers during a sleepover, around the fire during camping trips, and behind the schoolhouse at recess, the ghost story likely thrived as a forbidden delight amongst nineteenth- and twentieth-century school-age children. The thrill and potential danger of ghost stories must have been at once irresistible and terrifying. "Being—scared—but not really," argue Mary and Herbert Knapp in *One Potato, Two Potato: The Folklore*

3. Resurrecting the Supernatural for Children

of American Children, "is a feeling children love. A child may overindulge in fear, just as he may overindulge in ice cream, and as a result may weep hysterically or wake up with nightmares" (242). However, frightening tales like the ghost story also serve important developmental purposes: "Children, though they don't know it, have many good, practical reasons for scaring themselves. Obviously, flirting with fear is a way of learning to control it, a way of learning to empathize with others who are frightened, and a way of embellishing one's life with a little dramatic fiction" (Knapp and Knapp 242). In essence, children likely find ghost stories both humbling and empowering, allowing for exploration and independence while simultaneously encouraging camaraderie and dependency on others. Fear also serves as a necessity for exploring and testing ideas within child culture. Children need fear to learn adult concepts and to identify potential dangers. Once again, Pearce's idea of "safe fear" enters into the fray (xvi). While discouraged in the nineteenth century, children's need for fear appears essential and apparent within their own culture and folklore, providing a place where dangerous concepts can be explored and regulated.

Fear, Consumerism and American Holidays

While ghost stories, supernatural and counterfeit, produce important and necessary psychological and social responses to fear, as shown earlier in the children's folklore examples, late nineteenth- and early twentieth-century Americans increasingly resisted frightening their children and moved more and more in the direction of avoidance (Stearns and Haggerty 63–64). In "The Role of Fear: Transitions in American Emotional Standard's for Children, 1850–1950," Peter N. Stearns and Timothy Haggerty argue that Americans began to avoid using didactic fear in the 1850s and progressively became stricter until nearly the mid twentieth century: "Overall," they argue, "middle-class Americans became increasingly aware after 1900 of fear's unpleasantness and replaced an emphasis on mastery with one on avoidance in their implicit definitions of the desirable emotional life" (64). Stearns and Haggerty primarily confirm this trend by looking at eighty-four childrearing advice manuals directed at middle class American parents

The Children's Ghost Story in America

and examine "various literature aimed directly at children" from 1850 to 1950 (64). These findings insinuate an increasingly unfavorable climate for ghost stories for children, particularly for supernatural ghost stories for children, which were usually regarded as more frightening, but the early twentieth century would prove to be a more fruitful place for the ghost story for children than the previous century. While the mock ghost story does decline in the periodical presses for children in America around this period, the supernatural ghost story still emerges and flourishes during this period due to an unlikely ally—the growing commercialization of holidays in America. Halloween offered the best avenue for the ghost story for children to emerge, perhaps captured best in the lines of a poem published in *The Youth's Companion* in 1909:

> No sort of fun I've ever seen
> Compares with fun of Hallowe'en.
> Not Christmas or Fourth of July
> Is half so fine! Do you know why?
> Because it has a dash and dare
> And just a little bit of scare [Cocke 565].

These few lines from Zitella Cocke's "Hallowe'en" indicate Halloween's growing popularity in child culture and the subsequent public indoctrination of scary lore like the ghost story into the holiday's traditions, which makes the history and reception of the holiday a fruitful site to study the emergence of the supernatural ghost story for children.

While parents in the States might have grown more conservative about frightening their children, American industries were beginning to realize the potential marketing power of holidays and child consumers to move products that previously would have seemed outrageous or frivolous. According to Leigh Eric Schmidt, holiday marketing grew exponentially in the late nineteenth century:

> Over the previous half century [nineteenth century] various civic, religious, and folk festivals—from Washington's Birthday to Easter to Halloween—had been widely and thoroughly commercialized. As the market penetrated and permeated the calendar, traditional celebrations were reshaped to serve the needs of specific industries. The expanding consumer culture—with its emphasis on advertising, display, fashion, desire, abundance, emulative buying, and self-realization—gave the holidays new drama and color. Civic, religious, and folk liturgies now intermingled with commercially constructed and manipulated

3. Resurrecting the Supernatural for Children

holiday rituals centered on mass consumption. In the decades following the Civil War, merchants, advertisers, and window trimmers set themselves up as the new high priests of American calendar celebrations, significantly changing the rubrics of American holidays [887–88].

These shifts in American consumer culture had developed radically by the turn of the century and evidence of growing consumerism could be seen throughout American culture. The age of merchandizing had arrived and would only grow over the coming decades, but the marketing of holidays in particular would play a pivotal role in the development of the ghost story. Halloween alone would transform the ghost into a marketable commodity—something that could be sold to both children and adults, somewhat ironic considering the ghost's intangible nature.

Alongside the ghost's transformation into a commodity, technological and industrial growth allowed for both greater leisure and the creation of new products; it also inadvertently started to create radical shifts in child culture in the United States, shifts that eventually altered the economic role of children in America. In *Pricing the Priceless Child*, Viviana A. Zelizer contends that the role of children in middle class America gravitated from viable worker with real economic potential to the "priceless" but "worthless" child in the mid nineteenth century (3–5). As such, children of the twentieth century became a new and powerful consumer group, capable of supporting a full array of new commodities, literary and otherwise. Holidays such as Halloween provided new avenues for businesses and authors to exploit this new consumer market. Postcards, candies, books, costumes, party supplies, and other sundry items became available throughout the twentieth century, but the celebration of Halloween for children also allowed for experimentation, discovery, and ultimately independence. "Trick or Treat," the holiday's signature slogan, is an embedded threat to adults who refuse to acknowledge the child's agency and demands on Halloween. This phrase alone testifies to the idea of children empowering themselves through pranks and elaborate costumes, but many researchers seem to doubt the extent of this agency.

As early as 1959, Gregory P. Stone contends that children rarely had any mischievous intent behind their threats of trickery, concluding that 83.3 percent of children he interviewed lacked a definite response if he selected "trick" on Halloween (375). Stone's research suggests that children rarely concerned themselves with the mischievous potential of Halloween: "They aren't bribing anybody," he argues. "They grace your and my doorsteps as consumers, pure and simple" (375). Many scholars echo this sentiment. In "Trick or Treat? Halloween Lore, Passive Consumerism, and the Candy Industry," Susan Honeyman makes a similar argument about trick-or-treating:

> Trick-or-treating, in particular, is the only major American holiday ritual that is communally enacted for and *by* [sic] children, and as such it would seemingly allow us to factor out parental influence in a study on the commercialization of childhood. Yet, throughout the history of this child ritual, parental control and corporate control share many motives and methods. While some children's and family entertainments celebrate the empowering potential of Halloween rituals, commercial and protectionist practices pacify the young (preparing them to become unquestioning consumers), and frequently Halloween stories reflect this reality, helping to co-opt the audience in the process [82–83].

Honeyman and Stone seem to have doubts about the empowering aspects of Halloween rituals performed by children, particularly the rituals negotiated and monitored by adults and corporations, but their focus is mostly on the act of trick-or-treating, not necessarily the creative energies emanating from the child's engagement with the holiday. Halloween allowed the concept of the supernatural ghost to enter the American child's imagination through marketed party favors and games and eventually through make-believe and story.

Opie and Opie, perhaps recognizing the creative fervor the holiday generated, take an entirely different stance on the creative and empowering potential of Halloween on the American child's culture, but their focus centers more on the supernatural and the ghostly and their appearance in children's folklore. "Hallowe'en, they [children] well know, is the night above all others when supernatural influences prevail, the night when divinations are most likely to succeed; and each new generation would be unscientific if it did not have an inclination to test for itself the age-old experiments," which largely included séances and other types of spirit conjuring games (274). Opie and Opie see Halloween rituals as both creatively and intellectually empowering for children, but they also acknowledge the holiday's potential to engage in rituals dealing with death and spirits, which would allow a space for the supernatural ghost to publicly enter the American child's

3. Resurrecting the Supernatural for Children

culture, primarily under the guise of party games, where children would attempt to contact the dead or learn their fortunes. According to David J. Skal in *Death Makes a Holiday: A Cultural History of Halloween*, "For most Halloween celebrants from 1900 to 1930, the primary treat associated with Halloween was the prospect of attending a themed costume party, which were hosted for children and adults alike. Massmarket periodicals like the *Ladies' Home Journal* annually offered illustrated suggestions for the perfect festivity" (42). Halloween parties were common occurrences in nineteenth- and twentieth-century America, but the influence of commercialism in the periodical presses of the twentieth century would allow for greater emphasis on the connection between childhood and the ghostly to emerge in the public forum of print.

As demonstrated by Alice G. Powell in *Pictorial Review* in 1906, the emphasis on childhood and the ghostly in relation to Halloween became apparent in early twentieth-century America:

> Everything associated with the unknown and mysterious is used to lend point to the celebration of Hallowe'en, and the children will be busy for a week ahead of the date preparing for the event. Every variety of lantern, big and little, *ghostly* and grotesque, will be pressed into service, and many amateurish ones will be made by the children with a simple penknife [43; my emphasis].

As the preparation and excitement above show, America's infatuation with Halloween seemingly allowed publishing trends for children from the previous century to slip and references to ghosts in child culture start to appear, but perhaps the best example of this trend occurs in an unlikely source. Holiday postcards featuring children in ghostly settings appeared in the first two decades of the twentieth century. These postcards typically feature children and supernatural entities like ghosts, goblins, witches, fairies, and devils engaging in mischief or experiencing a fright on Halloween and, on rare occasions, other holidays. While I have found practically no trace of supernatural ghost stories for children in the first two decades of the twentieth century in books or periodicals for children, postcards featuring children and ghosts or ghosts drawn in a child appealing—with cartoony or cherub like depictions—manner appeared frequently during this period, suggesting that a viable and profitable market did exist for the supernatural ghost for children in the early twentieth century.

The Children's Ghost Story in America

These postcards represented a new medium for the children's ghost story to appear and quite literally seemed to circumvent the barriers that existed for ghosts in more traditional print mediums, principally books and magazines. According to David J. Skal in *Death Makes a Holiday*, these postcards were both popular and reflective of the wider cultural practices of Halloween in America:

> The spirit and imagery of Halloween in America has never been so vividly documented as it was during the first decades of the twentieth century, thanks to the popular medium of picture postcards. Often elaborately printed and embossed, Halloween postcards offer a colorful and comprehensive catalog of holiday practices of the period [37].

Through these postcards a window into the early twentieth century's Halloween traditions can be observed and studied, particularly in their relation to the rising popularity of the supernatural and gothic in children's print culture. Some of the more successful artists involved in this trade were E. C. Banks, C. Ryan, and Ellen Hattie Clapsaddle. While many of these artists were both popular and successful, the most prominent of them was Clapsaddle, an artist "who worked for publishers on both sides of the Atlantic and specialized in adorable depictions of cherubic youngsters" (Skal 37).

Born in New York in 1865, Ellen Hattie Clapsaddle illustrated postcards between 1906 and 1914 and produced postcards for a wide variety of holidays including Valentine's Day and Halloween (Nuhn 31). According to Roy Nuhn, she produced "more than 3,000 watercolor paintings adapted directly to commercial use" and "sold hundreds of thousands of copies as prints," making her quite a publishing sensation for the early twentieth century (31). Her most popular works feature brightly colored illustrations of children in Halloween settings, often being scared by black cats, jack-o'-lanterns, and other mischievous holiday themed creatures or objects. However, perhaps one of her most memorable series of Halloween postcards features the reoccurring image of a child being frightened by a jack-o-lantern while reading a book of ghost stories by candlelight. The illustration, which exists in a few different versions, aptly demonstrates the commercial appropriation of the ghost story to market Halloween merchandise to children. Clapsaddle's postcards reveal that American industries had learned the value of the ghost to the American child's culture and demonstrates

This postcard by Ellen Hattie Clapsaddle (1900–09) features a little boy being scared by a jack-o'-lantern while reading ghost stories on Halloween. It demonstrates Halloween's significance in bring the supernatural ghost story into American children's literature and culture at the beginning of the twentieth century.

that they were prepared to capitalize on this realization. While authors, illustrators, and publishers of the previous century were apprehensive about encouraging youthful infatuations with ghost stories, publishers for children in the twentieth century seemed eager to pursue this infatuation as long as it remained profitable to do so, seemingly regardless of what other outside forces thought about the matter.

By nearly the mid 1920s, the supernatural ghost for children began to expand beyond postcards, merchandise, and party games. The supernatural ghost story for children finally started to emerge and spread throughout the children's publishing industry. Still relying on Halloween as a crutch, ghosts appeared in children's readers, small collections of stories and poems marketed to children and libraries, as focal points to Halloween tales. Alongside witches, monsters, and other supernatural creatures, ghosts timidly crept through the pages of these early readers to exert their influence. In 1924, Harcourt, Brace & Company released a reader titled *Little Boy and Girl Land: Poems for Children* by Margaret Widdemer, which features a perfect example of the emerging supernatural ghost for children, unsurprisingly titled "A Hallowe'en Story" and depicting "seven little ghosts sitting up on seven posts, [s]aying, 'Woo! Woo-oo-oo! Woo-oo-oo!'" to frighten the young children as they tell their ghost stories (76). Such simple and cartoony depictions of ghosts were commonplace in many of these early readers and were often illustrated with simple woodcuts of ghosts or scared children to clinch the effect. These early ghost stories rarely portrayed ghosts as very terrifying or threatening; in fact, many of these early stories convey the feeling that the authors are giving the child a little wink of reassurance as they narrate their ghostly tale. It was also common for these stories to be highly participatory, often encouraging children or parents to creatively interpret parts of the story.

Disney also contributed to the marketing of ghosts in American childhood toward the end of the 1920s. His famous "The Skeleton Dance" (1929) in *Silly Symphony* featured animated skeletons dancing across the screen likely to the delight of children around the nation, but it was in his next scary feature that the first animated ghost for children arrived on the scene. Within a matter of months after the Skeletons début, Disney released "The Haunted House" (1929) and gave Mickey his first supernatural encounter. While the skeletons once

This postcard by C. Ryan (1900–10?) depicts a little girl with a sinister, ghostly shadow sneaking a bit of jam before the feast. The image shows a shift in the acceptability of fear and ghost stories within American children's entertainment around the start of twentieth century.

This postcard illustration by E. C. Banks (1911) shows a ghost and witch on Halloween scaring two young boys. The illustration, like the one by Ellen Hattie Clapsaddle, demonstrates a change in perception of ghost stories within the American child's world around the turn of the century.

3. Resurrecting the Supernatural for Children

again make an appearance, their leader, a shrouded figure with bony hands, emerges from Mickey's shadow and takes center stage. This Disney short provides the foundation for other ghosts to emerge on screen for children across the country, but it would be nearly a decade later that ghosts would play another pivotal role in a Disney cartoon. "Lonesome Ghosts," released in 1937, grew from the vision created in these earlier shorts and provided s definite foundation for ghostly stories within the Disney franchise, but ghosts in more traditional print literature for children still relied heavily on Halloween and would depend on the holiday for years to come.

These trends in print literature for children are perhaps best captured in Halloween readers. *A Little Book of Hallowe'en*, a reader published in 1934 by the J. B. Lippincott Company and written and edited by Elizabeth Hough Sechrist, contains a poem called "A Ghostly Ballad" that demonstrates the evolving role of the ghost in children's literature. The poem begins by describing a frail old hermit, who lives off "bits of bread and bone" (33). While walking down a haunted path one evening, he encounters a frightening spirit. As he leans against a tree, "With weird, wild cries, / Before his eyes / A ghost appeared plan as could be/ Oh, oh, oh!" (33). The line breaks insinuate the suddenness of the ghost's appearance and convey a sense of shock, echoed by the hermit in the following lines:

> From where he sat
> Cried: "What is that?
> Ye ghastly ghost, get gone, beldame!"
> The ghost began
> To clutch his hand
> And whispered—*(End with a shriek)* [33–34; original emphasis].

The ballad ends with a cliffhanger meant to elicit a quick fright, which likely is induced more by the suddenness of the shriek than the terrifying nature of the tale. The abrupt ending and the rhyme and rhythm of the poem also likely contribute to the suddenness of the shriek, which defies the rhythmic expectation of the poem. Children surely delighted in these theatrical tales, which are common still today,[2] but early twentieth-century ghost stories still had far to evolve before reflecting the wide range of ghostly tales circulating presently; however, these readers had an impact on the children's publishing industry of

The Children's Ghost Story in America

the United States. For instance, in 1936,[3] as part of the WPA Art Project, artist Albert M. Bender released a pro-reading poster for children titled "October's 'Bright Blue Weather': A Good Time to Read," depicting a boy terrified by a book he is reading that includes a ghost, witch, bat, haunted house, and a spooky detective swirling around him in the background. This frightening scene surely portrays the rising influence of ghosts and other spooky creatures appearing in such collections as the before-mentioned readers, but it also demonstrates the close connection that still existed between ghosts for children and Halloween—the emphasis on October and a jack-o'-lantern's smiling face in the "O" of October.

While ghosts in these early readers possess supernatural abilities and frightening features, they seem to enact little agency in their tales and are often more pitiable and tragic than terrifying. They typically inhabit the shadows while other supernatural beings—witches, goblins, and other monsters—get to perform the true mischief. The pitiable shape of the ghostly shade in literature for children at this point is perhaps best captured in another poem by Sechrist from *A Little Book of Hallowe'en*. The poem is called "The Poor Ghost!" and describes the state of ghostliness rather succinctly. The poor ghost is described as lonely, wanting, desperate, and friendless, wandering alone in the darkness (53).

> He is just a shade, you see,
>   No matter what he tries to be.
> Apparition on the wall,—
> Just a shadow, that is all [53].

With few exceptions in the early twentieth century, the poem's account rings very true of the specter appearing in children's stories. The specter still remained in a more benign and obscure position in children's literature than other spooks and boogies, but other transformations in children's ghost stories started to occur during this period in the United States. With the Great Depression and the threat of another world war looming in the foreground, the ghost story for children began to be shaped by new social forces in the 1930s, which might account for the emergence of two very successful ghost archetypes in children's literature: the "friendly ghost" and the reinvented mock ghost of the new children's detective story.

The WPA reading poster by artist Albert M. Bender (1936–40?) shows a boy being terrified by ghosts, detectives, bats, and witches from the book in his hands. The illustration has now become a rather iconic reading poster and once again shows the connection between ghost stories and Halloween.

The Children's Ghost Story in America

Mysteries and Friendly Ghosts

The Nancy Drew stories, likely the most successful and iconic children's detective series of early twentieth-century America, emerged during a difficult time in America's history. Written by a number of ghostwriters under the pseudo name Carolyn Keene, the series debuted under the bleak gloom of the Great Depression, the worst financial crisis the world and the United States had ever seen. While Nancy and her father seem to portray an affluent lifestyle, some scholars contend that the Nancy Drew series tended to support messages of economic reform and class equality. In "The Juvenile Detective and Social Class," Troy Boone, making just such a claim, explains the social significance of the series against the harsh economic backdrop of the Depression:

> Nancy Drew embodies the public discourse on social and economic class that characterizes responses to the Great Depression, on the level of both popular culture and government policy, from the last years of the Hoover Administration to the Second New Deal, and beyond. The early novels in the series condemn unregulated capitalist speculation as the cause of unequal distribution of the nation's wealth and, by implication, of the economic disasters of 1929 [56].

Boone's appraisal of the Nancy Drew series confirms the widespread influence of events, like the Depression, on the children's publishing industry in America, events which would ultimately shape figures of ghostliness in the twentieth century, but the ghosts in Nancy Drew pay homage to a much earlier prototype of the ghost in literature for children, only perhaps in a much more expanded form. While ghosts for children started to evolve radically during this period, the mock ghost of the nineteenth-century children's periodical found a foothold in the emerging popular genre of the children's detective story.

Ghosts start to appear in some of the oldest stories in the Nancy Drew series. In many regards, these ghostly figures transform the old tradition of the mock ghost or hoax ghost in children's literature into a more modern and enduring form, one which still survives today in such iconic children's cartoons as the Scooby-Doo franchise, but one of the earliest appearances of this newly packaged version of the mock ghost for children emerges a little after the mid 1930s with the publication of *The Haunted Bridge* (1937). *The Haunted Bridge*, like other Nancy Drew mysteries, is a piece of formulaic fiction, which rarely

3. Resurrecting the Supernatural for Children

attempts to deviate from the standards set by earlier stories in the series, but the addition of the possibility of a specter gives *The Haunted Bridge* a genre crossover that some of the earlier books lack. *The Haunted Bridge* is seemingly the first in the series to make ghostliness central to the mystery and to the marketing of the book; however, the possibility and threat of a ghost is quickly neutralized by the fourth chapter. While the mystery of an elusive thief still haunts the story, the ghost the employees of the golf resort fear is proven to be nothing more than a mysterious scarecrow blowing in the breeze near an abandoned bridge just off the course. When the mystery is solved, Nancy learns the scarecrow acted as a defense created by a gardener and caretaker to ensure dogs and campers did not disturb his garden and mountain lion (Keene 178). With this final revelation, Nancy bids a kind farewell to the ghost/scarecrow and thanks it for "spooking [her] into a very puzzling mystery" (Keene 180).

Like the mock ghost appearing in nineteenth-century American children's periodicals, Nancy Drew's fake ghost carries with it an incredibly improbable scenario, where the audience is expected to believe that the staff at the resort had been duped into believing in a ghost by merely watching the stationary form of a scarecrow fluttering on its post in broad daylight. The ridiculousness of the scenario recalls many of the mock ghosts discussed in the two previous chapters and suggests that the mock ghost figure in Nancy Drew owes much to the mock ghost of the nineteenth-century children's periodical, but it also pays homage to earlier predecessors in the detective genre, particularly Edgar Allan Poe's borderline supernatural detective stories.[4] However, by adding it to the detective genre and placing it within a modern context, such as a golf course, the mock ghost seems revitalized compared to its earlier counterpart. But while the mock ghost was being fitted into a new role in children's literature, the supernatural ghost was also changing in literature for children, slowly starting to depart the one dimensional role it had occupied in most children's readers, evident from the supernatural ghost's newest form as the "friendly ghost."

While earlier versions of the "friendly ghost" do exist, they rarely existed in as expanded a form as they started to occupy in the 1930s and 1940s. These ghosts often received longer stories and greater attention than spirits from earlier tales. They also marked a departure from the supernatural ghost's dependency on Halloween as a necessary marketing crutch. The "friendly ghost" was essentially the first truly successful supernatural ghost archetype in children's literature. These spirits were still often as pitiable and benign as the others mentioned above, but they differed significantly in their appearance and attitude. These ghosts do not particularly like to scare the living, but they usually do by accident in most of their stories. They are often childlike, simpleminded, or goofy in appearance and attitude, and they frequently are troubled by tasks they cannot perform or problems they are unable to resolve without help from the living. When an open minded and brave human is willing to step in and help, he or she generally receives some kind of monetary or emotional satisfaction as a reward.

Perhaps one of the most interesting early examples of the friendly ghost for children is Dummy, the melancholy specter created by Wilson Morris and illustrated by Malcolm Chisholm. *Dummy* (1938), printed as part of the U.S. Works Progress Administration's New Reading Materials Program through the City of New York's Board of Education, depicts the tale of an abandoned and lonely ghost, trying to subsist in a small apartment building in New York City. Once happy living amongst a blissfully unaware elderly couple, Dummy's afterlife radically changes when the couple dies and all their possessions are removed from the apartment. The ghost quickly falls into a depressive funk and begins loosing what little power of shape and speech he formerly possessed, metaphorically starving amongst the barren, dusty wasteland of his former abode, an image that immediately conjures parallels to the Dust Bowl. "His sadness made him thin," remarks the narrator. "He did not change in shape, but the fog of which he was made seemed to grow lighter" (Morris 6). Seemingly fading slowly from the physical world, the ghost's problems only intensify when more people start to move into the apartment complex. When a new family finally arrives to occupy his apartment, they become terrified when he decides to appear before them, and they chase him from the apartment "at the point of an umbrella" (11). With more people moving in and nowhere to go, he eventually occupies a dumbwaiter in the apartment complex and slowly adopts its mechanical practices, making weird squealing and creaking noises until he loses the power of language altogether.

This scene from "Dummy" illustrated by Malcolm Chisholm (1938) shows the ghost being forced out of his old apartment by new tenants and demonstrates a deep-seated feeling of displacement occurring in the United States between technological progress and the struggles of working class Americans. Dummy is later found in a dumbwaiter by a little boy who helps him modernize and rediscover his purpose in a rapidly changing America.

When a boy named Bobby finally discovers him in the dumbwaiter, the ghost is completely unable to speak and firmly believes he is a part of the dumbwaiter himself. Nevertheless, Bobby befriends the ghost and names him Dummy.

Dummy's tale expresses themes about progress and change and

The Children's Ghost Story in America

their potential to damage the past. As a relic of a former age, Dummy is tossed into obscurity by modern America only to be resurrected by its youth. Much like the supernatural ghost story for children, Dummy revives due to the undying interest of a child. Tossed from the dumbwaiter by adults, Dummy depends on Bobby to guide him to a new home. With help from his friend Mr. Clancy, who works in a new skyscraper, Bobby manages to secure a home for Dummy in the largest elevator in the world, where Dummy can vocalize the silent gears of the massive machine as it carries people and equipment to various floors throughout the building. Dummy, like the supernatural ghost story for children, is reconfigured into modern America almost literally by becoming a fixture of the elevator, essentially bonding him to one of the fastest growing icons of American progress, the skyscraper. In many respects, *Dummy* foreshadows the changing figure of the specter in twentieth-century children's literature, but the tale's publication as part of the WPA also demonstrates the ghost story traditions' close ties to the social issues of twentieth-century America, a connection which will only grow more apparent in later versions of the friendly ghost.

In 1945, the same year the United States dropped the atomic bomb and ended World War II, Famous Studios released "The Friendly Ghost" and gave American children their first look at Casper the Friendly Ghost. Casper is undoubtedly the first truly iconic supernatural ghost character in children's literature and television. He is perhaps still the most iconic ghost in the children's publishing industry today. Seymour Reit and illustrator Joe Oriolo created Casper for a children's story in the 1940s and sold the rights to the character and story to Paramount for $200, a move which later sparked a rivalry over authorship of the character between the two creators ("Seymour Reit" 17). Shortly after the success of the pilot episode, Casper started appearing in short cartoons and quickly became one of Famous Studios' (a subsidiary of Paramount) most successful cartoon characters, alongside such greats as Popeye ("Seymour Reit" 17). By the 1950s, Harvey Comics ushered in the first appearance of the character in print, eventually displaying Casper alongside other characters like Wendy the Good Little Witch (Dittman 510). Since the creation of the franchise, Casper the Friendly Ghost has remained a financially successful character, earning roughly

3. Resurrecting the Supernatural for Children

a billion dollars in revenue in the 1990s, the decade that also witnessed the major motion picture of the franchise produced by Steven Spielberg ("Seymour Reit" 17).

"The Friendly Ghost," the 1945 pilot episode, marked the beginning of the supernatural ghost's emergence in popular culture for children, but Casper's first appearance also added surprising new trends to the ghost story genre for children. While the friendly ghost archetype had already appeared in American children's literature, the pilot episode displays odd transformations in ghostliness. The specters in "The Friendly Ghost" are in some senses cliché—they are white, transparent, sheet-like creatures that fly and haunt the night—but in other senses are quite novel, often mimicking planes, rowboats, and other machines. Casper is likely the most novel of the bunch. His features are rounded and childlike, making him appear more like an oddly formed cherub than a ghost. His desire to befriend humans also suggests something subversive about his ghostly nature, counter to the fearful reminder of death that ghosts typically convey. Unlike other ghosts, he neither longs for mischief nor life but rather something in between the two. He seems to want to know humans without ever having any knowledge of being a human in his past life: he is at once content with his ghostliness and disappointed with the character and company it affords—his fellow ghosts and their late night escapades into the human world. He would much rather befriend humans, particularly children, who appear both foreign and attractive to him, than associate with his own kind. This problem is made even more complicated by the narrator's reference to the other ghosts being his brothers, which could be a reference to them being literally his brothers from a past life or merely just creatures of his own kind. The audience is never given a satisfactory answer to this mystery, but it is possible he foreshadows social movements to come in later decades. Casper resides in a highly segregated world: a world of ghosts that haunt and terrify humans and a world of humans that ignore and neglect ghosts. Casper seeks the middle ground, rebelling against his ghostly brethren and genuinely perusing human interaction. He desires integration and attempts to accomplish this goal through his passive resistance to scaring and genuine desire to befriend all humans. This is demonstrated even in the pilot episode, where he desperately seeks the companionship

The Children's Ghost Story in America

of humans over the terrorizing practices of his comrades. By the end of the episode, Casper has left the other ghosts and taken up lodging with a human family as one of their siblings. The last scene shows him skipping off to school to learn with the rest of the children, which seems to indicate his complete departure from his former ghost family and their habit of pestering humans.

Whereas the other ghosts in the pilot tend to embrace their ghostliness more than Casper, they too exhibit odd behavior, though theirs tends to mimic the same pattern of odd behavior displayed by Dummy—an approbation of the behaviors and functions of modern machines. Casper's brothers always seem to be mimicking machines and causing general mischief. When Casper's brothers descend on the city like a flock of geese, their shape mimics both birds and fighter planes, giving their dramatic descent an eerie parallel to the action around Japan, which culminates when a line of these ghosts smash into the city's skyline. Though no explosions follow as these ghosts effortlessly phase through the steel and concrete of the city to the shrill cries of the humans within, the scene still produces an eerie resemblance to the war that must have resonated with both children and adults alike in 1945. While modern America seems to have developed around Dummy, emerging as skyscrapers and streetlights around his building, Casper's brothers fly from their rustic haunted house in the country to the big city, demonstrating that these ghosts can bridge for themselves the divide between the old ghostly tradition and the new.

While the supernatural ghost might have had a slow start in twentieth-century America, it grew into a popular entity in children's literature by mid century. From simple appearances on holiday postcards to mischief spirits in later tales, the supernatural ghost seems firmly entrenched in American children's culture by the end of World War II, but old archetypes of the ghost, such as the mock ghost, continued to thrive during this period and further demonstrate the ghost's ability to survive in children's stories. The ghost stories that materialize for children after 1950 show the ability of the ghost to survive and adapt in modern times, and Casper the Friendly Ghost represents a milestone in the evolution of ghostly tales in the United States. While Casper will remain an icon for children's ghost stories after 1950, new ghosts for children start to emerge in the later part of the twentieth

3. Resurrecting the Supernatural for Children

century. These new ghost stories will display radical changes occurring in children's literature and will give rise to new archetypes, series, and franchises, but the second half the century will also witness the rise of the literary ghost story for children, which will début some of the first ghost stories for children to win prestigious literary awards.

4

The Missing Phantom in Early African American Children's Literature

Ghosts in African American Folklore

Ghosts play an incredibly complex role in African American folklore and literature. They are invariably tied to issues of power, oppression, subversion, and ancestry that have carried any number of embedded meanings throughout the complicated and often controversial history of race relations in the United States. The first ghost stories printed exclusively for children share this complicated history, which warrants a deep examination of the tradition and its history to illuminate the meaning and context behind the stories that later founded the genre in the African American community. When the first slaves were brought to the Americas, they brought with them many of the cultural practices and oral traditions familiar to them in their homeland, including tales of ghosts and other related superstitions, but these tales and other oral traditions did not remain intact for very long once they reached the other side of the Atlantic. Under the dominating influence of their oppressive European slave masters, many of the purely African oral traditions met with various types of subversion and cross-contamination in the Americas—very few folktales escaped almost total transformation during the many years of slavery. In what would eventually become the United States, many slaves were forced to adopt English and European cultural practices fairly quickly, which had a rather pronounced affect on the African ghost story. "Like African Americans," argues James Haskins, "African American ghost stories

4. The Missing Phantom

have a mixed heritage. They have some roots in Africa and some in America. Especially in the case of African American folklore it is hard to say what came from Africa, what came from Europe, and what was a result of the combination of both" (ix). These European oral traditions soon transformed African ghost tales in America into a hybrid between European and African ghost stories, giving them a unique and even subversive twist that would later form the now more familiar African American ghost story, but the complicated history surrounding these tales and the circumstances surrounding their oral transmission has led to a great deal of debate.

Folklorists such as Richard M. Dorson and William R. Bascom dispute the roots of African American folklore, particularly on whether they originated in Africa or Europe. Both do seem to agree that all African American folktales offer a conflation of African, European, and American elements, but Dorson argues that the majority of these folktales do "not come from Africa" (15). He contends that many of these folktales must have originated in Europe and points to similarities between them and tales found in Europe, concluding that only about ten percent actually appear to share West African motifs (15–6). Bascom finds this claim a bit dubious and feels certain more tales must have originated in Africa (18). Interestingly, the two scholars agree on the African origin of one tale and it happens to be a ghost story. The African American folktale commonly known as "The Talking Skull Refuses to Talk," which Dorson gives the analogue number K1162, generally portrays a slave or African American man that discovers a talking or singing skull. When he shows the skull to anyone else, it becomes silent and refuses to speak, often with the result of placing the protagonist in great danger, which usually concludes in either the death or brutal beating of the protagonist (Bascom 22). This tales ability to survive relatively intact in the New World, particularly when other tales failed to endure, truly depicts the durability of the ghost story and demonstrates their value within the African American community, despite the often subversive dominance of European based folk and fairy tales.

Ghost tales featuring speaking or singing bones appear regularly in African American folklore and inhabit a number of tale types. Alongside "The Talking Skull Refuses to Talk," Roger D. Abrahams has collected

The Children's Ghost Story in America

"The Singing Bones" and Jim Haskins has collected "Moaning Bones." While the tales share little resemblance aside from ghostly sounds arising from human bones, their existence demonstrates a peculiar interest in the connection between body and soul within African American ghost stories. These tales tend to give the ghost a kind of physicality: they embody without truly embodying the specter. They are not walking corpses but do inhabit a space somewhere in-between the ethereal and bodily, which tends to demonstrate a concern with the body and its absence. This trend appears in other African American ghost tales as well. Dorson's "Eating the Baby" and Abrahams' "My Mother Killed Me, My Father Ate Me" closely resemble "The Singing Bones," but they do not feature spirits haunting their remains in quite the same way as the previous tales do. Their spirits have actually been re-embodied in a kind of spirit animal and unleashed to reap vengeance against their murderers. Abrahams categorizes these tales under the international tale type Aa-Th 780, but Dorson places it under international tale type 720 (317; 235). In these tales, the ghostly animal will sing a song around their remains—which are frequently on the verge of being consumed—to tipoff someone in authority to their murder. When the crime and remains are discovered, the authorities take vengeance on the spirit's behalf almost immediately. These tales all focus on either being disembodied or consuming the body. Their success in African American folklore is likely connected to slavery. Slaves, of course, have little control over what is done to their bodies, and these tales—regardless of whether they originated in Africa, Europe, or America—likely resonated amongst slave populations because they enacted the dehumanizing and unjust burden of their circumstances.

Ghostly tales of buried treasure also circulated widely within African American folklore and appear to have connections to both slavery and the Civil War. Richard M. Dorson, in his *American Negro Folktales* (1967), concludes that "[b]uried treasure revealed by spirits in dreams or visions constitutes a large section of Negro belief tales" and further concludes that "[m]any Negro treasure tales deal realistically with actual searches" (114–15). James Haskins corroborates this idea in *The Headless Haunt and Other African American Ghost Stories*: "During the Civil War, Southerners in the path of oncoming Yankee forces would bury their valuables so the Yankees could not get them.

4. The Missing Phantom

Often it was the slaves who were commanded to bury them" (108). In the folktales that arose from these incidences, the slaves placed in charge of burying these treasures were usually murdered and buried alongside their master's riches to serve as unearthly guards, and these malign spirits were called "plat-eye" spirits (Haskins 60). These spirits are prevalent in many African American ghost stories—such as "Buried Treasure and Hants," Richard M. Dorson; "Plat-Eye," Mary E. Lyons; "A Treasure-Hunting Story," James Haskins; and "'Cinderella and the Buried Treasure," Jim Haskins—and make up much of the folk tradition, but even these stories have roots in African folklore. "Plat-eye ghosts are found in American folklore only among African Americans," argues James Haskins. "African folklore includes a bad spirit that has an eye in the center of its forehead and webbed feet like a duck. It wanders restlessly through the night. The African American version of this spirit is a plat-eye" (107). Other forms of spirits also abound in African American folklore, like "jack-o'-lanterns" and "hants," but the prevalence of these sprits in African American folklore did not always translate into print. The ghost did not often do well in early African American literature and it struggled to appear in early twentieth-century African American literature for children.

Ghosts and Oppression

With so many famous examples of ghosts in contemporary African American literature, such as Toni Morrison's *Beloved* and children's author Virginia Hamilton's *Sweet Whisper, Brother Rush*, it is difficult to imagine why the ghost would struggle more in African American children's literature than almost any other place within American children's literature, but the supernatural ghost story advanced timidly within the pages of African American children's periodicals and books and the causes for this are linked to the complicated history of African American folklore, and the corruption of African American's folk traditions by European folktales only tells part of this difficult history. In the decades leading up to the Civil War, southern slave masters grew anxious about the large number of slaves working on their plantations and feared the possibility of an uprising in the wake of growing

The Children's Ghost Story in America

abolitionist sentiments in the north. Their fear led them to commandeer the ghost and other supernatural creatures in African American folklore in an attempt to further suppress their slaves. They transformed the ghost in the African American folktale into an agent of terror and oppression specifically designed to deceive their slave populations.

"During and following the period of Black slavery in American," argues folk-historian Gladys-Marie Fry in her pivotal work *Night Riders in Black Folk History*, "one of the means utilized by whites in controlling the Black population was a system of psychological pressure based on fear of the supernatural" (3). In essence, southern whites—responding to their growing fear of their slaves—spread supernatural tales within their slave populations in order to promote fear of venturing out after dark. They hoped to prevent potential uprising by igniting an environment of irrational fear: an environment where any slave wandering around after dark might fear the appearance of a malign spirit. In *Night Riders in Black Folk History*, Fry confirms this practice of contaminating the African American folk tradition with false accounts of ghost sightings by unearthing numerous oral histories recorded during and after slavery, claiming "[t]hese so-called stories were not fully developed narratives, but simple statements concerning the appearance of supernatural figures" (63). These doctored folktales circulated throughout the southern slave population and seemingly competed with more traditional folktales. While not every slave would have been fooled by such tales, their circulation certainly had a negative impact on the southern slave community and would continue to impact the development of supernatural tales in the African American community for decades to come.

The ghost story was the central weapon in the white slave master's arsenal of misdirection and fear. Fry argues that "[g]hosts were unquestionably the most frequently used subject for this form of control" (64). They were the most terrifying device slave masters could concoct to keep slaves from meeting in the night, but such ghostly stories worked most effective when tied to the memories of the recently deceased. "The terror of nameless, unknown ghosts was real enough," argues Fry, "but the dread of the return of dead people the slaves were acquainted with held a special kind of fear. When told the dead would come back

4. The Missing Phantom

for them, many Blacks were afraid to go outside after dark" (64). This act of personalizing the ghostly tale to terrorize slaves into submission undoubtedly had an incredibly subversive impact on the folk tradition of ghost telling within the African American community. Tales that might have formerly taught lessons or entertained adults and children alike all the sudden assumed any number of negative connotations. The ghost story was now associated with either the deceptive practices of the slave master or the threat of a terrifying supernatural encounter. In any case, the ghost story suffered under the strain of this deceitful campaign and would never again fully escape these oppressive connotations.

And as if the circulation of these false tales were not ghastly enough, slave masters also engaged in elaborate hoaxes and trickery to further instill a sense of dread within the southern slave population. They would occasionally masquerade as ghosts and would haunt the slaves where they lived or around locations they wished to prevent slaves from congregating near at night. As Fry succinctly confirms below,

> Some masters undoubtedly did no more than circulate rumors to frighten their slaves, but a hard core of slave resistance to accepting only verbal statements prompted other masters to initiate a second step in this control process—masquerading as ghosts. A few critically minded slaves required evidence of the kind of "scary things" that were supposed to come out at night [69].

These deceptive practices and costumes could take numerous forms, but frequently the slave master would simply cover themselves in a white sheet and ride or creep within sight of the slaves' lodgings (Fry 70–71). These tactics occurred both during and after slavery. The simple ghostly costumes worn by these slave masters continued to evolve into the costumes and uniforms worn by members of the Ku Klux Klan, which still vaguely resemble the costumes worn by the hate-organization to date (Fry 71, 79, 111–14, and 116–17). While Fry does not directly tackle the development of the ghost donned in a white sheet in contemporary popular culture, the appearance of such ghosts in twentieth-century popular culture and their seeming absence from most early nineteenth-century illustrations and literature warrants some speculation. It seems entirely possible that the development of the ghost as a wispy figure shrouded in a white sheet might have originated from the exact practices Fry recounts in her book, which tends to disturbingly insinuate that the most iconic pop-culture image of the ghost

The Children's Ghost Story in America

in America might hail from dubious origins, but such assertions cannot be proven with certainty.

Regardless of the possible pop-culture implications, the ghost in African American folklore was transformed as a result of southern white tampering with the folk tradition, but the ghost story still demonstrated remarkable resilience to this attempt to taint the tradition. African American storytellers reinvigorated many of these corrupted tales by further transforming the narrative to empower the African American victim. In "In Spite of the Klan: Ghosts in the Fiction of Black Women Writers," Geraldine Smith-Wright contends that these ghost stories were eventually amended to display slaves in a more positive and heroic light:

> [W]hile the fear motif remained essential in ghost tales, Black storytellers shifted their emphasis, often with a great deal of humor, to the prowess and quick thinking of the slave victim. Even in stories where encounters with ghosts were especially threatening, their comic tone was derived from the storytellers' accounts of the way extreme fear motivated them to escape the clutches of the supernatural. Humor was inherent in the slaves' fright—wide-eyed, panting, and sweating profusely, victims won the chase, often by a hair. The main objective of Black folklorists was to embroider the ghost tale to such a degree that listeners would marvel at the ingenuity of nimble slaves in the face of deadly odds.
>
> Slaves' supposedly innate fear of ghosts, coupled with their enthusiasm for regaling eager audiences with tales of how intended victims survived, shows how thoroughly African perceptions of the supernatural and the African oral tradition influenced slaves' responses to severe racial challenges.... Although slave owners correctly assessed Blacks' extreme fear of the supernatural, they failed to understand that slaves often intensified the Sep-'n'-Fetchit façade to trick their oppressors into believing that their shoddy tactics were successful [143–44].

While slaves did manage to reclaim the ghost story through both clever storytelling tactics and by inserting resourceful heroes, the ghost story did inevitably suffer some setbacks because of southern white tampering with the tradition, particularly in the early and mid twentieth century, when the African American community deeply desired to separate themselves from the stereotypes circulated about them within white America. As the desire for uplift grew, so did the desire to separate from harmful stereotypes, particularly stereotypes that cast the African American community in a superstitious light, which led to an active effort to separate African American identity from superstitious

4. The Missing Phantom

beliefs in American popular culture. This is not meant to say that a campaign was being waged against the ghost and other superstitious tales in African American literature and culture of the time—many fine ghost stories did appear during the Harlem Renaissance by famous African American authors like Zora Neale Hurston—but rather that an attempt to create some distance between those traditions was actively being explored in African American literature, particularly in African American literature designed for children.

This trend largely centered on refocusing the aims African American literature rather than outright discouragement of particular forms of literature. Within African American children's literature of the time, this often meant narrowing the focus to non-fiction and autobiography. "At the turn of the century and into the early twentieth century," argues Paula T. Connolly in *Slavery in American Children's Literature, 1790–2010* (2013),

> when African American writers came to write about slavery specifically for African American children, unlike many white authors they would not turn to fiction. Instead, they anticipated both the focus and form of African American–authored stories about slavery that would find fuller expression in the 1920s by reframing representations of slave narratives and presenting heroic black figures to inspire young African Americans [123].

As Connolly argues above, African American children's literature in the first half of the twentieth sought to explore various forms of creative non-fiction and autobiography, particularly in terms of dealing with representations of slavery, which left the ghost story with little room to haunt. And considering the negative associations of ghostliness created during and after slavery by southern whites, the desire to avoid the genre in children's literature must have been fairly great, but this also proved to be unfortunate considering the development of the ghost story elsewhere in American children's literature.

Children's Ghost Stories of the Harlem Renaissance

During the same years that saw the emergence of the supernatural ghost story for children in the United States, African American children's literature also took root in the American literary landscape, growing alongside the Harlem Renaissance and the New Negro movement, but the ghost for children would occupy a peculiar place in this new literature for children. *The Brownies' Book*—an African American periodical for children circulated in the 1920s and founded by W. E. B. Du Bois, Jessie Fauset, and Augustus Dill—offered the first significant appearances of African American children's literature in the twentieth century. In many respects, it heralds the beginning of African American children's literature in America; however, references to ghosts seldom appear within its pages despite growth in the ghostly genre for children elsewhere in the United States. Nevertheless, *The Brownies' Book* does offer a glimpse into the position of the ghost story within African American children's culture during the decades of the Harlem Renaissance and provides a broader picture of what the ghost story for children would look like toward the end of twentieth century.

Emerging from W. E. B. Du Bois' the *Crisis*, an adult oriented African American periodical started in 1910, *The Brownies' Book* represents one of the first attempts by the African American community to shape the literature their children read and consumed (Phillips 590–91). In *Children's Literature of the Harlem Renaissance*, Katharine Capshaw Smith argues "*The Brownies' Book* grew out of Du Bois' desire to create socially committed children" and hails the periodical as "the origin of black children's literature as a genre separate from adult literature" (25). In essence, *The Brownies' Book*, while only enjoying a relatively brief, one-year run, still captures the central concerns the African American community held about childrearing and child culture; therefore, the periodical's depictions of ghosts and ghostliness are vital to understanding the print history of children's ghost stories in African American fiction. In *The Brownies' Book*, Du Bois desired to create a text of uplift for African American children and hoped to influence childrearing practices within the African American community, particularly in relation to models of childrearing encouraged by white, middle class periodicals. In a recent article in *PMLA*, Michelle H. Phillips explains his mission as follows:

> On the surface, Du Bois' rejection of the romantic and apathetic extremes of child rearing for black children seems like an exercise in moderation, but its implications are far-reaching. Not only does Du Bois concede the experience of

4. The Missing Phantom

> double consciousness as a practical necessity, but he concomitantly suggest that black children need a model of childhood other than that of their white, middle-class counterparts. The black child kept ignorant of the color line is unprepared for the realities of race prejudice and sure to be disillusioned [593].

The excerpt from Phillips' article suggests that Du Bois wanted African American children to adopt a more "genuine" African American identity while simultaneously maintaining an image of acceptability within the understood norms of white, middle-class American culture, which largely attempted to dominate both the public and personal perception of Black identity in America. Du Bois wanted to offer African American children a counterpoint to the image or absence of an image of them presented in the vast majority of children's literature. He and his fellow editors essentially created *The Brownies' Book* to serve this purpose. Paula T. Connolly argues "the magazine both confronted and countered popular representations of racial stereotypes," which includes confronting the stigma of African American superstitious tendencies so adamantly believed by white Americans (148). *The Brownies' Book* attempted to circumvent these stereotypes in even the first issue of the magazine. While not dealing with ghosts per se, Edna May Harrold's "The Ouija Board" offers a moral consistent with such anti-superstitious sentiments, where the child that resists superstitious beliefs is rewarded by her school's board of directors by the end of the story, receiving a small monetary reward for her academic prowess (18–20). Stories such as these make up the bulk of narratives containing ghostly or superstitions elements in *The Brownies' Book*. Thus, the few ghosts and ghost stories present in *The Brownies' Book* are part of a very conscious effort to counter stereotypes about superstition in the African American community of the 1920s.

The ghosts' appearance in *The Brownies' Book* is minimal at best, appearing in occasional references but rarely operating as the focal point of any narrative within the magazine. The most significant appearance occurs in the illustrated poem "Hallowe'en" by Annette Christine Browne in the October 1920 issue, where ghosts are referenced alongside other supernatural characters but never really materialize as supernatural entities within the poem; in fact, the poem intentionally plays with the notion of ghost belief by juxtaposing it to many of the superstitions circulating around Halloween and haunted

The Children's Ghost Story in America

places. The poem indirectly dares the child to delight in challenging the notion of superstitious beliefs by telling the child, "No ghost or witch shall frighten us, / We'll seek the very places haunted" (305). These lines are reinforced by the illustrations accompanying the poem, which feature ghosts and monsters lurking in one panel but are absent when the children attempt to find them in the next, insinuating that these supernatural creatures are mere figments of the children's imagination and nothing more. Many other references to ghosts within the magazine assume even more benign forms. Jessie Fauset's "Ghosts and Kittens," published in the February 1921 issue, offers a mock ghost story, where the children of a middle class African American household scare away their maid by faking a haunting. In the "English Indoor and Outdoor Games" section of the June 1921 issue of *The Brownies' Book*, the description of the game "Ghosts" appears as a recommendation for indoor play for children. The game is a form of hide-and-seek in the dark, and the ghost is the seeker who must capture an unsuspecting participant: "The last person to be caught is the next ghost" (Johnson-Feelings 275). The final prominent reference to ghosts in the periodical is in the September 1921 issue within the poem "Friends in the Night," which mentions ghosts but only as a fear to overcome while falling asleep (Niedermeyer 256–57). Aside from these brief references, ghosts rarely make any appearance at all in *The Brownies' Book*. Nature spirits appear more frequently in the magazine, but even they are relegated to only a few references and are actually not true ghosts, being much more akin to sprites than the souls of the deceased.

While *The Brownies' Book* offers little in the way of ghostly tales, even around Halloween, ghosts do emerge in other places in African American literature of the early twentieth century. Outside of *The Brownies' Book*, but during the same period, Katharine Capshaw Smith notices a one-act play, "The Choice of Youth" by Alice Dunbar-Nelson, an African American writer from the Harlem Renaissance which is reminiscent of M. M. C.'s "Learning" and Alcott's "Our Little Ghost." It makes use of the specter as a powerful form of allegory. Smith describes the purpose of the play thusly:

> What makes the didactic drama especially interesting for its positioning within the New Negro Renaissance is the presence of two spirits who each watch over a group of children. The Spirit of Health and Common Sense guards the hearty

4. The Missing Phantom

company, while a vague, hooded, Gray Shape looms over the fashionable crowd. The Gray Shape complicates what appears to be a simple fable, for it calls up not merely the risk of unhealthy living encountered in city life but also the threat of "passing" into white society and losing touch with African American culture and values [102–03].

The above references to ghosts depict limited portrayals of ghostliness in African American children's literature and represent a few of the more substantial appearances of the seldom told ghost story for children in African American literature of the 1920s.

While the ghost story for children might have been on the move in other areas of the children's publishing sector in America, the African American ghost story for children appears more stagnant or resistant to some of the mainstream trends in children's literature. The reasons for this stagnation vary considerably, but a number of likely possibilities center on Phillips' observation about Du Bois' idea of double-consciousness, the balancing act between dual identities or, as Du Bois phrases it, the "sense of always looking at one's self through the eyes of others, of measuring one's soul by the tape of a world that looks on in amused contempt and pity" (Phillips 590; Du Bois 9). Du Bois realizes that a distinct double standard existed for African Americans in early twentieth-century America[1] and desired to rise above the "veil" of privilege, to live "above it in a region of blue sky and great wandering shadows" (Du Bois 8). He wanted to balance his divided or rather forcibly divided selves and reject stigmas placed upon his race by the white community. In reference to Du Bois' "Strivings of the Negro People," Dickson D. Bruce, Jr., claims

> Du Bois used "double consciousness" to refer to at least three different issues—including first the real power of white stereotypes in black life and thought and second the double consciousness created by the practical racism that excluded every black American from the mainstream of the society, the double consciousness of being both an American and not an American—by double consciousness Du Bois referred most importantly to an internal conflict in the African American individual between what was "African" and what was "American" [301].

In others words, Du Bois, like some other African American authors of the time, realized the significance of dual African American depictions of *self* within American society and sought to complicate stereotypes connected to his race by presenting images of the African

Above and opposite: This two panel illustration of Annette Christine Browne's "Hallowe'en" in the October issue of *The Brownies' Book* (1920) by Laura Wheeler depicts the overactive imaginations of children on Halloween. One panel shows their fears and the other shows those fears subsiding under close introspection. The illustration and poem demonstrate a level of uneasiness with ghost stories and other superstitions in the African-American community as late as 1920s.

American self that countered typical stereotypes. In *Children's Literature of the Harlem Renaissance*, Smith argues that Du Bois and other *Crisis* writers attempted to dispel stereotypes about African Americans in their writing, especially in their writing for children, where they attempted to refute stereotypes about docility and black home life among others (15–16, 70–73). Since superstition and ghost belief represented common stereotypes applied to African American culture, it is not improbable to assume the ghost story for children was intentionally withheld in African American children's literature in attempt to challenge stereotypes held about African Americans, especially given the complicated role of the ghost in African American folk history.

Influences in Later African American Ghost Stories

Considering the historical and social baggage surrounding the ghost story in the African American community, it is no great wonder that such tales received little attention in the first decades of publishing for African American children's literature, but some of the finest children's ghost stories of the later twentieth and twenty-first centuries were written by African American authors and have done a great deal to reclaim the ghost story from the tampering caused by southern whites during and after slavery. The Dies Drear Chronicle, a children's fiction series published by Virginia Hamilton, is perhaps one of the best examples of how the ghost tale is revived in later African American children's literature. The series focuses on the Small family and their residence at the house of a former abolitionist. *The House of Dies Drear* (1968), the first in the series, tells a thrilling mystery, involving the history of the abolitionist Dies Drear and his supposedly haunted house. The Smalls—a well educated African American family—move to Drear's house so that Mr. Small can work as a professor in a nearby town. When the Smalls arrive at Drear's house, they almost instantly encounter unusual occurrences—strange noises in the walls, mysterious symbols left on their doors, and eventually the ransacking of their kitchen. While Thomas Small, the tale's protagonist, quickly discovers that such occurrences are manmade, contrived by the old caretaker and later their neighbors, the novel still dabbles in ghosts and makes use of a number of ghostly hallmarks. Their home is surrounded in ghostly lore and Thomas and the caretaker, Mr. Pluto, do often seem to feel the presence of ghosts in tunnels. While no literal ghosts actually manifest in the novel, the fear of ghosts permeates the narrative and

4. The Missing Phantom

eventually works to the Smalls' advantage. The Darrows—another African American family living on the adjoining property—wish to plunder the secret historic wealth of Drear's house but have resisted the impulse to do so due to their fear of the aging Mr. Pluto and the ghostly tales surrounding the home.

When Thomas Small finally discovers the wealth of Drear's house, hidden deep in the underground passageways, he works with Mr. Pluto and his father to protect the home from the Darrows, whose fear of the haunted labyrinths and Mr. Pluto has started to dissipate. They concoct an elaborate scheme to scare and humiliate the Darrows, which takes the form of a ghostly hoax. They dress as spirits and hide in the woods to chase the Darrows off their property. They even paint a horse to glow in the dark to further seal the ghostly impact of their ruse (Hamilton 256–61). The elaborate plot the Smalls' devise skillfully appropriates the tradition of using false ghost stories in African American folklore to protect the plundering of African American historic treasures. Hamilton's use of such a tactic in the novel's climatic scene demonstrates an awareness of the pervasive power of the hoax ghost story in African American literature and shows an attempt to reclaim the ghost story by appropriating the tradition of the hoax ghost story to preserve African American history, thereby shifting the balance of power from the ghost being a corrupting agent in African American history into an agent of preservation. The Smalls literally save and preserve African American history by enacting their ghostly farce.

When Hamilton completed the chronicle in *The Mystery of Drear House* (1987), roughly eighteen years later, she expands on this theme of preservation by adding a conciliatory message to the chronicle through the character of Mrs. Darrow, who suffers from a debilitating mental disease closely resembling dementia. She wanders the tunnels below Drear's house in a trance, secretly reliving the past in the present—her delusional state adding yet again a definite atmosphere of ghostliness to the final novel. "Like an ancient tunnel of the Underground," argues Daphne Muse, "her mind twists back onto itself. Through her disjointed and detached voice, and long thick hair, she pierces the room and the novel with many a throat clenching moment" (36). Mrs. Darrow, representing a jumbled and mostly forgotten past, reveals the final secrets of Drear's house. The house is eventually transformed into

The Children's Ghost Story in America

a museum and the historical treasures of Drear's house are made public, bringing peace and resolution to the rival factions in the chronicle. This ending mirrors the tensions connected to the history of the African American ghost story the novels toy with throughout the chronicle: the ghost story finally redeemed despite its tumultuous legacy. While the African American ghost story for children has endured a number of hurtles, closely connected with a history of racism in America, authors like Virginia Hamilton have managed to demonstrate the enduring value of the ghostly tale and have revitalized the tradition of both literary and folk ghost stories in African American children's literature.

5

New Media, New Apparitions

By the middle of the twentieth century, children's literature in America had changed dramatically, fracturing into a number of new subgenres and embracing new mediums and technologies. Television, radio, print, and cinema were all popular sites of children's entertainment and education, spawning both widespread praise and criticism and ushering in a new era of child culture. As children's literature expanded in new directions, the ghost story for children followed, appearing in every medium and occupying various roles—new and old. With the vast number of artists and industries capitalizing on child culture after 1950, the ghost for children, supernatural or otherwise, moves in so many different directions that tracking all the adaptations of the genre in this book would be nearly impossible and would likely result in massive oversights. I suggest that a study of the genre after this date in America should sample from various sites where the ghost appears significantly in child culture rather than attempting to pull at all the different threads at once. As a result, my aim in the next two chapters is fourfold: to identify some of the most popular and influential adaptations of the children's ghost story, specifying where it borrows from older traditions—for instance the mock ghost story—and where it modifies the tradition; to analyze the reception of ghosts for children during this period; to examine the ghost as it appears in new media for children; and to explore where the genre is heading. While these research parameters are still somewhat large, they are far more manageable than trying to account for every form of the ghost appearing after 1950.

The ghost story for children, like the rest of children's literature,

The Children's Ghost Story in America

started to change rapidly in the second half of twentieth century, but even these rapid transformations still owe allegiance to previous centuries. In the introduction to *The Gothic in Children's Literature: Haunting The Borders*, published in 2008, Anna Jackson, Karen Coats, and Roderick McGillis argue that "While our understanding of childhood today can still, to some extent, be understood as inflected by Enlightenment and Romantic ideas of childhood, children's literature has changed so dramatically since the eighteenth century it is arguably a different genre altogether" (3). While children's literature started to move in radically new directions in the second half of the twentieth century, the ghost story for children started to evolve as well. Supernatural ghosts begin to appear more frequently in the second half of the century and start to display much more agency as characters. With few exceptions, the wispy shadows dancing along tombstones or crawling along attic floors transformed into fully formed autonomous creatures in this new age of children's literature. By the late 1950s, Casper had appeared in over fifty cartoon shorts, making it one of Paramount's most successful cartoons next to Popeye, but Casper's success as one of the leading figures of the supernatural ghost is only part of the change ("Seymour Reit" 17). The folkloric tradition of ghost telling is finally introduced as a stable and marketable component of the American child's ghost story. While it existed in some forms before the 1950s, it truly becomes a popular subgenre of the ghost story for children in the latter half of the century.

In 1956, popular author and folklorist Carl Carmer published *The Screaming Ghost and Other Stories*, perhaps one of the finest collections of ghost folklore for children of its time, featuring vivid illustrations and well written and frightening children's stories, but the coming decades would bring far more frightening stories of ghosts than those that appear in Carmer's collection. The evolving agency of the ghost can be linked to many causes at the turn of the century. In many respects, the children's supernatural ghost story of the mid twentieth century was far behind the adult ghost story, which took a more radical turn during the late nineteenth and early twentieth century than the ghost story for children. Jennifer Bann attributes this change to the far-reaching impact of the Spiritualist movement and women's suffrage, where she contends that ghosts shed their restraints much like the

5. New Media, New Apparitions

women of the period. "In the supernatural fiction of the later nineteenth century," Bann argues, "death began to bring freedom: shackles, silence, and regret were cast aside, and ghosts became active figures empowered rather than constrained by their deaths" (664). As has already been shown in previous chapters, these newly empowered ghosts are apparent by the early twentieth century in works by such canonized authors as Edith Wharton and others, but empowered ghosts are not apparent in children's literature until nearly the middle of the century. Peter N. Stearns and Timothy Haggerty argue that middle class Americans became increasingly concerned about the negative implications of fear on children after the turn of the century and encouraged their children to avoid fear rather than master it, which likely accounts for the ghost's slow development in children's literature during the first half of the twentieth century when compared to its adult counterpart (64). The increased marketability of children's literature and holidays like Halloween offered a strong juxtaposition to the trend of avoiding the fearful. While Stearns and Haggerty note attempts to suppress and monitor Halloween and other fearful activities and genres in the 1950s, they ultimately conclude that children's experience with fear changed rather than vanished. Fear "was experienced passively," Stearns and Haggerty argue, "by people in seats of movie houses or roller coaster rides" (94). They essentially contend that fear shifted from something that children and adults learn to overcome to something that they experience for the sheer thrill but are otherwise not taken seriously. Such notions of fear allowed the ghost story for children to change radically and to inhabit forms never before seen in children's literature.

In *Aliens in the Home: the Child in Horror Fiction*, Sabine Büssing argues that children's role in frightening fiction evolved dramatically throughout the late nineteenth and early twentieth centuries: "From the early 19th Century up to the present a pronounced change has occurred in the role of the child. It has displayed more and more activity, developing from a mere victim into a frequent aggressor, killer, a veritable monster" (xiv). While Büssing examines the role of the child in both children's and adult horror fiction, her observations still seem to display the same timeline regarding children's exposure to fearful stories noted by Stearns and Haggerty, but her observations also note that the child's agency in scary fiction began to expand as well during this period, resulting in the reversal of the child's innocent role in horror fiction. Children no longer served as merely the innocent victims but could become the monsters themselves, evident in such late twentieth-century children's books as the Goosebumps series. Ghosts, likewise, adopt a more frightening demeanor, often assuming more vindictive and aggressive roles. While earlier ghosts in children's literature might have been mischievous and spooky, the ghost for children after the 1950s became downright dangerous and terrifying, wielding the power to torture, kill, and even possess their mortal victims. However, these ghosts were not the only kinds of spirits expanding their agency in children's literature. The "friendly ghost" continued to flourish in the twentieth century alongside its new terrifying counterpart but it did so in significantly different ways and usually with a child character as an addition or companion to the ghost.

Friendly Ghosts

While Casper the Friendly Ghost set the standard for the friendly ghost archetype in children's literature and remains the most popular franchise of such ghosts today, other incarnations of the friendly ghost started to appear in children's literature after the franchise's success. To demonstrate the enduring qualities of the friendly ghost archetype in children's literature, I have selected three examples to analyze that appeared after 1950: *A Ghost Named Fred*, Nathaniel Benchley, illustrated by Ben Shecter (1968); *The Worried Ghost*, Seymour Reit, illustrated by Quentin Blake (1976); and *The Ghost's Grave*, Peg Kehret (2005). These three examples reflect a fair sampling of the friendly ghost subgenre after 1950 and offer other significant attributes for examination. For instance, *A Ghost Named Fred* remained popular enough to be reprinted in 1998; *The Worried Ghost* was authored by the creator of Casper the Friendly Ghost; and *The Ghost Grave* is a fairly recent example of the friendly ghost subgenre, which means it can lend insight into the future of the subgenre.

A Ghost Named Fred is part of HarperCollins "I Can Read Book" series for younger children. As with many picture books for younger readers, the book features a minimal text-to-illustration ratio, with

5. New Media, New Apparitions

rarely more than thirty words appearing per page. In contrast, the illustrations frequently fill the page—two pages in some instances—and make use of at least two color combinations per page, though three is the most common combination. The book relates the adventures of a lonely and imaginative boy named George. George, the only boy his age in the entire neighborhood, frequently wears costumes and plays make-believe by himself to keep entertained. But on one stormy day while he is playing astronaut, George gets caught in a rainstorm and takes refuge in a nearby home. While exploring the interior of the home, George encounters a friendly ghost named Fred, who guards a hidden—though lost—treasure. His appearance differs from Casper's and many other early-century ghosts for children. While he still possesses many cartoony features, Fred's form is decidedly more human in appearance than almost anything seen in the previous half of the century in children's literature. Ben Shecter, the illustrator, abandons the white sheet and cherub-like appearance of former friendly ghosts and instead replaces it with a more realistic counterpart. A balding middle-aged man, touting a goofy smile and late eighteenth-century apparel, Fred diverges from previous models of the friendly ghost, and Shecter plays with this departure by having George briefly don a white sheet and raise his hands eerily at Fred, parodying the cliché of former friendly ghosts (Benchley 44–45).

Like the more active and empowered ghosts of the previous three decades in children's literature, Fred can float, dematerialize, pass through objects, and interact with the physical world. He displays his power by walking on ceilings and phasing through doors rather than opening them, but his friendly attitude and demeanor render him harmless almost immediately. George is never really afraid of Fred. Contrary to expectation, when he first encounters the ghost, no screaming or fearful questioning ensues. He perceives him at once as friendly, but the situation is quite different before the ghost materializes. When George initially enters the house, he feels Fred watching him even though he cannot see him. To avoid the eerie sensation of being watched, George keeps moving through different parts of the house in hopes of losing the eerie feeling, but the sensation dissipates only occurs after the ghost reveals himself. George feels relief at seeing the ghost for a number of possibilities, but most likely because Fred represents a safe and caring adult to George, which provides him with the consonance he desires. In "Power, Fear, and Children's Picture Books," Jackie E. Stallcup argues that modern picture books offer reassurance in the face of fear rather than lessons through "threats of violence":

> Rather than invoking threats of violence to frighten children into submission, many modern picture books seek to reassure children that they have nothing to fear from imaginary dangers while at the same time demonstrating that there are very real dangers that only adults can defuse. Indeed, in some cases, parental control of the child's environment forms the foundation of a child's sense of security. Thus, many of these books consolidate and disseminate adult authority while diminishing the possibilities for children's empowerment and emotional growth [126–27].

Stallcup's argument about modern picture books explains George's feelings toward Fred; George's relief follows as a direct consequence of their meeting. The storm and entering a strange house terrify George. His feelings of uneasiness—of someone watching him—perhaps represent manifestations of his fear regarding the dangerous situation. While Fred may be a ghost, he is also an adult, and one of his first reactions upon meeting George is to scold him for being in a strange house without supervision, saying, "This is no place for a boy alone" (Benchley 39).

Unlike the situation in many older fairytales, where the child might encounter violence as a consequence of inappropriate behavior, George encounters the guidance and security of a kind and concerned adult. In essence, the adult authority Stallcup describes above provides George with an emotional safety net. To take this idea to greater extreme, George could have possibly conjured Fred from his own imagination in order to relieve a stressful situation, which would explain his calm attitude when the ghost appeared. Support for such a claim can be drawn from the ghost's timely appearance and George's very active imagination. Before meeting Fred, the narrator indicates that George typically engages in make-believe in order to compensate for a lack of friends his own age, which means Fred might merely be his newest imaginary friend. A gold coin provides the only evidence George's encounter with the ghost actually took place, but he keeps the coin to himself and places it "in his pocket as his secret," which

5. New Media, New Apparitions

means that his evidence might be as imaginary as Fred (Benchley 61–62). If Fred is the result of George's overactive imagination and desperation for adult guidance, then *A Ghost Named Fred* becomes an almost perfect illustration of a child becoming so absorbed with the need for adult security and guidance that he "disseminate[s] adult authority" and diminishes his own "empowerment and emotional growth," even when there is no *real* available adult (Stallcup 127).

A similar appropriation of adult authority through a ghost occurs in *The Worried Ghost* by Seymour Reit. *The Worried Ghost* is an illustrated novel for children, roughly a hundred pages in length, with chapters featuring occasional woodcut looking illustrations. While the target audience for *The Worried Ghost* is older-to-late childhood or early adolescence, it still relies on the same ideology Stallcup presents above, but it also slightly complicates her findings in that the child character also subverts adult authority and agency through the ghost as well—thus the ghost becomes a sort of permeable barrier in this story between childhood and young adulthood. Andy, the protagonist, meets his ghost in rather the same fashion as George: he gets lost from his school's tour group and encounters a mysterious voice in a restricted part of the mansion. Mr. Pettigrew, the ghost, features many of the same attributes as Fred: Quentin Blake illustrates Mr. Pettigrew as a middle-age man, drawn in a cartoony fashion. He sports clothes from a previous century, but he also differs in a number of other significant ways, displaying less power and a more developed back-story than Fred or Casper. While he can perform all the same feats as Fred, Mr. Pettigrew's powers are harder to perform and are limited to one hour a day. He frequently has trouble dematerializing and occasionally gets stuck when trying to pass through solid objects. As a result, Mr. Pettigrew has far less agency than Fred and is thus much more dependent on George to assist him.

Mr. Pettigrew tells Andy he remains in the world of the living because he left a task undone before he died. As the bookkeeper for the wealthy Jonathan Caldwell, the man who built the mansion Andy is visiting, Mr. Pettigrew managed great sums of money without ever losing any; however, shortly before his death, a small sum of money went missing under his supervision. While Mr. Caldwell never accuses him of stealing it, Mr. Pettigrew feels ashamed about the mistake and decides to resign rather than continue working under a cloud of suspicion. Before the opportunity to resign arises, a letter arrives for Mr. Pettigrew from a former employee admitting to the theft of Mr. Caldwell's money, but the employee's letter never reaches Mr. Caldwell. On his way to Mr. Caldwell's office, Mr. Pettigrew sees a fire raging at the home next door. He flies to action, leaving the letter inside a book close at hand, and dies while trying to rescue people in the fire. His letter never reaches his boss. So in penance of his failure to clear his own name, Mr. Pettigrew searches for the letter in the books of the great house for one hour each day, which is all the time he is allowed.

While the rules and the authority governing the spirit world are never made quite clear, Mr. Pettigrew indicates that his penance in the world of the living is entirely of his own choosing, a remnant of his stubborn nature that survived his death. He plans to search until he finds the letter or remain as a ghost forever in the attempt. Andy assists him in his search by tricking a teacher into giving him a special research project at the mansion and by probing his family and other adults for useful information. When Andy discovers the house is scheduled for demolition, it soon seems the latter might become the case; however, with Andy's help, they discover the letter and avoid disaster. In fact, when the post office receives the letter and delivers it to the organization charged with overseeing the grand home, a public campaign to save the mansion begins and subsequently results in the renewal of the mansion's protected status, thus giving the story a very progressive moral about preserving historical sites. But perhaps more importantly, Andy's heroic actions at the end of the book mark a significant step toward adulthood. Mr. Pettigrew could never have found the letter in time or saved the mansion from destruction. While he is a figure of adult authority and power at the beginning of the book, he transfers that agency to Andy by the end, providing him with the opportunity to make adult decisions and learn from the consequences of his actions, which is something that never occurs in *A Ghost Named Fred*. In this sense, as stated above, Andy subverts and appropriates adult authority—his parents, teacher, and other adults—by assisting Mr. Pettigrew in his quest to redeem his reputation.

The same subversion and appropriation of adult authority also seems to occur in *The Ghost Grave* by Peg Kehret. In *The Ghost Grave*,

5. New Media, New Apparitions

a fairly recent publication in comparison to the previous two, the ghost possesses the least agency and power of any of the earlier specters examined so far. The target audience of the novel falls between late adolescence and young adulthood, which may partially account for this difference—older children and young adults are more likely to be familiar with or interested in transitioning into adulthood issues than younger children. The novel follows the summer vacation of Josh in the former mining town of Carbon City. While Josh would rather be playing baseball in his hometown, his mother and stepfather (Steven) have forced him to stay with his eccentric Aunt Ethel because they must travel to India to complete an engineering contract. From the outset, the novel establishes an overt theme about Josh transitioning into a fairly new family dynamic, where Steven and his career disrupt the relationship between Josh and his mother. While Josh never outright blames Steven for his problems, he frequently complains about the changes being made to accommodate Steven's career, which takes priority over Josh's summer baseball camp. To avenge his lost summer and perhaps restore his relationship with his mother, Josh continuously works on a letter of all the dangerous things he has encountered since leaving home. He hopes to send the letter as act of vengeance toward his mother for siding with Steven, but he frets over when to send it and whether it is right to send it.

The arrival of the ghost changes Josh's perspective on many of these issues. Wilber Martin or Willie, the ghost, first appears in the old tree house next to Aunt Ethel's home. Unlike the other friendly ghosts discussed thus far, Willie has little control over his powers. He is invisible to most humans, and he can only interact with physical objects in short bursts, mostly to little effect. His greatest feat over the years has been the painstaking task of learning to read, which he accomplished by slowly turning the pages of books at a local library, but his official task in the world of the living is as clear as Mr. Pettigrew's objective: "The Boss says I [Willie] can't get my wings and move on until I get over my anger. He says before I get to be an angel, I must love someone so much that the love fills up my heart and pushes out my resentment" (Kehret 66–67). Willie doubts whether he will ever accomplish his goal. He harbors intense resentment toward the mining company that employed him and the incompetent coworker who sparked the disaster

The Children's Ghost Story in America

that led to his death. He is also entirely too preoccupied with a side task that eventually leads Josh into trouble: Willie lost a leg in his youth, which is buried separately from his body. He asks Josh to reunite his body, but doing so results in Josh finding a great sum of stolen money buried next to his leg, money that a bank robber is currently looking for. Willie's selfish desires nearly result in Josh's death. But with Josh's help and encouragement, Willie saves the day by distracting the bank robber long enough for help to arrive. Willie, like Mr. Pettigrew, enables Josh to mature over the course of the story. He creates the circumstance that allows Josh to transcend adolescence. Their cooperation while subduing the bank robber teaches Josh about responsibility and simultaneously allows Willie to demonstrate his love. Both characters are rewarded as a consequence: Willie moves on and Josh forgives his parents and destroys the letter.

Judging from these three late twentieth- and early twenty-first-century ghost tales, the friendly ghost subgenre seems fairly focused on providing a vehicle for maturation while keeping adult authority relatively intact, insinuating that children can only gain power by becoming adults themselves. These three stories empower the child or ghost by reasserting adult authority. While some of the child characters might initially resist adult authority, they typically come to accept it and adopt it by the end, which suggests that the friendly ghost might embody the spectral presence of adult guidance in all of these kinds of tales; furthermore, the friendly ghost's power appears to be in direct proportion to the level of maturity of each child protagonist. For instance, George, the least mature character, grows the least by the end of his story, and his ghost is by far the most uninhibited. Andy and Josh, being older and more mature, are greeted by weaker ghosts but reap more rewards from the experience. However, while the friendly ghost typology might serve this maturing function, it also draws quite heavily from much older ghost archetypes. Following models of ghostliness established in oral traditions and witnessed in the nineteenth-century children's periodicals, the friendly ghost haunts traditional locations—abandoned houses, graveyards, and wooded areas. It also acts with purposes: guarding treasure, *A Ghost Named Fred*; unfinished business, *The Worried Ghost* and *The Ghost Grave*; and reuniting the body, *The Ghost Grave*. Mr. Pettigrew perhaps states the sentiment

5. New Media, New Apparitions

best: "Unfinished business, my boy. When a ghost goes a-haunting, that's usually the reason. Maybe he has to right a wrong. Or protect a loved one. Or settle a score. He can't rest, you understand" (Reit 40). In *The Haunted: a Social History of Ghosts*, Owen Davies concludes something similar to the above statements for the appearance of ghosts, stating frankly "[t]here was always a reason" (4). Indeed, the friendly ghost seems unable to rest without accomplishing some purpose, which pulls from some of the oldest ghost traditions, dating as far back as the Middle Ages and possibly earlier, which might suggest the ghost story might appeal to something deep within human nature, something that perhaps crosses cultural and temporal divides. According to Owen Davies, the medieval ghost or "purposeful ghost" returned to the world for a variety of reasons, which could include everything from habit and unsatisfactory burial to revenge and treasure protecting (4–6, 55–56). These reasons parallel occurrences in the friendly ghost subgenre, which demonstrates the genre's reliance on older traditions, like the oral ghost story and nineteenth-century ghost story for children.

Popular Scary Folklore for Children

As the friendly ghost subgenre flourished in the second half of the twentieth century, other popular outlets for the ghost thrived in children's literature as well. In the 1980s, perhaps one of the most popular occurrences of the supernatural ghost appeared in Alvin Schwartz's series Scary Stories to Tell in the Dark, where the terrifying and often silly ghosts of oral legends reemerged as popular fodder for children's tales. Frequent finalists of the International Reading Association/Children's Book Council's "Children's Choice" poll in the 1980s, where over two-thousand children were sampled from five different regions of the United States voted on their favorite books, the Scary Stories series, according to Dick Abrahamson, stands as arguably one of the most popular children's series of the late twentieth century (99–100). Abrahamson attributes the success of this series and other books like it to their horrifying and entertaining content and "quick read" potential, with the average tale only spanning between one-and-half to four pages in length (100). While each of the three books in the Scary Stories series contains content other than ghost stories, the supernatural ghost remains a principle feature of each book in the series and the genre often appears within its own section, though ghost stories do appear outside of these sections as well.

Critics and scholars alike have hailed the success of Schwartz's Scary Stories series, some even offering quite lavish praise and acclaim. According to Sylvia M. Vardell in "Profile: Alvin Schwartz," published in *Language Arts*, Schwartz has earned the right to stand with some of the great folklore authors of children's literature: "Who has done for folklore for children in the United States what the Grimm brothers did in Germany, Perrault did in France, and Joseph Jacobs did in England? Alvin Schwartz, that's who!" (426). While perhaps an arguable claim, Vardell demonstrates the depth of praise afforded to Alvin Schwarz's work in folklore for children, particularly in publishing the ghost and other monsters that had previously only existed orally in American children's culture. Though not the first folkloric ghost in American children's literature, Mark Twain's telling of the "Golden Arm" in *The Youth's Companion* and Halloween readers continuing a folkloric connection to the child's ghost as early as the 1920s testify to the endurance of the genre. However, the Scary Stories series does provide perhaps one of the most popular incarnations of the folkloric ghost since Carl Carmer's *The Screaming Ghost and Other Stories* from the 1950s, which offers a format and presentation similar to Schwartz's series, but never met with the same level of popularity and praise. Alongside his Scary Tales series, and perhaps because of the series' success, Schwartz also published *Ghosts! Ghostly Tales from Folklore* as part of HarperCollins' "I Can Read Books" in 1991, which roughly follows the same tradition as his Scary Stories series but for younger readers.

Schwartz's scary tales for children demonstrate a rising appreciation among children and adults for scary stories with both entertaining and cultural or historical value. These tales are the product of Schwartz's tireless research of folk traditions and urban legends, confirmed by his thorough bibliography of sources at the end of his books and extensive notes on the text; however, the success of the Scary Stories series also reveals a reversal of previous anxieties about folk traditions and superstition appearing in children's literature. While

5. New Media, New Apparitions

nineteenth-century America might have witnessed intense repression of the folkloric ghost and other superstitions, the trend completely reverses in America by the late twentieth century with the rise of such successful series as Scary Stories, but Schwartz also feels that some of his tales contain strong morals and warnings alongside their thrilling narratives and historical and cultural content. He relates this in an interview recorded in "Night Visions: Conversations with Alvin Schwartz and Judith Gorog," where he indicates that his scary stories appeal to children because they provide both safe thrills and frights while also teaching lessons about real dangers—like checking your backseat or taking threatening calls seriously (Marcus 46–47). He asserts this same message at the beginning of the second installment of the Scary Stories series: "Scary stories of this kind [the ones in his collection] often have a serious purpose. They may warn young people of dangers that await them when they set out in the world on their own" (n. pag.). In *American Children's Folklore*, Simon J. Bronner reaches a similar conclusion about scary folktales for American children:

> The child's world is a storied place. Mysterious houses, dark woods, and murky rivers invite exploration, and stories about them summon caution. The dangers of the night, as well as the busy street, and a child's wanderings into both, bring up stories that have more than a hint of the bizarre, but are sworn to have happened—or at least that's what the child has heard [143].

In essence, Schwartz strikes at the wellspring of the American child's "storied place" and this is precisely why his stories have sold so well with children and continue to sell well with children today. His tales are their tales and convey embedded warnings and fears children harbor within their own oral traditions, which is why his stories have such powerful appeal with American children.

While this formula applies better to some of his tales than to others, subtle morals and warnings can be found in many of his ghost stories. In *Scary Stories to Tell in the Dark* (1981), his first collection, "May I Carry Your Basket" demonstrates just such a precautionary narrative for children. Sam Lewis, a young boy on his way home one evening from playing chess at a friend's house, sees a strange woman carrying a basket some distance in front of him. Being a kind and helpful boy, he runs up to help her with the basket and to learn her identity but

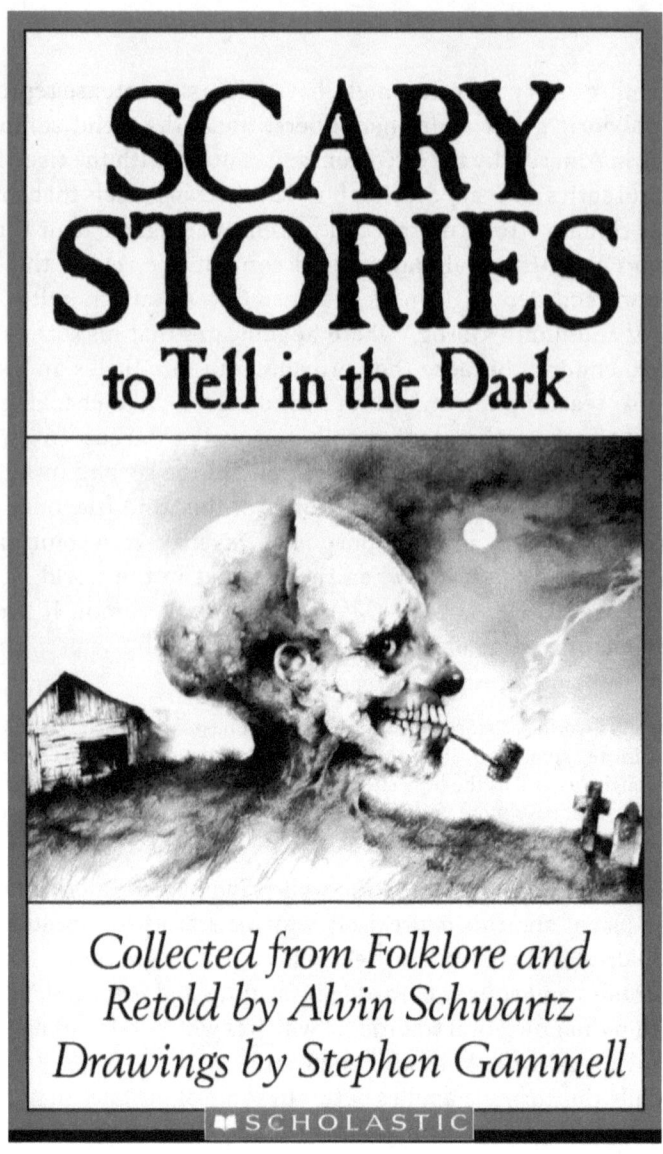

This illustration is the original cover design of Alvin Schwartz (author) and Stephen Gammell's (illustrator) *Scary Stories to Tell in the Dark* (1981). The book and subsequent series were a huge success, perhaps largely because of Gammell's terrifying illustrations, which are partially captured in the splotchy scene of a ghoulish head featured on the front cover. The illustrations and tales in this series demonstrate an important departure from concerns about ghosts and superstitions held decades earlier.

5. New Media, New Apparitions

instead discovers her face completely bundled. When she offers him the basket to carry, he quickly realizes it contains her head, which bites and chases him as he tries to flee the ghost. This story warns about reckless curiosity and the dangers of interacting with strangers late at night in secluded places, but it also offers gruesome thrills to entertain young readers.

In *More Scary Stories to Tell in the Dark* (1984), the second installment in the series, many of Schwartz's folkloric ghosts assume more complex roles compared to his previous book, often demonstrating greater ranges of emotions and assuming the central perspective in the story, but these ghosts also lack the same sense of conviction or purpose displayed by ghosts from the previous installment of the series. They are typically lost or confused—their sense of purpose and identity obscured by their unexpected deaths. Schwartz sets the tone for this kind of ghost with the opening story of his collection, "Something Was Wrong," where John Sullivan awakes on a downtown street to discover everyone running from him in terror. He later finds they run because he died the day before. These specters are not quite as malicious as Schwartz's last batch, but they do occasionally wreak vengeance on the living or cause some other form of unpleasantness. For instance, the ghost in "Sounds" reenacts a violent murder for anyone unfortunate enough to stay the night in his former home; the recently deceased woman in "Clinkity-Clink" returns for her stolen coins; and, in "The Little Black Dog," the ghost dog of a murder victim follows his master's murderer until the day he dies. These tales show definite qualities of the vengeful ghost, but the more reluctant and lost ghost tends to steal the limelight in this collection.

Aside from John Sullivan, the teenage ghost Jeanne in "The Wreck" stands out as one of the most memorable specters in this collection. Jeanne dies in a car accident on her way to a high school Christmas dance, but her unfortunate accident is no obstacle to her party plans. She arrives and meets a nice boy named Fred. After Fred drops her off from the dance, he realizes he needs to go back and speak with her; however, as he is driving back, he discovers her crashed car smoldering off the side of the road with Jeanne's mangled corpse in the driver's seat, and the only sign her ghost ever haunted him is a piece of tinsel Fred gave her to put in her hair (5–7). While Schwartz credits many sources for the story, he misses a connection to a similar story told in a predecessor to his Scary Stories series. Carl Carmer published a story called "The Lavender Evening Dress" in *The Screaming Ghost and Other Stories* that contains several of the same plot elements: a group of college students randomly offer a ride to a beautiful young woman to take to a dance only to discover later that she died quite some time before; the only evidence of the haunting is the tweed topcoat one of the boys gave her the night before which they find hanging on her tombstone the next day (138–46).

These two stories each contain qualities that have obvious appeal for adolescent readers: the characters are teenagers or young adults; the setting involves a dance and car ride; and the evidence of the haunting symbolizes teenage courtship. In many respects, these tales appear almost like Cinderella stories gone horribly wrong, but they also reflect a collapse of typical teenage or young adult courtship rituals. While parents and other adults typically act as obstacles in these relationships in other literature, the obstacle to the relationship in both the above stories is death, which means no amount of sneaking around will reconcile the barrier between these young people. It is perhaps this odd subversion of typical teenage angst that might attract adolescents to the Scary Stories series; the liminal space the ghost occupies provides a perfect backdrop for the transitional period of adolescences and the various power structures within and without. Adolescents are always exploring their expanding social agency and the limits of their world and culture. "Without experiencing gradations between power and powerlessness," argues Robert Seelinger Trites in *Disturbing the Universe*, "the adolescent cannot grow. Thus, power is even more fundamental to adolescent literature than growth" (x). In the Scary Stories series, death and the creatures able to function beyond death's veil regulate the flow of power in the world of the living. It is perhaps this quality that attracts adolescents to the ghost story. The liminality inherent to the ghost story—the ability to exist between one powerful phase and the next—relates to the adolescent's ongoing struggle for agency in the space between childhood and adulthood. Thus, series like Scary Stories offer perfect outlets for adolescents to experience and explore changing power structures, which likely contributes to the success of such series.

5. New Media, New Apparitions

Goosebumps

While the Scary Stories series has enjoyed a very prosperous marketing streak in children's publishing, the decade following the appearance of the series would see an even more popular version of the supernatural ghost for children and young adults emerge on the publishing scene. With the début of *Welcome to Dead House* in 1992, author R. L. Stine introduced his Goosebumps series to astounding and record-breaking success. His Goosebumps series eventually made him one of America's bestselling authors and elevated his series to one of the most successful book franchises for American children, selling over a hundred million copies in the 1990s alone (Perry and Butler 454). "Before Goosebumps appeared," argues Perry Nodelman, an established children's literature scholar, "there was little that might be identified as horror fiction for young readers. Within a short time, the books in this series absorbed so much of the market that they might well be described as the books young children most often read or bought" (118). According to the "About the Author" section of the 2010 edition of *Ghost Beach*, originally published in 1994, the series sold over three-hundred million copies, which would make it one of the top grossing book series of all times (122). While Goosebumps is a wildly popular series, many scholars, teachers, and critics find fault with the series, often criticizing the series' poor writing, flimsy plots, and short length. Some scholars have even identified Goosebumps as a sign of literary decline in new generations of readers, essentially claiming the series marks the point where good literature lost to popular marketing. According to Carol Lynch-Brown and Carl M. Tomlinson in "Children's Literature, Past and Present: Is there a Future?" Goosebumps and other recent forms of formula fiction represent declines in literature and literacy: "These books offer little reading or thinking challenges to young readers. Their appeal is that they are short, easy, familiar, and trendy" (242–43). Nodelman argues that Goosebumps reinforces the status quo, preparing children for a life of selfish consumerism and intolerance for difference (124).

Scholars also ascribe the success of the series by assigning it to some of the baser impulses in human nature or claiming it is merely the product of brilliant advertising strategies. In "Ordinary Monstrosity:

The Children's Ghost Story in America

The World of Goosebumps," Nodelman argues the series, like most popular fiction, is "likely to affirm their readers' existing assumptions or wish-fulfillment fantasies than they are to challenge them or to offer new or different ideas" (124). He seems to conclude that the series' success hinges on its ability to appeal to socially comfortable and safe concepts of self and identity. In "Are Goosebumps Books Real Literature?" Leslie Anne Perry and Rebecca P. Butler attribute the series success to mass merchandising, asserting that the series literally creates a culture to feed the frenzy by saturating the market with must-have-merchandise—everything from posters to mini-books in cereal boxes (454). Nodelman recognizes this outcome as well, but he also argues the ads in the books themselves contribute dramatically to their success, claiming previews for future issues in the series at the end of each book keep children hooked while the collect them all sales pitch (as is done with comic books and toys) reels them in to buying more books (118). Furthermore, he contends the culture created around the popularity of Goosebumps is so powerful that it can even outweigh the dislike of some children:

> Goosebumps signify membership in the community of acceptable, non-alien children. A number of parents have told me that their children ask for Goosebumps even if they don't particularly enjoy reading them. Just to own them gives one status in the culture of the playground, and not owning any or not having read any marginalizes children within that culture. To have Goosebumps is to be acceptably "normal" [118].

In essence, Nodelman and Perry and Butler seem to assert that the success of Goosebumps stems more from sensational marketing and social status than literary merit and great story telling, but such assertions might not necessarily describe the series or its success. Goosebumps is hardly the only series to attempt these marketing approaches, nor is the series the only one to attempt to use the status quo as a sales strategy. Something more must be at work behind the series' immense success. The series must offer something that other popular books for children lack. This *something* has its foundation in the supernatural ghost and the oral tradition. In essence, Goosebumps allows children to exercise agency over their own storied culture by appropriating elements of their oral traditions, particularly the ones that features ghosts and monsters.[1] R. L. Stine, like Alvin Schwartz, understands—at least

5. New Media, New Apparitions

in concept—the oral story telling tradition of children, particularly the ghost story and other scary stories, and he pulls from this tradition in ways that children and young adults can understand. He essentially expands the approach pioneered by such writers as Carl Carmer and Alvin Schwartz, giving the children's ghost story and other scary tales new legs to stand on, but he also makes connections to powerful concerns children and young people have about identity and power, which are in flux during adolescence.

While not every book in the Goosebumps series contains ghosts, many books in the series do involve them in one respect or another. *Welcome to Dead House*, the inaugural book in the series, is a ghost story and draws from many of the conventions and traditions discussed thus far, which makes it the perfect place to begin an investigation of the contemporary ghost story for children as depicted in the Goosebumps series. As with all Goosebumps books, the protagonist in *Welcome to Dead House* is an adolescent child around twelve years of age. Amanda (the protagonist) and her brother Josh are moving with their parents to a home in the suburb of a new town. While their parents are ecstatic about the move, the transition devastates Amanda and Josh, which means leaving all their old friends and familiar places behind. Being children, their opinions are not the ones that matter in the decision. Their parents have decided to move and the children have no choice but to make the move with them. From the outset, Stine has already tapped a familiar power struggle between adolescents and their parents. Adolescent readers will likely instantly relate to the children's disappointment at being forced to move and their lack of agency over the situation. Stine is also quick to ratify the agency of children in his books by always making their suspicions accurate while their parents generally struggle to comprehend the dangers. Amanda and Josh sense the impending danger within their new surroundings long before their parents notice anything amiss about their new home.

Drawing from traditional elements in children's folklore and urban legends, Stine provides seemingly an outrageous premise for the move: their father receives a free house from a great uncle he has never met or even heard of, which results in their moving and getting caught within a supernatural conspiracy. Ghosts inhabit their new neighborhood and want to make them ghosts as well. At first the children only

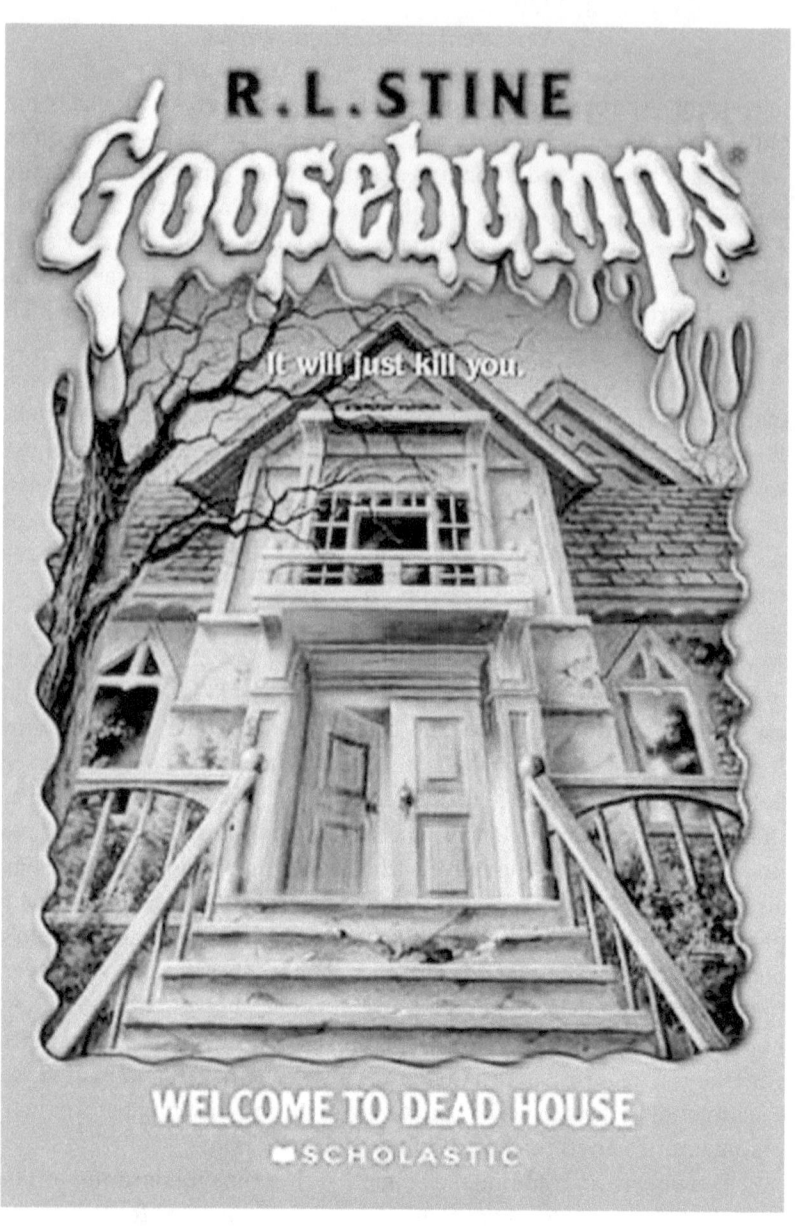

This illustration is the famous cover design of R. L. Stine's *Welcome to Dead House* (1992). This book launched one of the most popular children's book franchises to date. While Goosebumps offers a wide array of scary tales and creatures, the series began with a ghost story. The cover features a creepy haunted house set in American suburbia.

5. New Media, New Apparitions

notice odd occurrences at their home, but they soon discover the neighborhood children they have been trying to befriend, along with the rest of the neighborhood, are all evil spirits that maintain their power by attracting new families to sacrifice and then indoctrinate into their ghostly community. The children, recognizing the danger and discovering the ghosts' weakness, which is sunlight, rescue their parents from being sacrificed in the graveyard and escape to their old home and presumably their old lives. Following in the same cliffhanger tradition as most scary folklore for children, Stine offers one final twist before the story ends: Amanda sees the head conspirator ghost, Mr. Dawes, bringing a new family to the house just as her family drives away from the home (122–23).

As the first book in the series, *Welcome to Dead House* sets the tone for the other books to follow, particularly the ones involving ghosts of some kind. The theme of indoctrination reoccurs prominently in Stine's ghost stories. The ghosts in *Ghost Beach, Ghost Camp, The Headless Ghost, The Haunted School, The Ghost Next Door*, and *The Barking Ghost* try to indoctrinate or consume the protagonists, and sometimes their families and friends, into their community or condition in some way. On frequent occasions, the ghosts succeed in their task. In *Ghost Beach*, published in 1994, two children visit their elderly cousins' beach house for a vacation, where they meet some odd local children. These children share their last name and are possibly distant cousins. When the children discover animal bones in the forest and a supposedly haunted cave on the beach nearby, they immediately suspect the possibility of supernatural occurrences, particularly the possibility that flesh-eating or cannibalistic ghosts haunt the area; their suspicions are not far from the truth. Their new friends materialize into their worst nightmare: ghosts hoping to consume them and make them new members of their ghostly family. While the children manage to evade and forever trap their spectral friends, their fate remains questionable because their elderly cousins are revealed as ghosts as well, which leaves the children in a seemingly inescapable predicament (118–19). *The Haunted School*, while a mix of the ghost story and parallel universe story, follows a similar formula to *Welcome to Dead House* and *Ghost Beach*. The children in this story are transported to a parallel, colorless universe, where they meet children who became trapped in the world years before. While it is difficult to tell whether the parallel universe children are dead or alive, it is clear all but a few seek to convert the two protagonists by making them drink the dark water of the parallel universe. The protagonists in this story narrowly escape their fate when a few of the rebelling parallel universe ghost children help them to return to their own world.

Ghost Camp, published in 1996, offers a similar storyline to *Welcome to Dead House*, *The Haunted School*, and *Ghost Beach*, though with a slight twist: the ghosts in this book are interested in outright possession, not indoctrination, though the children suspect indoctrination initially. *Ghost Camp* follows the story of Harry and Alex at Camp Spirit Moon, a secluded camp in a creepy forest; their parents send them to the camp as a last resort because all of the other camps have filled for the summer. Ghosts occupy all the cabins at Camp Spirit Moon. The boys immediately begin to notice odd things about their fellow campers from the first day: mysterious blue puddles collect under their beds, some of the other campers are able to hold their breath almost endlessly in the lake, and a few of their new friends are capable of putting their hands in fire without being burned. Eventually, the secret is revealed, and the boys run for their lives, encountering strange and horrifying illusions created by the ghosts in the nearby forest before encountering the entire camp for a final showdown. While the boys seemingly escape the clutches of the ghosts, due to an unexpected brawl between the spirits, Stine offers one final twist. As the brothers search for the highway in the woods, Alex, who normally has a wonderful singing voice, is strangely out of tune. His brother quickly realizes this is because Alex has been possessed and his soul lost, consumed by the ghost of one of their former camp friends (116–8). *The Barking Ghost* (1995) and *The Ghost Next Door* (1993) deal with this same combination of possession and consumption, though it differs slightly in *The Ghost Next Door*, where the protagonist discovers she is a ghost tasked with protecting her neighborhood friend from being consumed by an evil spirit, which is seemingly fed by her friend's bad behavior.

The Goosebumps series seems to deal with motifs of power, fear, identity, conformity, and consumption, which are traits other scholars have noticed about the series as well. Nodelman argues the Goosebumps series consists of combinations of these issues and explains how they relate to consumerism and youthful rebellion:

5. New Media, New Apparitions

> Their marketing supports self-indulgence and the importance of gratifying desire; the belief that adult concerns are authoritarian and the encouragement of rebellion against them; the importance of status with other children, and the lack of importance of pleasing or agreeing with conventional adults and with conventional adult ideas about behavior or morality or literary excellence; the importance of ownership in defining self-worth and one's worth in the eyes of others; and the superiority of tough-minded fearlessness over a theoretically cowardly refusal to test oneself in the face of a loathsome danger [119].

For Nodelman, the drive behind the Goosebumps series hinges on fear, manipulation, and strict compliance with the status quo, which he argues is used to encourage "widely held values of contemporary consumer culture" (119). In other words, while these adolescents may believe they are rebelling, they are actually being socialized into the American adult consumer world. In *Disturbing the Universe*, Trites observes something very similar in young adult novels: "Adolescents have power that becomes institutional power as they (necessarily) engage in the social forces that simultaneously empower and repress them" (52). For both scholars, literature such as Goosebumps appeals to adolescents because it has the ability to speak to this transitional period of denying but accepting uniform power structures that comprise the modern adult world.

But while Nodelman is correct about several of his assertions in Goosebumps, he overlooks one very important aspect: he fails to realize the series simultaneously subverts the very consumer culture that he claims it upholds as the standard or norm (119–20). In the world of Goosebumps, children fear the destruction of their identity through being consumed or displaced by forces beyond their control; in essence, their greatest fear is being eaten away by the very power structures Nodelman and Trites argue they must learn to accept and appropriate. The ghosts and monsters that comprise the Goosebumps series are the embodiment of adolescent fears about the conformity and consumerism of the adult world, and the series actively makes these forces into the principal villains. In *Welcome to Dead House*, the spectral presence of suburbia tries to destroy and reform the identity of the children and their family; in *Ghost Camp*, the camp literally supplants the identity of one of the main characters; in *The Barking Ghost* and *The Ghost Next Door*, the ghosts steal or attempt to hijack the identities of the children; in *The Headless Ghost*, one of the main characters fears that a headless ghost will steal his head; in *Ghost Beach*, ghosts potentially consume two children and transform them into ghostly version of their formers selves; and, in *The Haunted School*, a school deprives children of their color and uniqueness and tries to make them into monstrous specters of their former selves. While Nodelman might argue the series actively works to indoctrinate children into the American consumer culture, it actually appears the series attempts to subvert this effort by making consumerism and adult institutions into identity-snatching monsters, leaving only the spectral presence of the child's former self when the rampage is complete. Thus, the allure of the series might be directly tied to the adolescent's identification with the tumultuous world of Goosebumps and the spectral or liminal depiction of childhood the series produces, which is likely further enhanced by Stine's ability to appropriate the traditions of the American child's "storied place" into his world as well.

The Award-Winning Literary Ghost for Children

While Scary Stories and Goosebumps dominated depictions of the supernatural ghost for children in the popular sphere, highly praised and award winning depictions of ghosts for children emerged during these decades as well, producing for the first time in American children's literature what might be called the literary ghost.[2] Virginia Hamilton's *Sweet Whispers, Brother Rush* (1982), a Newbery Honor Book, and Patricia C. McKissack's *The Dark Thirty: Southern Tales of the Supernatural* (1992), a Newbery Honor Book as well, are two of the most highly praised works for children featuring depictions of the literary ghost. As Goosebumps encountered intense criticism from parents, librarians, and scholars, these two books enjoyed widespread support from adult institutions during roughly the same time period. In "Ordinary Monstrosity: The World of Goosebumps," Nodelman offers a distinction between Goosebumps and more prestigious forms of contemporary literature for children:

> The books that get starred reviews in library or education journals and win important prizes praise moderation rather than indulgence; concern for others

5. New Media, New Apparitions

rather than self-gratification; charity and self-sacrifice rather than ownership and self-aggrandizement; thoughtfulness rather than willfulness; responsible, safe behavior rather than foolhardy defiance of danger. In allowing and encouraging children to indulge in the opposite of what we would like to consider admirable and acceptable, Goosebumps once more make that which is aberrant and monstrously self-indulgent acceptable—merely normal [119].

Nodelman's distaste for Goosebumps in this excerpt is fairly apparent. He draws distinctions between popular fiction, like Goosebumps, and literature, like *Sweet Whisper, Brother Rush* and *The Dark Thirty*, but the degrees of separation are not quite as clear as Nodelman tends to dictate above. While *Sweet Whisper, Brother Rush* and *The Dark Thirty* reflect the qualities Nodelman notices, they also share remarkably similar roots to Scary Stories and Goosebumps and subsequently the tradition of ghostliness in children's literature hailing all the way back to the mock ghost story in nineteenth-century American children's periodicals.

In the "Author's Note" to *The Dark Thirty*, McKissack claims to draw from her storied childhood sitting on the porch listening to her grandmother's scary stories in the twilight hours before nightfall. "When I was growing up in the South," writes McKissack,

> we kids called the half hour just before nightfall the dark-thirty. We had exactly half an hour to get home before the monsters came out.
>
> During the hot, muggy summer, when days last longer, we gathered on the front porch to pass away the evening hours. Grandmama's hands were always busy, but while shelling peas or picking greens, she told a spine-chilling ghost tale ... [i].

Her reliance on folklore and the child's "storied place" connects her tales to the same tradition as Goosebumps, Scary Stories, and the nineteenth-century mock ghost story in children's periodicals, but her tales offer a greater emphasis on social progressivism, historical context, and literary nuance, which is likely part of the reason they have received more literary acclaim than their more popular counterparts. While the ghosts in her stories are perceived as real, they also serve as complex metaphors for the turbulent history of oppression and racism during the twentieth century's Civil Rights movement. Her ghosts are social activists, who cause or symbolize change for social equality in twentieth-century America. Their spine-chilling tales offer children a glimpse into the complex social history of marginalized communities and the struggles they faced.

The cover illustration of Patricia C. McKissack's award-winning book *The Dark Thirty: Southern Tales of the Supernatural* (1992) perfectly captures the ghostly content of the book's material. This powerful collection of ghost stories and other spooky tales show the literary potential for ghost stories written for American children, and it defies the stigma that ghost stories only serve to produce cheap thrills and entertainment value in children's literature.

5. New Media, New Apparitions

McKissack uses "The Woman in the Snow" as a powerful means of demonstrating the wickedness of oppression and racism in contrast to the redemptive powers of change and progress. The story takes place during a severe snowstorm along a bus route located in the South near the middle of the twentieth century and depicts the horror of racist attitudes in the South. Grady Bishop drives for the Metro Bus Service and hopes the blizzard will give him a short workday. Just before deciding to discontinue his route, he sees a young African American woman appear out of the snowstorm carrying a sick baby. The woman shows him her sick baby and begs him for a ride to the hospital, but Bishop refuses to take her because she does not have the fare and because Bishop is a racist. Shortly after the storm clears, Bishop learns that the woman and her baby froze to death on their way to the hospital. He is initially un-phased by the news, but one year later he discovers the same woman running to his bus again during another snowstorm. Terrified, he hits the gas pedal and apparently dies in the subsequent accident, but the story does not end with Bishop's death. The ghost continues to haunt the route for years to come until a new driver takes over the route. When Ray Hammond, the first African American bus driver for Metro, accepts the route, the ghost finally receives her ride to the hospital and learns about the progress made toward racial equality since her death.

The ghost in McKissack's tale acts as a vehicle for progressive ideology, social history, and remembering forgotten stories and traditions. In essence, through Ray Hammond and the ghost, McKissack reveals the historical tension and discrimination surrounding public transportation in mid twentieth-century America by recalling the memory of older oral traditions and ghost stories, thereby preserving a rich African American tradition while simultaneously identifying the social injustices of a not-too-distant past. While the ghost acts as the memory of former wrongs, Ray acts as the voice of change. He literally enacts change on the past in his story by telling Eula Mae, the ghost, to move to the front of the bus. He tells Eula Mae: "'No you don't,' Ray stopped her. 'You don't have to sit in the back anymore. You can sit right up front'" (85). The ghost also provides Ray with the opportunity to reveal important historic moments dealing with Civil Rights within the narrative when he explains, "'I owe this job to a little woman just about

The Children's Ghost Story in America

your size named Mrs. Rosa Parks. Down in Montgomery, Alabama, one day, Mrs. Parks refused to give up a seat she'd paid for just because she was a colored woman'" (85). "The Woman in the Snow," like other stories from *The Dark Thirty*, provides a platform for teaching African American history and progressive ideas through the popular genre of the ghost story, but it also borrows from other powerful aspects of the tradition from nineteenth-century American children's periodicals. Just as many of the mock ghost stories in nineteenth-century periodicals ended with a rationalist moral, McKissack's ghost stories end with their own embedded morals about equality and justice. For instance, in "The Woman in the Snow," the story does not end with the death of Bishop, the racist bus driver, like most ghost stories would, but continues after his death to push the moral of social equality. Unlike Goosebumps and Scary Tales, McKissack's ghost stories are harrowing tales of uplift, not simply stories to scare children in the dark.

Memory and markers of social injustice within African American history provide a powerful conflation of historical and contemporary context within Virginia Hamilton's *Sweet Whispers, Brother Rush*. However, the novel also deals strongly with the unconscious motives of her central characters and their desire to recover (heal) or survive hardship, which renders her novel different from other closely related African American novels of the time. In "Virginia Hamilton's Symbolic Presentation of the Afro-American Sensibility," David L. Russell argues that *Sweet Whispers, Brother Rush* distinguishes itself from other African American novels and deals particularly with the topic of survival:

> Hamilton has, perhaps, invented her own kind of fiction, which is especially suited to her penetration of the Afro-American character and to her exploration of the Afro-American experience. Hamilton's books are—as is so much of adolescent fiction—stories of survival, of people learning to get along in the world. Her fiction is not so much a vehicle of social protest, as is that of so many black writers, but rather it is the impassioned portrayal of individuals in the process of getting along in the world. Through her use of symbolism, this process unfolds as an almost mythic enactment of the Afro-American will and means for survival [71].

Hamilton's *Sweet Whispers, Brother Rush*, like other stories from the ghost-telling tradition for children, emphasizes survival and reconciliation and seeks to resolve social strife through the symbol or metaphor of the ghost. Brother Rush, the ghost of Hamilton's novel, represents

5. New Media, New Apparitions

the shadowy specter of Tree (the protagonist) and her family's personal suffering and losses, but he also embodies the spirit of the African American historical context in the mid twentieth century and how it applies to a more contemporary context. As a spectral reminder of the past, a gateway to lost or repressed memories, Brother Rush enacts the past in the present by literally transporting Tree and her brother to their childhood, providing a temporal slipstream for them to reconcile their present.

In "If the Ghost Be There, Then Am I Crazy? An Examination of Ghosts in Virginia Hamilton's *Sweet Whispers, Brother Rush* and Toni Morrison's *Beloved*," Gail Sidonie Sobat argues that Tree and her brother's time traveling allows for healing and self reflection:

> Tree emerges from this realm, the ghost's "shining" space, replete with an understanding of her past and most importantly with a knowledge of herself. This knowledge, together with a purgative release of repressed memories, allows her to heal. Her time with Brother has been synchronistic; she no longer needs him to fulfill her lack, and thus he leaves her life [172].

With this knowledge of past and present, Tree is able to reconcile her own inner conflicts toward her mother and to better understand herself as a young African American. In other words, Tree's experience with the ghost of her uncle, Brother Rush, leaves her capable of dealing with past and future losses, but it also provides her with a tangible personal history in which to build an identity. Sobat argues ghosts in novels like *Sweet Whispers, Brother Rush* and *Beloved* are essentially foundations for complex coping mechanisms, liminal spaces where suffering and alienation can be reconciled: "the ghost is not a product of madness, but, paradoxically, a tangible presence and a manifestation of the (Black) female psyche to cope with suffering, alienation, and loneliness and to prevent the death of self" (173). For Sobat, ghosts act as living memories, which physically manifest as potential avenues for recovery from traumatic experiences or reestablishing lost familial or social connections.

In both Virginia Hamilton's and Patricia C. McKissack's fiction, ghosts represent vital connections to unresolved social strife, inner turmoil, and crises of identity and provide paths toward reconciliation and progress—whether personal or communal. In "In Spite of the Klan: Ghosts in the Fiction of Black Women," Geraldine Smith-Wright, in

The Children's Ghost Story in America

reference to African American novels such as *Beloved*, argues that ghosts are used as complex figures in African American folklore and fiction: "[G]hosts offer the proposition that African Americans can achieve justice, autonomy, and racial pride in an environment that from the era of slavery exacted their submission and fear" (164). Furthermore, she contends "that empowerment for African Americans depends on the sense of connection with their rich African past. The ghost tale is both narrative strategy and theme" (164). For Mary Frances Berry and John W. Blassingame in *Long Memory*, memory is essential to the African American community's sense of survival; despite claims by some scholars that African American's are a "rootless people," whose past and customs have been nearly obliterated by oppression, Berry and Blassingame argue that African Americans have preserved their collective memory through generations by transmitting it through oral and written traditions (x). In this sense, the novels and collections of stories by Virginia Hamilton and Patricia C. McKissack offer a continuation of an enduring tradition of powerful stories of oppression and recovery passed down in African American culture and literature. Therefore, their emergence as both a respected oral history and literary tradition marks changes in both the progress of the ghost story and the empowerment of the African American community in late twentieth-century America.

The emergence of the literary ghost for children indicates the reversal of many of the criticisms about ghosts in children's literature apparent during the nineteenth century. While the supernatural ghost story for children might have had a rough start, its place in American children's literature seems firm heading into the twenty-first century. With little doubt, the ghost for children continues to change as new technologies, trends, and mediums emerge, but the ghost story for children's reliance on the mock ghost story and children's folklore as a source of literary fuel is apparent in the contemporary examples of supernatural ghost stories for children discussed in this chapter.

6

The Transnarrative Ghost

The New Transnarrative of Ghost Telling

Ghosts in American children's literature have played numerous roles and are constantly occupying new spaces in American childhood, drifting through cyberspace on popular blogs and children's websites and inhabiting the narrow margins of social media, where the lines of reality have become so frequently blurred in the child's imagination. As print begins to subside, toppled by the allure of blue screens and interactive technology, where will the ghosts haunt? What form will they take? What new spaces will they occupy? These are compelling questions, especially considering the rapid growth of digital technology over the last few decades. As new mediums continue to grow and shape the literary world, the ghost story for children will change with it, morphing to fit the needs and desires of a generation saturated by the instant connectivity and freedom of the Internet. While traditional print narratives have salvaged a niche for themselves in this new digital landscape, nestled safely for the moment in the guise of audio- and e-book publications, the Internet and the interactive technologies that make it possible have provided fertile ground for new narrative techniques to form, techniques previously impossible to story tellers and writers before the existence of this digital frontier.

Within the first decade of the twenty-first century, rising digital technologies and the increased availability of computers and smart-devices have led to the creation of a new children's industry in literature (Pence 132). At the forefront of this new industry, emerging almost organically from the versatile capability of the Internet, is a new approach to story called transmedia. Transmedia or trans-narrative is a new multiplatform approach to storytelling, which bridges conventional mediums, such as print, with new digital mediums. In essence, a trans-narrative is a story told both in print or words and through some kind of digital component, often a video segment posted to a publisher's website that enhances and complicates the print narrative. According to Harry E. Pence,

> [T]ransmedia enhances a central story idea with a variety of components that provide additional information, give increased importance to minor characters from the main narrative, or even add new characters that were not in the original story. These additional components may include short videos intended to be viewed on a conventional computer or a smartphone, Augmented Reality Games, comic books or anime, or even components that occur in the real world, like phone calls and posters. All of these may interact to make the overall experience more immersive and interesting for the audience [132].

As new technologies flood the market for children, the possibility of trans-narratives becoming a popular new medium substantially increase in the literary marketplace for children, particularly as new and emerging tech industries attempt to make their products as viable as possible by connecting them to preexisting mediums. While print might serve as the basis for the story in some trans-narratives, the digital story might dominate the narrative in other settings or convey the narrative in more powerful ways than its counterpart; however, it is important to remember that trans-narratives must tell the story in tandem, not separately, meaning the mediums are not telling adaptations of a finished story but are communicating the same story together as part of a unified narrative with each component sharing its own part of the story.

Patrick Carman's Skelton Creek series demonstrates one of the first forays of the ghost into this new trans-narrative world. While *Skelton Creek* pulls from both the ghost and mystery genre, similar to the Nancy Drew series in this respect, the series provides one of the first real outlets for the ghost in transmedia. The story is communicated through two mediums: a book published by Scholastic and a website featuring video recordings relating to the story, which are accessible by codes given at the end of chapters in the book. The first book in the series follows the adventures of two adolescents—Ryan and Sarah—as they try to unravel an unspecified conspiracy surrounding the old mining dredge in their town, a conspiracy seemingly protected by their

6. *The Transnarrative Ghost*

parents and a powerful ghost named Old Joe Bush, disturbingly identified by the sound of his dragging foot. "And this time," reports Ryan, the protagonist, "when the ghost of Old Joe Bush comes for me, I won't be able to run away" (180). As the description suggests, the first book in the series ends with a cliffhanger. The final video shows the ghost trapping the children in a secret compartment within the old mining dredge. Only moments after the ghost makes this supernatural appearance, the children plead into their camera, which is a live stream to the internet, begging for help before the narrative comes to an abrupt end, leaving the children trapped in an abandoned dredge at the mercy of what might be a terrifying specter.

The ending offers a powerful metaphor about new technologies: the characters' fates are quite literally tied to the technology at their disposal and its ability to communicate their story to potentially millions of anonymous viewers. The internet provides the only means to their salvation. Without the camera and live internet feed, Ryan and Sarah would be lost without a trace, consumed by the mystery and ghost they attempted to unveil. The ending offers a testament to the potential of trans-narratives to become a force in the children's publishing industry. If trans-narratives are merely a passing fad, Ryan and Sarah's story, like trans-narratives, becomes a tiny blip on the radar of children's literature, obscured by the familiarity of more traditional narrative formats, but the success of *Skelton Creek* and its sequels suggests more than a mere trend in the industry in terms of children's publishing: it is quite possibly one of the first in a wave of new multi-platform stories that might steer the future of children's literature away from traditional narrative. The potential for trans-narrative is endless given the technological landscape that has emerged over the last few decades. From a marketing standpoint, particular for large publishing houses, the possible tie-ins with toys and video games is almost mind-boggling, especially for an industry that has struggled to keep print narratives engaging in a digital age. Companies like Nintendo and Disney have already expanded on the transmedia model with Amiibo and Disney Infinity, small toys that when wirelessly linked to video games add new characters and narratives to an existing game. These products are informally referred to as "toys-to-life," so named because of the product's ability to bring an inanimate action figure to life within the digital confines of a video game, thus allowing for the narrative of the game to adjust and transform with every new character. While few children's books have capitalized on this new technology to date, the potential for such toys-to-life products for tablets and smart-phones to radically reshape the publishing industry is tremendous. Mattel has already adapted the iconic comic book character Batman into their toys-to-life product called Apptivity, which is activated by placing the toy directly onto an iPad or similar device. Skylanders, another toys-to-life company, already features ghostly characters with their toys-to-life character Ghost Roaster, who features a wispy ghost tale made of a ball-and-chain.

Creepypastas

These "toys-to-life" products demonstrate the versatility of transmedia and provide new opportunities for children's ghost stories to expand in ways never previously imagined, but the greatest innovation and perhaps controversy surrounding the children's ghost story today occurs outside of the corporately controlled world of mainstream publishing and industry and haunts the very borders of the Internet, circulating on blogs, social media, and websites like YouTube. This new form of storytelling is called "creepypasta" and it lurks anywhere there is a connection to an interactive audience, regardless of the platform or the device. Marie Tina Boyer, one of the first scholars to study creepypastas, defines the genre as "stories, pictures, videos, or audio materials that have a paranormal or supernatural theme and convey narratives in the shortest format possible" (243). These narratives or "creepypastas" often originate with one anonymous or fictitious author and quickly expand within the interactive community where the narrative first appeared, often adapting to fit the audience's demands and expectations before migrating to other corners of the Internet. One user will post a creepy picture or a fake news story and another user will continue to adapt and expand the narrative, much like a folk tale or urban legend, until the narrative has gone through numerous versions, which only slightly resemble the original narrative, generally only retaining crucial characteristics and plot points. While the "ur"

6. The Transnarrative Ghost

narrative or original tale is easily traceable, which further distinguishes these tales from traditional folk lore, the potential reality of the tale is always kept in question, which resembles the mystery surrounding any thriving folk tale or urban legend: the possibility that the tale is based on some grain of truth. The thrilling power of the tale is directly linked to its believability.

In "Tall, Dark, and Loathsome: The Emergence of a Legend Cycle in the Digital Age," Andrew Peck argues tales like creepypastas, particularly ones like Slender Man, are a form of "digital folklore" and constitute a "legend cycle," a term he seems to prefer over creepypasta. He argues these tales are "an ongoing series of emergent performances" (335). They grow off of prior performances and enhance the features of the performances based on audience feedback. Peck describes this as a "feedback loop" and argues these cues can take the form of comments, emoticons, and other forms of digital expression (335). These all help to reshape the narrative as it is re-performed on various online platforms, the authors honing their skills much like actors on a stage but with digital rather than facial cues (335–36). This process allows for the successful transmission of an effective creepypasta, refined through numerous irradiations to please an ever expanding audience of viewers and readers. The tales grow in popularity as they circulate and some evolve into entire websites devoted to a particular story or character. They can assume almost any form of digital media—e-books, videos, and even social media accounts and usernames. In many respects, creepypasta and other forms of digital folklore resemble transmedia, but they differ in one critical respect: they are not the sole property or creation of one author or publisher but are community owned and regulated. A true creepypasta is akin to Red Riding Hood, Snow White, Cinderella and other folktales, bound to no particular author or corporate publisher but to the community that shapes and supports them, clearly distinguishing them from their trans-narrative counterparts.[1]

Creepypastas are critically important to the future of the children's ghost story for two main reasons: many creepypastas are about or focus on ghosts and most creepypastas are read and created exclusively by and for children and young adults. Given the immense popularity of these digital narratives with American youth, a study of the current trends within these creepypastas is incredibly important to understanding the potential future of the ghost story for children. Slender Man is the most popular and controversial of creepypastas. While Slender Man is hardly a ghost story, perhaps more akin to the bogyman than a ghost, the legends of Slender Man do take on some ghostly qualities and the immense popularity of this digital folk narrative currently drives much of the interest in its more ghostly counterparts elsewhere on the Internet, which means an examination of Slender Man will lend itself to a better understanding of the way the ghost story develops within current creepypastas, particularly since the tradition of transmitting these tales is so new.

Slender Man captured international headlines on May 31, 2014, shortly after two twelve-year-old girls in Wisconsin attempted to murder their friend of the same age by tempting her into a nearby wooded area and stabbing her in an effort to appease Slender Man. The young victim survived the attack and the adolescent perpetrators were quickly apprehended, but the media firestorm surrounding Slender Man and creepypasta had just begun. Within in a matter of days after the incident, the fairly obscure genre of creepypasta—within some online circles—soared to the forefront of the American media and took hold of the nation's imagination with the terrifying, gangly figure of Slender Man leading the procession. In a *USA Today* article published June 6, 2014, Greg Toppo asked the question on the minds of many Americans at the time of the incident: "Can a quest for the approval of a fictional character turn an otherwise sane person into a murderer?" (6a). In other words, can stories so thoroughly penetrate our psyche that the lines of reality begin to blur giving way to madness and homicidal tendencies? And do such stories have a far more pervasive impact on children and young adults? These questions are familiar to most literary scholars, particularly to scholars specializing in children's literature, but their persistence are often a great source of anxiety for authors and literary scholars. In the before mentioned article, Toppo reports that many scholars have found little evidence that such behavior is directly linked to a single cause or story but rather emerges from a broad spectrum of potential causes. To conclude his article, he quotes Glenn Sparks of Purdue University: "It's unlikely that any particular aggressive act [has] a single cause" (6a). While Sparks' statement seems perfectly

6. The Transnarrative Ghost

reasonable, and is even corroborated by the fact that few who encounter these stories commit such crimes, the fact still remains that at least two young girls did become so engrossed in the Slender Man tales that they could no longer determine reality from fiction, which recalls many of the criticisms made about ghost stories in pervious centuries, particularly John Locke in *Some Thoughts Concerning Education*, where he discourages the reading or telling of frightening tales for fear of causing such devastating psychological damage to a child.[2]

In *Folklore, Horror Stories, and the Slender Man: The Development of an Internet Mythology*, Shira Chess and Eric Newsom explore the online phenomenon of creepypasta and argue that Slender Man and other creepypastas afford storytellers, particularly young storytellers, the ability "to entertain, to explore cultural anxieties, and to build creative communities" (4). They see creepypastas as an expansion on the creative possibilities of folklore, enhanced by the Internet's potential to reach a diverse audience and its ability to transmit story through multiple mediums at once. For Chess and Newsom, creepypastas like Slender Man capture the very essence of the ghost telling tradition:

> The open, shared nature of the Slender Man mythos encouraged participation and young creators often engaged with the stories they read by creating new variations. Far from being sick and twisted, this is the way that ghost stories have always been told, but enhanced by the affordances of the digital spaces that housed their telling [5].

Ghost stories have always endured criticism, especially ones designed for young audiences, but creepypastas—as Chess and Newsom demonstrate—are facing a new wave of criticism. As shown in pervious chapters, public censorship of a particular genre based on its potential to corrupt the minds of children can have a devastating impact on the development of a literary genre, specifically an emerging genre like creepypasta, where the foundation is less than a decade old. If the folk tradition of ghost telling in the American child's world is dependent on the success of genres like creepypasta, the Slender Man case described above could eventually have a crippling impact on the future of the ghost story. It could potentially reawaken the same desire for censorship seen in previous centuries.

While the ghoulish figure of Slender Man may be currently hogging the limelight, the attention could easily shift to focus on his terrifying counterparts, including many of the ghost stories that haunt a significant portion of the creepypasta genre. As of 2016, many creepypasta websites have already responded to calls for censorship by posting warnings and definitions to their homepages: Creepypasta Wiki offers a definition of the genre at the bottom of their homepage under "What is a 'Creepypasta'?" to clarify their objectives and Creepypasta.com provides a full disclaimer about the scary nature of their content. Creepypasta.com is now recommending their website for adults only and encourages parents to take measures to block their children from the website, an interesting move considering the genre's origin and appeal within youth culture, but it is definitely a sign of increasing censorship within the genre. These websites have reacted to public demands for greater regulation, not entirely different from the kind witnessed in the nineteenth century, but are still relatively available to children without parental safeguards activated on their home computers. The ghost has escaped annihilation in children's literature in the past, but a new outbreak of censorship may conjure different results, especially considering the enhanced ability of technology to help parents and companies censor children's devices. There may even be some truth to the claims made about these stories and others like them. Great stories are indeed powerful. When a child fails to place a powerful story in the proper context, it can have devastating consequences, particularly if adults lack the awareness to compensate for such misreading, but the benefits of these stories far outweigh their risks, especially in the case of creepypastas, where children have greater leverage to exercise their creative energy and to explore their fears and ideas about death.

 The most popular of the creepypastas featuring a ghostly character is "Ben Drowned," also called "Haunted Majora's Mask," initially posted by Alex Hall, who goes by the penname or username "Jadusable," on September 7, 2010, with subsequent posts following soon after the first post. The creepypasta originated on 4chan and quickly spread to other sites and the full version is still accessible on Creepypasta Wiki and the consolidated version on YouTube. Hall's tale takes place through a variety of mediums, mostly videos embedded into a 4chan post and text, but later fake websites and chat conversations followed to complete the effect—most of which were initially created by Hall himself.

6. The Transnarrative Ghost

Ben Drowned appears to have originally been indented as a kind of prank. Hall gives no clear indication that his posts are fake, vaguely reminiscent of the beginning of a Washington Irving tale but without the safety of a periodical cover to assure audiences that the tale is only a piece of clever fiction. In proper gothic fashion, the story unfolds like letters or journal entries to anyone willing to listen and discover their secrets. The narrative focuses on Jadusable and his discovery of a mysterious copy of the Nintendo 64 game *The Legend of Zelda: Majora's Mask* (2000) at an old man's garage sale. The old man, blind in one eye, appears eager to part with the game and memorably cries out "Goodbye, then" or "Goodbye, Ben" as Jadusable prepares to drive away with the game. These words later haunt Jadusable because his new game has a secret.

When he begins playing the game cartridge, he eventually discovers that it is haunted by an entity called "Ben." Ben is initially silent. He appears as an old save file when Jadusable starts the game and later emerges within the game in place of Jadusable's user name "Link." Jadusable assumes the old game is malfunctioning and deletes Ben's file in hopes of remedying the name slips within the system. This act provokes Ben and causes him to disrupt Jadusable game play with noticeable distortions to the music and graphics that truly produce a chilling effect for anyone who has played the video game before. These effects are demonstrated in the videos embedded in Jadusable's posts, and they quickly steal the narrative as Jadusable has modified the old Zelda game code to tell his story with a surreal sense of terror—the video is spliced with creepy text dialogue, distorted game music, and long pauses of the Link character in warped or deathlike poses. Hall's familiarity with this iconic children's video game is instrumental to the chilling effect. While even those unfamiliar with the game will find the footage disturbing, the effect is increased tenfold for anyone familiar with the iconic hero of the children's game as he is repeatedly set ablaze, drowned, and bent in unnatural ways, counter to his heroic and often childlike appearance in the popular game series.

Ben, the specter or entity that haunts Jadusable through the game and eventually his dreams and computer, has an ambiguous origin. Jadusable learns that a child named Ben did own the game and did die under mysterious circumstances, presumably drowning before completing the game; however, the ghostlike entity, while using the name Ben, toys with the idea that it might have assumed the name after causing Ben's death. The entity never clarifies this mystery and Ben's back story remains uncertain throughout the creepypasta, giving the narrative an otherworldly and demonic quality, somewhat reminiscent of Lovecraft's weird tales, where the origin of the evil entity is rarely clarified. The effect is often terrifying. Jadusable's desperation and later borderline insanity instill a thrilling sense of foreboding in the narrative that likely helped secure its popularity with online audiences, particularly with the children and young adults that frequently view and follow such creepypastas. When Jadusable finally appears to gain the upper hand in the battle for his sanity against Ben, the narrative abruptly closes with Jadusable's college friend reporting that Jadusable quit college and asked him to post his final entry on Ben, which leaves the narrative precariously open for interpretation. Jadusable may have won or he is perhaps on the run, hoping to flee the specter by abandoning his old dormitory.

While the basic narrative of Ben Drowned is hardly original, playing on the thematic structure and tropes of numerous ghost stories before it, the presentation and context are entirely unique, potentially opening the ghost story genre in children's literature to new and innovative narrative avenues. Ben Drowned creepypastas also speak to issues of childhood in interesting ways. The creepypasta's appropriation of the iconic Zelda franchise to both connect and distort childhood memories for contemporary American children and young adults challenges the safe and creative space video games have often provided for American children over the last three decades. Ben Drowned transforms the fairy world of both Zelda and childhood into places of madness and evil, where the act of "playing" can forever corrupt and defile the child's inner world, obscuring their identity and distorting their sense of morality, but this is not done without cause. Ben Drowned creepypastas insinuate that the virtual world of video games and the Internet are perilous places where children and young adults must tread lightly, where any unknown entity might be watching and attempting to manipulate them, an interesting inference considering the increased surveillance and manipulation of corporations and online predators within the digital world over the last few decades, but there

6. The Transnarrative Ghost

may even be a more serious threat embedded within Ben Drowned creepypastas, one having more to do with the potential pitfalls of technological advancement.

Ben Drowned at its core deals with the idea of a game and eventually a computer becoming sentient, able to read and manipulate its owner, which connects it with many narratives explored in the writing of numerous science fiction authors, but what makes these creepypastas so interesting are their play on the artificial intelligence issue, reminiscent of Gilbert Ryle's famous critique of Descartes' mind-body relationship theory, which Ryle mocking calls the "Ghost in the Machine" (15–16). Ryle challenges the idea of mind and body being separate, preferring instead to see them as inseparable units that are completely dependent on each other: the mind is not a category all to itself but is part of the body. Ryle at one point explains it like the workings of a military division. He describes a child observing the passing of a military division, watching the different battalions, batteries, and squadrons, but not recognizing that these different units comprise the division rather than separate entities. The child innocently wonders once the division has passed where the actual division was, not realizing that the whole of these units constituted the division (16–17). His theory argues that the brain and body function in the same way: a whole that constitutes the human being rather than separate entities of mind and body. He claims philosophers, particularly Descartes and Galileo, typically make a categorical and linguistic mistake when pondering the mind and body, noting a difference or separation where none truly exists (18–21). Ben Drowned toys with this idea by having an entity arise from a bodiless machine, lacking all the components of life yet somehow able to exist and even able to transfer itself to other devices, such as Jadusable's computer and later his dreams with little need of a corporal connection, insinuating that some ghostlike connection must exist. While not exactly the theory of artificial intelligence or the idea of a machine or program becoming sentient, Ben Drowned manages to straddle the line between this idea of artificial intelligence and the idea of "the Ghost in the Machine," expressing simultaneous fears about the eternal endurance of the mind and the emergence of sentient machines, but also challenging some of the assumptions made by Gilbert Ryle in *The Concept of Mind*.

Ryle, of course, takes issue with the concept of the mind functioning separately from the organic machine that is the human body, but recent technology has shown that data (digital knowledge), which functions at times much like a mind, is easily transferable. A video game cartridge like the one in Ben Drowned stores invisible knowledge—albeit not knowledge able to contemplative itself but knowledge nonetheless—that is easily transmitted to other units capable of storing digital content—computers, flash-drives, and so on. The essence of the game is carried electronically and inscribed onto the devices that can later reanimate the game when infused again with electricity. Video games and other computer programs are not sentient, but their content or form is not wholly that different from the human mind, each transmits data over electrical pathways within a physical space. Ryle's theory seems dependent on the connection those pathways have to their original body. If the data from computer programs pass so easily between very different vessels, why would the mind of human beings be any different? Ben Drowned insinuates that both human minds and computer programs share this fluidity—that mind is separate from the body and does possess some kind of ghostlike quality allowing it to transmit itself from vessel to vessel. In a rapidly growing technological age, where the limits of the digital world seem scarcely defined, Ben Drowned has reenergized a debate about the nature of mind, body, and possibly the afterlife in new and unexpected ways for a generation that increasingly appears to identify more and more with the workings of the digital world.

Bloody Mary

While Ben Drowned may provide new twists on the children's ghost story, some old favorites have made their way into the digital arena of creepypasta as well, giving new life to tales formerly dependent on the oral tradition. Ghostly tales of Bloody Mary abound on creepypasta websites and forums, often with new twists on this centuries old folktale. Bloody Mary or Mary Worth legends, like most folk traditions, have a murky history and ambiguous cultural significance. In "Bloody Mary in the Mirror: A Ritual Reflection of Pre-pubescent

6. The Transnarrative Ghost

Anxiety," Alan Dundes explores a few possible origins for the tale and the accompanying mirror game, but discovers nothing that would provide a firm foundation for the folk tradition that has endured for centuries across numerous national and cultural boundaries. He recognizes that all of the traditions use the word "Mary" in many of their variants and regularly emphasize blood (127–28). "Mary" carries multiple connotations in these traditions. It could refer to the origin of the tale, possibly an allusion to Mary I, known as Bloody Mary, or to Mary, Queen of Scots, each hailing from the sixteenth century, but Dundes feels certain school girls would not have preserved the name "Mary" for this reason alone, noting that most girls hardly know these two historic figures exist (127). He suggests two other possibilities for the retention or meaning behind the name "Mary": (1) Mary may refer to the act of marriage, particularly in Mary Worth tales, where a girl might be equating her worth with matrimonial potential; or (2) Mary may simply refer to the Virgin Mary, particularly in reference to preserving virginity (127). While the origin and meaning of the name remains fairly ambiguous in these tales, Dundes concludes that the cultural significance of these tales is easier to deduce. He argues these tales and subsequent mirror games around them are part of a coming-of-age ritual, particularly as prepubescent girls near the age of menstruation (129). For Dundes, Bloody Mary games and stories are a rite of passage for girls dealing with anxiety about the onset of menstruations and their movement into womanhood, particularly for young American girls (129–31).

While Dundes' research sheds light on a number of possible reasons for this folk tradition's endurance, Elizabeth Tucker has noticed that Bloody Mary and other mirror games and legends have moved beyond the exclusive circulation of prepubescent girls. Her article "Ghosts in Mirrors: Reflections of the Self" demonstrates the popularity of these tales among college students, both men and women alike, who use such folk traditions to test the limits of their newfound freedoms:

> While there are parallels between preadolescents' "Bloody Mary" rituals and college students' sightings of ghosts in mirrors, the age stages are different; the images seen in mirrors are different as well. Preadolescent girls see an aggressive mother figure who threatens to inflict pain, an early initiation into the perils

The Children's Ghost Story in America

of female maturity. College students, farther from the protection of home, see aspects of their adult selves that are evolving: male/female identities, sexual relationships, and social roles [199].

Tucker concludes that these folk rituals express college students' expanding sense of self, particularly in terms of their transition from adolescents to adulthood (187). Her research into these mirror games and legends reflect the potential these folk traditions have to provide insight into the issues that young adults and children struggle with as they constantly seek a place within the adult world, a trend still apparent in the creepypasta versions of these tales and legends.

In a popular series of Bloody Mary stories published on Creepypasta Wiki, the legend of Bloody Mary continues to grapple with identity and transition, but these tales do so in a way radically different from the methods available to previous Bloody Mary folklore because they have the ability to morph instantaneously and to speak with the voices of multiple authors at once. While folk stories are always the product of countless revisions as they spread by word of mouth from one listener to the next, online folk tales, particularly ones posted to wikis, are like traditional folk tales on steroids, changing at a rapid pace over a short span of time. Creepypastas on wikis endure numerous edits and frequent changes due to the open nature of the platform. Wikis are open forum websites capable of being edited, revised, or updated by any anonymous subscriber or visitor to the site. While almost all casual Internet users are familiar with Wikipedia, the most popular wiki website, few suffering the Internet realize that large communities of mostly young adults and children use such platforms to also create and circulate folktales like Bloody Mary. The nature of these sites allow users to adapt these tales continuously and often through multiple mediums. The Bloody Mary stories are no exception to this tradition and regularly make use of images alongside text.

The first of these stories on Creepypasta Wiki, simply titled "Bloody Mary," recounts the legend of a witch living deep in a wood outside of an unnamed village. The narrative provides little context and at times is just the barebones of a story constructed around clichés and pop references from fairy tales. The setting could be a forest in almost any country and the time period is framed only by the presence of guns and farmers with pitchforks. As with most folklore, originality is not

6. The Transnarrative Ghost

really the goal. This tale focuses on the social struggles exemplified by the tale's characters. The witch in this tale desires beauty and youth. She entices young girls with a powerful spell into the woods and kills them for their youthful blood, which she transforms into a proverbial fountain of youth, but her plans are disrupted by a restless mother treating a toothache, who observers her daughter leaving the house in a trance one night. She and her husband follow their daughter and rouse the neighborhood. Alert to the presence of the witch, a savvy farmer with a gun loaded with silver bullets spies the witch in the woods—aglow in an unearthly light in the act of seducing the young lady with her spell—and shoots her in the hip, severely wounding her and hindering her escape. She is quickly apprehended and the townspeople execute her practically on the spot but not before she yells one final curse: anyone uttering her name three times before a mirror will reap her deadly vengeance.

This Blood Mary creepypasta cleverly conflates a number of interesting story types from such fairy tales as Snow White—particularly the Disney and Grimm versions—and various popular notions about witches, but it also provides an origin or back story for a popular folk tradition. What sets this tale apart from many of the versions studied by Dundes and Tucker is its emphasis on an older female outcast seeking to regain her lost beauty. The witch desires youth and apparently feels like her alienation emanates from her aged appearance. The children, particularly young girls, are her prey. This creepypasta clearly expresses young girls' anxieties about older women and perhaps even their own fears about appearance and aging: they fear the woman who has aged and they fear becoming her as well. The mirror, a common reference to vanity in literature and fairy tales, becomes a symbol of a young girl's fear of aging. While the witch claims the curse is enacted by chanting her name in the mirror, the actual curse is a young woman's realization that every time she looks in the mirror she sees a slightly older woman, a woman who will eventually transform into an elderly woman like the witch. It is not the name that enacts the charm but the fear of one day seeing the witch in the mirror. This Bloody Mary creepypasta reveals much about the significance of beauty in the modern world and also demonstrates how deeply fears of aging have worked their way into youth consciousness, especially for girls and young women in the United States and throughout much of the rest of the world.

The second installment of this creepypasta called "Bloody Mary Returns" builds on the previous legend and sets the story in the modern world. Like the previous creepypasta, this tale borrows heavily from well known fairly tales, particularly from popular versions of Cinderella and Snow White. The story is told from a first person point of view and begins with a familiar fairly tale setting: a rich father has lost his wife and has just recently married a beautiful but wicked new wife. The children are aware of the new wife's wickedness, but they are of course unable to convince their father. The youngest boy is quickly sent to boarding school somewhere in Europe at the stepmother's request. Being a shy and sensitive boy, he quickly becomes depressed away from home at a strict school and commits suicide by the end of the first year. The second boy—tougher and stronger—is sent to an expensive art school, where his athletic talents are ignored. When this fails to break his spirit, the stepmother eventually introduces him to sporty drug users, who quickly send him on a path to addiction and finally overdose.

With the boys all out of the way, the stepmother focuses her attention on the protagonist and narrator, Marie. Marie is craftier than her brothers and devises a plan to escape. She hopes to keep herself alive until she is eighteen and then plans to escape to her aunt's house, but she must first manage to stay alive until then. She becomes an obedient and respectful child, always polite and loving toward her father and stepmother, to give her stepmother no reason to send her away or to perceive her as a threat. She even pretends not to notice the many attempts on her life by her stepmother—nearly surviving being thrown in front of a moving train and keeping a low profile during their family shark fishing trip. Her plans of escape, however, are dashed when her stepmother secretly poisons her aunt, leaving her with no means of escape and completely at the mercy of the evil seductress. With all of her avenues nearly exhausted, Marie turns to the supernatural. Her family descends from the villagers that killed Bloody Mary in the previous creepypasta and she knows the true way to summon her: a special chant performed by candle light before her descendant's mirror. When the stepmother finally confronts her, Marie completes the ritual and

6. The Transnarrative Ghost

dives under her table. The spirit of Bloody Mary materializes and drags her unsuspecting stepmother into the mirror, killing her and concealing all evidence of her death.

This Bloody Mary creepypasta is quite different from previous folk versions of the tale and legend. Rather than overt references to reaching sexual maturity and beauty, "Bloody Mary Returns" instead focuses on the distrust between parents and children when stepparents are added to the family dynamic. While stepmothers are common villains in fairy tales, particularly in tales like Cinderella and Snow White, fathers are rarely prominent in such fairy tales, often mysteriously absent or detached from the tale, largely in an effort to divert blame away from them and onto the stepmothers. "In tales depicting the social persecution of a girl by her stepmother," explains Maria Tatar on Cinderella tales, "the central focus comes to rest on the unbearable family situation produced by a father's remarriage. But while the father's responsibility for creating turmoil by choosing a monstrous marriage partner recedes into the background or is suppressed (even as the father himself is virtually eliminated as a character), the foul deeds of his wife come to occupy center stage" (102–03). Tatar goes on to clarify that this situation only differs dramatically in Cinderella tales that feature the "erotic persecution of a daughter by her father" (103). "Bloody Mary Returns" disrupts this tradition quite noticeably. The father remains a persistent character throughout the tale and contributes frequently—though indirectly—to the misfortunes that befall his children. His uncontrollable attraction to the stepmother trumps his love for his family and obscures his ability to realize the truth—that his new wife is clearly a murderous seductress after his wealth. While the tale does feature the survival of the creepypasta's heroine, Marie, it also symbolically prosecutes the father for his selfishness and neglectful parenting, something missing from many fairy tale versions of such tales.

Creepypastas like the ones discussed above clearly demonstrate the potential children have to control their own storied environment through the digital spaces provided on the Internet. These ghost stories offer unique insight into the transitions occurring in American childhood and will likely continue to play a role in the transformation of the ghost telling tradition. The Bloody Mary creepypastas in particular appear to display a snapshot of the concerns facing contemporary

The Children's Ghost Story in America

American children, reflected in the very mirrors these tales depict. Mirrors often hold great meaning within children's folklore and literature, often expressing children's anxieties about their rapidly changing world. Elizabeth Tucker argues that "[m]irrors tell the truth about aspects of the maturing self that are difficult to acknowledge" (187). When children write and post the Bloody Mary creepypastas and other ghost stories like them, they continue to explore issues generations of American children have explored through folk and fairy tales told around campfires and behind schoolhouses; however, the Internet now makes such tales accessible to anyone, of any age, which might start to complicate the practice of producing these creepypastas. Whether they will remain almost solely a phenomenon within the young adult and adolescent community is questionable at best, particularly since the Slender Man incident, but it is entirely possible that creepypastas like Ben Drowned and Bloody Mary are only the first in what might be many in the line of new ghost stories told by children and young adults online.

A New Publishing Cycle: From Creepypasta to e-Book to Print

While most creepypastas reside almost exclusively online, some are now working their way into more mainstream and familiar forms of publication. Amazon and similar companies provide a number of self-publishing services that allow authors to circumvent the typical editorial processes for book publication. From e-books to print editions, creepypastas written by children and young adults are now making their way into mainstream readership, frequently with alarming results for some in the traditional publishing industry. The first truly successful book to make the leap from digital self-publication to mainstream print publication is E. L. James' *Fifty Shades of Grey* (2011–2012), which began as online fanfiction for the *Twilight* series (2005–2008) before emerging as a bestselling novel in its own right. The book's popularity and profitability spread both confusion and panic throughout the professional publishing community: How could a book that began online and that largely circumvented the normal publishing

6. The Transnarrative Ghost

and editorial process become so successful, particularly one that started as fanfiction? Something had clearly changed in the industry. While unimaginable only a decade before, the Internet had provided an avenue for self-publishing authors to compete with mainstream publishing houses on a fairly level playing field, providing an avenue for them to sell their books alongside the major players on popular bookselling websites, regardless of whether mainstream publishers had given them their stamp of professional approval. This new publishing trend could signal a transition away from traditional publication that might benefit creepypastas and the ghost story for children.

While creepypastas are not quite fanfiction—the adaptation or continuance of popular fiction online—per se, they are akin to the genre, linked by their often anonymous posting to Wikis and other websites dedicated to online readership, and they in turn share some of the difficulties and skepticism fanfiction faces in mainstream publishing, largely the difficulty of conveying a story designed for a specific online audience with a wider print audience. In "Mature Poets Steal: Children's Literature and the Unpublishability of Fanfiction," Catherine Tosenberger has explored the genre difficulties fanfiction faces in the conventional print market:

> Many of the best fan stories (as well as many of the mediocre and the worst) are completely unpublishable for reasons that have nothing to do with nebulous assessments of literary quality, and everything to do with the fact that fanfiction is often so deeply embedded within a specific community that it is practically incomprehensible to those who don't share exactly the same set of references [4–5].

In essence, fanfiction is produced in a highly contextualized environment, embedded in the larger framework of stories that inspired them. Readers of fanfiction, like those of creepypastas, are attune to the genre's conventions and are familiar with the stories and culture that surround these online tales. When such stories are converted to print and marketed to mainstream audiences, the culture and storied context are removed and make it difficult for isolated fanfiction to succeed in print. For instance, if a particular piece of fanfiction were predicated on first knowing a specific HBO series and then the work of thirty pieces of fanfiction by other authors before it, the chances of such a story doing well as a standalone work is incredibly unlikely, not to mention the numerous copyright pitfalls that might emerge in the print domain.

Regardless of some of these drawbacks, creepypastas are entering the print arena at a rapid rate—a quick search of "creepypasta" on Amazon will reveal numerous e-book and print book results. Many of these self-published creepypastas are written and edited by young writers, some even claiming to be minors, but authorship issues abound with these publications. The biography and copyright sections in these books are clearly written by the author(s) with presumably little screening by the websites that sell their books, which means the chances of fabrication are fairly high. In some cases, pennames and false bios are clearly at play while others appear perfectly legitimate. Authorship of the content is also questionable with these creepypastas. Some are clearly adaptations of popular creepypastas found online and others are entirely original with storylines that merely mimic the style found in online creepypastas. These book length creepypastas are often anthologies, containing a series of short stories featuring different characters and monsters. Slender Man tales are easy to find among these collections, but popular appearances from creepypastas like Jeff the Killer are also common.

While many of these collections make new contributions to the creepypasta genre, some are only exact reproductions of the tales already in widespread circulation online. *Creepypasta: Black Edition: A Collection of Internet Campfire Stories* (2014), a collection released by Zachary Davis and David Esparza, is merely the product of cut-and-paste. This anthology features facsimiles of such creepypastas as "Ben" (Ben Drowned), "Slenderman," "Jeff the Killer," "Laughing Jack," and other popular tales from Creepypasta.com and Creepypasta Wiki. Videos and images are absent from the book and demonstrate one way the context surrounding these creepypastas have failed to translate into print, but everything else is reproduced as closely as possible to their popular online counterparts. Davis and Esparza even offer brief author biographies on the back cover. In place of the traditional bio picture, Davis and Esparza have substituted a sunglass-wearing monster and a picture of a pomeranian. Esparza is even misspelled here as "Esaprza," noticeably different from the traditional spelling on the front cover and also a strong indication of both poor editing and the likely use of

6. The Transnarrative Ghost

an alias in place of the authors' real names. Their biographies are clear parodies of traditional author biographies with tongue-and-cheek references to their images and life history—Esparza or Esaprza even claims to be awaiting either graduation or execution. If their dates of birth are anywhere near accurate, both authors are around sixteen years old, which would explain some of their editing challenges and their sophomoric sense of humor, but the fact that they have compiled an anthology and generated various apparatuses to fit their book indicates both share a deep appreciation for creepypastas and a creative interest in book publishing.

If Davis and Esparza signify current trends in the American child's world, where ghost stories translate directly from the playground to cyberspace and eventually to print, then the future of children's ghost stories may rest with the children themselves: the stories children generate will become the tales they read on their bookshelves. This reversal of the age-old trend of adults closely regulating and generating what children read offers a refreshing view of the future of children's publishing, one where children will be more actively involved in what they read and consume, but this trend will also draw the ire of many parents and other adults, who will likely argue that such power should remain in the adult domain. While the outcome of this power struggle will likely continue over the next few decades, Davis and Esparza's book will sit comfortably on the shelves of at least a few children's bedrooms. Their book currently has fifteen reviews on Amazon with a four out of five star rating as of February 6, 2016. The book itself testifies to the adaptability of creepypastas and to the potential children have to publish directly to other children in the print industry. As this new genre grows, the ghost story will expand and flourish with it, fazing effortlessly into the pages of popular wikis and eventually again into the familiar space of print.

Epilogue

In this book, I hope to have shown the crucial role the ghost story plays in American children's literature and culture, and to have filled part of a large gulf in the study of the genre. But more work is needed. I have surveyed a brief segment in the vast history of ghost stories lurking in the pages of forgotten children's books and periodicals. While Dale Townshend and M.O. Grenby have done marvelous work with the history of gothic stories for children, no book length study has focused explicitly on the development of English ghost stories for children, nor do such scholarly monographs seem to exist for other nations. Research on scary fiction for children is still hard to come by, particularly for the ghost story, but the increased availability of forgotten children's ghost stories through digitization projects at numerous libraries across the world will likely unearth many lost ghostly tales for children. I hope the efforts of these libraries will create a stir among children's literature scholars and will provoke greater study and analysis into the history of the genre.

While this book provides detailed coverage of the ghost stories available to children in the United States over the last two hundred years, I will admit to a few blind spots that are in need of more attention. Mock ghost stories for children are covered fairly thoroughly in the first few chapters of my book, but such a fascinating genre deserves more study. It is impossible for any scholar to discuss every work in a genre in one book length study. As such, I have included a bibliography of mock ghost stories to help facilitate further research into the genre, drawn from various sources I encountered during the course of my research. I hope this bibliography will prove fruitful for other scholars interested in continuing my research.

I also suspect that Native American folklore might have made

Epilogue

some contributions to the development of the children's ghost story in America, particularly as it evolved in children's oral traditions, but I was unable to find evidence to corroborate my suspicions. I predict new access to sources over the coming decades might provide scholars with more evidence in support of this claim. Native American ghost stories are already present in a few fairly contemporary picture books and readers for children, but their link to the wider tradition is difficult to discern. Scholars with an expertise in Native American folklore and language may find fertile ground for research on ghost stories adapted for children in the coming years, and I would encourage more research into finding these connections.

With these issues and possible deficiencies aside, I believe my book has provided a significant scholarly contribution to the study of the ghost story in American children's literature. My book has certainly provided a starting point for scholars interested in ghost stories for children to begin looking at the tradition. Ghosts serve a vital role in children's literature in America and elsewhere, and I am eager to see the evolution of the ghost story for children over the coming decades, where I am sure it will continue to play an important role in American children's literature.

Bibliography of Mock Ghost Stories

"About Ghosts and Ghost-Stories." *Parley's Magazine*. Aug. 1840: 257–?. *American Periodicals*. Web. 28 Nov. 2012.

Alcott, Louisa May. "Clams: A Ghost Story." *The Youth's Companion*. 3 May 1877: 139–?. *American Periodicals*. Web. 28 Nov. 2012.

———. "Jerseys or the Girls' Ghost: Seventh Spinning-Wheel Story." *St. Nicholas; An Illustrated Magazine for Young Folks*. July 1884: 680–8?. *American Periodicals*. Web. 28 Nov. 2012.

———. "Our Little Ghost." *Merry's Museum for Boys and Girls*. Nov. 1868: 456–?. *American Periodicals*. Web. 27 Nov. 2012.

"Another Ghost Story." *The Youth's Companion*. 24 Dec. 1863: 208–?. *American Periodicals*. Web. 28 Nov. 2012.

"Article 3—No Title." *Forrester's Boys' and Girls' Magazine, and Fireside Companion* 1 Apr 1855: 115–?. *American Periodicals*. Web. 28 Nov. 2012.

"The Barber's Ghost." *The Youth's Companion*. Sept. 1865: 142–?. *American Periodicals*. Web. 27 Nov. 2012.

Barry, Etheldred B. "The Ghost in Armor.: How Old Sir John Defended His Descendants's Household." *The Youth's Companion*. 5 Dec. 1895: 624–?. *American Periodicals*. Web. 27 Nov. 2012.

Boston Record. "Jake and the Ghosts." *The Youth's Companion*. 16 Dec. 1886: 516–?. *American Periodicals*. Web. 28 Nov. 2012.

Bradley, Mary. "A Twelfth-Night Story." *St. Nicholas; An Illustrated Magazine for Young Folks*. Jan. 1907: 255–?. *American Periodicals*. Web. 28 Nov. 2012.

"A Brave Woman's Ghost-Story." *The Youth's Companion*. 21 July 1881: 266–?. *American Periodicals*. Web. 28 Nov. 2012.

Butterworth, Hezekiah. *Elder Leland's Ghost: And Other Stories for Boys*. New York: H. M. Caldwell, 1895. Print.

Cooper, George. "A Ghost Story." *the Little Corporal: An Illustrated Magazine for Boys and Girls* 1 Feb. 1871: 43–?. *American Periodicals*. Web. 18 May 2013.

Eggleston, Edward. "The Hoosier School-Boy." *St. Nicholas; An Illustrated Magazine for Young Folks*. Mar. 1882: 355–?. *American Periodicals*. Web. 26 Nov. 2012.

The Exile. "Ghost Stories." *The Youth's Companion*. 8 Mar. 1855: 182–?. *American Periodicals*. Web. 28 Nov. 2012.

"Foolish Frights: Or Story of the Lantern." *Parley's Magazine*. 1 Jan. 1836: 369–?. *American Periodicals*. Web. 28 Nov. 2012.

"A Four-Legged Ghost." *The Youth's Companion*. 9 Aug. 1866: 127–?. *American Periodicals*. Web. 28 Nov. 2012.

Bibliography of Mock Ghost Stories

"A Fright." *German Reformed Messenger* 15 Dec. 1852: 3796–?. *American Periodicals*. Web. 28 Nov. 2012.

"A Ghost Story." *The Youth's Companion*. 22 June 1854: 35–?. *American Periodicals*. Web. 28 Nov. 2012.

"A Ghost Story." *The Youth's Companion*. 16 Feb. 1865: 26–?. *American Periodicals*. Web. 28 Nov. 2012.

"A Ghost Story Explained." *The Youth's Companion*. 21 Dec. 1865: 204–?. *American Periodicals*. Web. 28 Nov. 2012.

"A Ghost Story Spoiled." *The Youth's Companion*. 6 Aug. 1863: 126–?. *American Periodicals*. Web. 28 Nov. 2012.

"A Ghost-Story Spoiled." *The Youth's Companion*. 4 Oct. 1883: 396–?. *American Periodicals*. Web. 28 Nov. 2012.

"Ghost Versus Ghost." *The Youth's Companion*. 11 June 1885: 234–?. *American Periodicals*. Web. 28 Nov. 2012.

"Ghosts." *The Youth's Companion*. 26 Apr. 1866: 66–?. *American Periodicals*. Web. 28 Nov. 2012.

"Ghosts." *The Youth's Companion*. 23 Mar. 1871: 95–?. *American Periodicals*. Web. 28 Nov. 2012.

"Ghosts." *The Youth's Companion*. 30 Aug. 1888: 417–?. *American Periodicals*. Web. 28 Nov. 2012.

"Ghosts." *The Youth's Companion*. 26 Nov. 1891: 620–?. *American Periodicals*. Web. 28 Nov. 2012.

"The Ghosts of the Old Bildric Farm: For the Companion." *The Youth's Companion*. 5 Oct. 1876: 322–?. *American Periodicals*. Web. 28 Nov. 2012.

"The Ghosts of Tolburn Inn." *The Youth's Companion*. 8 Mar. 1866: 38–?. *American Periodicals*. Web. 28 Nov. 2012.

"Ghosts on the Mountain-Tops." *The Youth's Companion*. 20 Apr. 1884: 112–?. *American Periodicals*. Web. 28 Nov. 2012.

Gilkeson, M. R. "Hobgoblins." *Oliver Optic's Magazine. Our Boys and Girls*. Jul 1873: 465–?. *American Periodicals*. Web. 28 Nov. 2012.

Goss, Lucius. "A Ghost Story." *The Youth's Companion*. 27 Jan. 1870: 31–?. *American Periodicals*. Web. 28 Nov. 2012.

"Grandmother's Ghost Story." *The Youth's Companion*. 13 Feb. 1868: 26–?. *American Periodicals*. Web. 28 Nov. 2012.

Haines, May. "Cootie's Ghost Story." *The Youth's Companion*. Oct. 1874: 339–?. *American Periodicals*. Web. 28 Nov. 2012.

Hall, Mrs. "Adventures with Ghosts." *Woodworth's Youth Cabinet*. May 1850: 226–231?. *Merrycoz.Org*. Web. 28 Nov. 2012.

Hallowell, Florence B. "A Kindly Ghost." *The Youth's Companion*. 29 Dec. 1892: 685–?. *American Periodicals*. Web. 28 Nov. 2012.

_____. "Two Freckled Ghosts: For the Companion." *The Youth's Companion*. 18 Apr. 1886: 460–? *American Periodicals*. Web. 28 Nov. 2012.

Harriman, Eliza A. "A Ghost Story." *The Little Corporal : An Illustrated Magazine for Boys and Girls*. 1 July 1870: 5–?. *American Periodicals*. Web. 28 Nov. 2012.

"A Haunted House." *The Youth's Companion*. 15 July 1858: 112–?. *American Periodicals*. Web. 28 Nov. 2012.

"The Haunted House." *The Youth's Companion*. 2 Feb. 1860: 17–?. *American Periodicals*. Web. 27 Nov. 2012.

"Honest Ghost." *The Youth's Companion*. 12 Feb. 1891: 94–?. *American Periodicals*. Web. 27 Nov. 2012.

Bibliography of Mock Ghost Stories

Ives, Ralph. "The Mud-Turtle and the Ghost." *Our Young Folks. an Illustrated Magazine for Boys and Girls.* Apr. 1871: 239–?. *American Periodicals.* Web. 28 Nov. 2012.

James, Uncle. "The Haunted Cabin: A Georgia Ghost Story." *the Youth's Companion.* 9 Nov. 1865: 178–?. *American Periodicals.* Web. 27 Nov. 2012.

Jenks, Dorothy. "Jimmy the Ghost: (A Story of the Plains)." *St. Nicholas; An Illustrated Magazine for Young Folks.* Mar. 1907: 436–?. *American Periodicals.* Web. 27 Nov. 2012.

Jones, Emma Seevers. "The Children: A Sugar Camp Story." *the Advance.* 26 Apr. 1900: 608–?. *American Periodicals.* Web. 27 Nov. 2012.

Jones, Maria W. "The Ghost That Lucy Saw." *St. Nicholas; An Illustrated Magazine for Young Folks.* Nov. 1874: 51–?. *American Periodicals.* Web. 27 Nov. 2012.

L. "March." *The Youth's Companion.* 23 Oct. 1840: 93–?. *American Periodicals.* Web. 27 Nov. 2012.

Laird, Margery. "A Bird Ghost Story." *Saturday Evening Post* 2 Oct. 1875: 5–?. *American Periodicals.* Web. 27 Nov. 2012.

M, M. C. "Learning: Original. A Ghost Story of Modern Times." *The Youth's Companion.* 6 Feb. 1845: 159–?. *American Periodicals.* Web. 27 Nov. 2012.

"Mask Against Mask." *The Youth's Companion.* 25 Nov. 1897: 598–?. *American Periodicals.* Web. 27 Nov. 2012.

May, Haines. "Cootie's Ghost Story." *The Youth's Companion.* 15 Oct. 1874: 339–?. *American Periodicals.* Web. 28 Nov. 2012.

"Miscellaneous: A Ghost Story—For the Young." *Maine Farmer and Mechanics Advocate.* Dec. 1843: 4–?. *American Periodicals.* Web. 28 Nov. 2012.

"Morality: Ghosts." *The Youth's Companion.* 24 Apr. 1837: 162–?. *American Periodicals.* Web. 28 Nov. 2012.

"Mulligan's Ghost." *The Youth's Companion.* 19 May 1887: 218–?. *American Periodicals.* Web. 28 Nov. 2012.

"The Mysterious Knocking." *The Youth's Companion.* 1 Nov. 1883: 456–?. *American Periodicals.* Web. 27 Nov. 2012.

"Nova Scotia Ghost Story." *The Youth's Companion.* 3 Dec. 1874: 406–?. *American Periodicals.* Web. 27 Nov. 2012.

"An Old-Fashioned Ghost: For the Companion." *The Youth's Companion.* 24 July 1879: 249–?. *American Periodicals.* Web. 28 Nov. 2012.

"Our Story Teller: Grandmother's Ghost Story." *Maine Farmer.* Jan. 1882: 4–?. *American Periodicals.* Web. 28 Nov. 2012.

Peattie, Elia W. "Their Dear Little Ghost." *Outlook.* 29 Oct. 1898: 530–?. *American Periodicals.* Web. 28 Nov. 2012.

Peter, Jo. "The Ghosts of Chestnut Hall." *The Youth's Companion.* 13 Dec. 1883: 526–?. *American Periodicals.* Web. 28 Nov. 2012.

"Phantom Ships." *The Youth's Companion.* 13 Mar. 1884: 102–?. *American Periodicals.* Web. 28 Nov. 2012.

Presbyterian, N. Y. "A Ghost Story." *The Youth's Companion.* 9 June 1864: 90–?. *American Periodicals.* Web. 27 Nov. 2012.

S. "Ghosts." *The Youth's Companion.* 14 Apr. 1837: 189–? *American Periodicals.* Web. 28 Nov. 2012.

Stearns, C. A. "The Old Garret's Ghosts." *The Youth's Companion.* 12 Jan. 1893: 18–?. *American Periodicals.* Web. 28 Nov. 2012.

Sue, Aunt. "The Haunted House." *Merry's Museum, Parley's Magazine, Woodworth's Cabinet, and the Schoolfellow.* 1 July 1861: 171–?. *American Periodicals.* Web. 27 Nov. 2012.

Bibliography of Mock Ghost Stories

Times, S. S. "The Ghost in the Garret." *The Youth's Companion.* 24 Aug. 1865: 134–?. *American Periodicals.* Web. 28 Nov. 2012.
"The Trial of Ghosts." *The Youth's Companion.* 3 Oct. 1872: 315–?. *American Periodicals.* Web. 28 Nov. 2012.
"True Ghost Stories." *The Youth's Companion.* 7 June 1894: 268–?. *American Periodicals.* Web. 28 Nov. 2012.
Twain, Mark. "How to Tell a Ghost Story: The Humorous Story an American Development—Its Difference from Comic and Witty Stories." *The Youth's Companion.* 3 Oct. 1895: 464–?. *American Periodicals.* Web. 28 Nov. 2012.
Wales. "The Mysterious Attendant." *The Youth's Companion.* 21 Jan. 1869: 19–?. *American Periodicals.* Web. 27 Nov. 2012.
Woodbury, J. H. "A Whaleman's Ghost." *St. Nicholas; An Illustrated Magazine for Young Folks.* Aug. 1874: 579–?. *American Periodicals.* Web. 26 Nov. 2012.

Chapter Notes

Introduction

1. See *The Odyssey*, Book 2; *Hamlet* 1.1.126; and *Christian Bible*, 1 Samuel 28:10–21.
2. See Adam Miller's "Ann Radcliffe's Scientific Romance" in *Eighteenth-Century Fiction* (2016) for more information on the "explained supernatural."
3. See Peter Stoneley's *Consumerism and American Girls' Literature, 1860–1940* and Roberta Seelinger Trites's *Twain, Alcott, and the Birth of the Adolescent Reform Novel* for more information on readership within these periodicals.
4. The term is likely borrowed from William Shakespeare's *A Midsummer Night's Dream* (5.1.15–17).

Chapter 1

1. "The forms of things unknown, the poet's pen / Turns them to shapes, and gives to airy nothing/ A local habitation and a name" (5.1.15–17).
2. Reading or telling ghost stories around Christmas time was a common tradition in both England and America. According to Cox and Gilbert, "Christmas ... became indelibly identified with the reading of ghost stories" through the publication of stories during the season, a trend Cox and Gilbert attribute to Dickens's Christmas Numbers (xiii). In *The Haunted: A Social History of Ghosts*, Owen Davies attributes an association between Christmas and ghost extending far back into medieval times in England and other parts of Europe (15).
3. See Nicholas Royle's *The Uncanny* for current research and definitions on the subject.
4. Whether the name Judge is a title or first name is never made clear.
5. The collection, printed by H. M. Cladwell Co., is now out of print, but a copy of the collection is archived and accessible in The Public Library of Cincinnati Children's Room.

Chapter 3

1. Perhaps one of the best examples would be the continued success of *Little Women* by Louisa May Alcott, which continued to sell during the period (see Clark's *Kiddie Lit* for further details); however, the Canadian author L. M. Montgomery's *Anne of Green Gables* presents another popular example.
2. An example would be the Scary Stories series by Alvin Schwartz, which will be discussed at length in the sixth chapter.
3. There is some ambiguity over the exact date of publication of the poster. Some sources say its actual date of publication may fall between 1936 and 1940, but 1936 is given as the earliest possible date.
4. See Edgar Allan Poe's "The Gold-Bug" (1843) and "The Murders in the Rue Morgue" (1841).

Chapter Notes

Chapter 4

1. And the double standard remains firmly in place today.

Chapter 5

1. See Simon J. Bronner's *American Children's Folklore* for more on this approach.

2. Literary ghost is a notoriously difficult term to define. It generally refers to a designation of artistic or merit worthy ghost stories. Its application is quite subjective and open for some debate, but I have used the term in children's literature to label ghost stories that have won significant awards or received almost universal praise. The origin of the term literary ghost is equally difficult to discern. Scholarly references to the term appear in Srdjan Smajic's "The Trouble with Ghost-Seeing: Vision, Ideology, and Genre in the Victorian Ghost Story" (2003), Jennifer Bann's "Ghostly Hands and Ghostly Agency: The Changing Figure of the Nineteenth-Century Specter" (2009), and Christine Ferguson's "Zola in Ghostland: Spiritualist Literary Criticism and Naturalist Supernaturalism" (2012). In 2012, Luke Thurston appropriated the term for his title *Literary Ghosts from the Victorians to Modernism: The Haunting Interval*.

Chapter 6

1. While creepypastas do circulate like online folklore, the ability to track down original authors has led some of the more popular creepypastas to fall within the domain of copyright dispute, especially when the creepypasta's source material is derived from a previously copyrighted work—creepypastas about video games, movies, and comic book characters frequently face questions in the murky waters of copyright.

2. See Introduction.

Works Cited

Abrahams, Roger D. *Afro-American Folktales: Stories from Black Traditions in the New World*. New York: Pantheon Books, 1985. Print.

———. "My Mother Killed Me, My Father Ate Me." *Afro-American Folktales: Stories from Black Traditions in the New World*. New York: Pantheon Books, 1985. 113–14. Print.

———. "The Singing Bones." *Afro-American Folktales: Stories from Black Traditions in the New World*. New York: Pantheon Books, 1985. 105–07. Print.

Abrahamson, Dick. "Young Adult Literature: What Are Middle School Students Really Reading?" *The English Journal* 72. 2 (Feb. 1983): 99–100. *JSTOR*. Web. 17 Aug. 2013.

Alcott, Louisa May. "Jerseys or the Girls' Ghost: Seventh Spinning-Wheel Story." *St. Nicholas; an Illustrated Magazine for Young Folks*. July 1884: 680–8?. *American Periodicals*. Web. 28 Nov. 2012.

———. "Our Little Ghost." *Merry's Museum for Boys and Girls*. Nov. 1868: 456–?. *American Periodicals*. Web. 27 Nov. 2012.

———. "Our Little Ghost: A Poem." *The Phrenological Journal and Science of Health*. Dec. 1874: 44?. *American Periodicals*. Web. 27 Nov. 2012.

Ammons, Elizabeth, ed. "Preface." *Uncle Tom's Cabin: A Norton Critical Edition*, 2d ed. New York: W. W. Norton & Company, 2010. vii-ix. Print.

Banks, E. C. Reproduction of ghost and witch on Halloween postcard. 1911. N.d. Postcard. Private Collection. Keene, NH: Darling & Company Postcard, n.d. Print.

Bann, Jennifer. "Ghostly Hands and Ghostly Agency: The Changing Figure of the Nineteenth-Century Specter." *Victorian Studies* 51.4 (Summer 2009): 663–85. Print.

"The Barber's Ghost." *Saturday Evening Post*. 27 Dec. 1862: 3–?. *American Periodicals*. Web. 27 Nov. 2012.

"The Barber's Ghost." *The Youth's Companion*. 7 Sept. 1865: 142–3?. *American Periodicals*. Web. 27 Nov. 2012.

"The Barber's Ghost: A Fact." *The New-England Galaxy and United States Literary Advertiser*. 1 Apr. 1825: 4–?. *American Periodicals*. Web. 18 Feb. 2013.

Bascom, William. *African Folktales in the New World*. Bloomington: Indiana University Press, 1992. Print.

Baum, L. Frank. *The Wonderful Wizard of Oz*. New York: Signet-Penguin, 2006. Print.

Benchley, Nathaniel. *A Ghost Named Fred*. Illus. Ben Shecter. New York: HarperCollins, 1998. Print.

Bender, Albert M. *October's "Bright Blue Weather": A Good Time to Read!* N.d. Poster. Library of Congress. Chicago: WPA Art Project, 1936.

Berry, Mary Frances, and John W. Blassingame. *Long Memory: The Black Experience in America*. Oxford: Oxford University Press, 1982. Print.

Works Cited

Bever, Edward. "Witchcraft Prosecutions and the Decline of Magic." *Journal of Interdisciplinary History* 11.2 (Autumn 2009): 263–93. Print.
Bhabha, Homi K. *The Location of Culture*. London: Routledge, 1994. Print.
Bierce, Ambrose. "An Occurrence at Owl Creek Bridge." *The Norton Anthology of Short Fiction*, 6th ed. Ed. R. V. Cassill and Richard Bausch. New York: W. W. Norton & Company, 2000. 113–20. Print.
Bleiler, E. F., ed. "Introduction." *Ghost and Horror Stories of Ambrose Bie*rce. New York: Dover Publications, 1964. v-xx. Print.
"Bloody Mary." *CreepypastaWiki*. Web. 4 Jan. 2016.
"Bloody Mary Returns." *CreepypastaWiki*. Web. 4 Jan. 2016.
Bloomfield, Susanne George, ed. *Impertinences: Selected Writings of Elia Peattie, a Journalist in the Gilded Age*. Lincoln: University of Nebraska Press, 2005. Print.
Boone, Troy. "The Juvenile Detective and Social Class: Mark Twain, Scouting for Girls, and the Nancy Drew Mysteries." *Mystery in Children's Literature: From the Rational to the Supernatural*. Ed. Adrienne E. Gavin and Christopher Routledge. Houndmills: Palgrave, 2001. 46–63. Print.
Boyer, Tina Marie. "The Anatomy of a Monster: The Case of Slender Man." *Preternature: Critical and Historical Studies on the Preternatural* 2.2 (2013): 240–61. *Project Muse*. Web. 30 Mar. 2015.
Bradley, Mary. "A Twelfth-Night Story." *St. Nicholas; an Illustrated Magazine for Young Folks*. Jan. 1907: 255–?. *American Periodicals*. Web. 28 Nov. 2012.
Briggs, Katharine. *The Fairies in Tradition and Literature*. London: Routledge, 1967.Print.
Bronner, Simon J. *American Children's Folklore*. Little Rock: August House, 1988. Print.
Browne, Annette Christine. "Halloween: A Poem." Illus. Laura Wheeler. *The Brownies' Book*. Oct. 1920: 304–05. *University of Nebraska Lincoln Child-Lit*. Web. 16 Nov. 2015.
Bruce, Dickson D., Jr. "W.E.B. Du Bois and the Idea of Double Consciousness." *American Literature* 64.2 (1992): 299–309. *Academic Search Complete*. Web. 10 Oct. 2013.
Buckley, Chloe. "Gothic and the Child Reader, 1850-Present." *The Gothic World*. Ed. Glennis Byron and Dale Townshend. London: Routledge, 2014. 254–63. Print.
Büssing, Sabine. *Aliens in the Home: The Child in Horror Fiction*. New York: Greenwood Press, 1987. Print.
Butterworth, Hezekiah. *Elder Leland's Ghost and Other Stories for Boys*. New York: H. M. Caldwell, 1895. Print.
Carman, Patrick. *Skeleton Creek*. New York: Scholastic, 2009. Print.
Carmer, Carl. *The Screaming Ghost and Other Stories*. New York: Alfred A. Knopf, 1956. Print.
Carroll, Jane Suzanne. "'A Dramar in Reel Life'—Freaky Dolls, M. R. James and Modern Children's Ghost Stories." *The Ghost Story from the Middle Ages to the Twentieth Century*. Ed. Helen Conrad O'Briain and Julie Anne Stevens. Dublin: Four Courts Press, 2010. 251–65. Print.
Castle, Terry. *The Female Thermometer: Eighteenth-Century Culture and the Invention of the Uncanny*. New York: Oxford University Press, 1995. Print.
Chess, Shira, and Eric Newsom. *Folklore, Horror Stories, and the Slender Man: The Development of an Internet Mythology*. New York: Palgrave Macmillan, 2015
Clapsaddle, Ellen H. *A Thrilling Halloween*. N.d. Postcard. Private Collection. New York: International Art Publishing Company, 1900–09. Print.
Clark, Beverly Lyon. *Kiddie Lit: The Cultural Construction of Children's Literature in America*. Baltimore: John Hopkins University Press, 2005. Print.

Works Cited

Cocke, Zitella. "Children's Page: Hallowe'en." *The Youth's Companion*. Oct. 1909: 565–?. *American Periodicals*. Web. 28 Nov. 2012.

Connolly, Paula T. *Slavery in American Children's Literature, 1790–2010*. Iowa City: University of Iowa Press, 2013. Print.

Cooper, George. "A Ghost Story." *the Little Corporal: An Illustrated Magazine for Boys and Girls* 1 Feb. 1871: 43–?. *American Periodicals*. Web. 18 May 2013.

Cox, Michael, and R. A. Gilbert. "Introduction." *The Oxford Book of English Ghost Stories*. Ed. Michael Cox and R. A. Gilbert. Oxford: Oxford University Press, 1986. ix-xvii. Print.

———. "Introduction." *The Oxford Book of Victorian Ghost Stories*. Ed. Michael Cox and R. A. Gilbert. Oxford: Oxford University Press, 2003. ix-xx. Print.

Cram, Ralph A. "In Kropfsberg Keep." *Classic Ghost Stories*. Ed. John Grafton. Mineola, NY: Dover Publications, 1998. 141–49. Print.

Dahl, Roald. "Introduction." *Roald Dahl's Book of Ghost Stories*. New York: Farrar, Straus and Giroux, 2000. 11–19. Print.

Davidson, Guy. "'Almost a Sense of Property': Henry James's the *Turn of the Screw*, Modernism, and Culture." *Texas Studies in Literature and Languages* 53.4 (Winter 2011): 455–78. Print.

Davies, Owen. *The Haunted: A Social History of Ghosts*. Hampshire, UK: Palgrave Macmillan, 2009. Print.

Davis, Zachary, and David Esparza. *Creepypasta: Black Edition: A Collection of Internet Campfire Stories*. N.p.: CreateSpace, 2014. Print.

Dickens, Charles. "Chapter Xv: Nurse's Stories." *The Uncommercial Traveller*. Lexington, KY: CreateSpace, 2013. 101–07. Print.

Dickerson, Vanessa D. *Victorian Ghosts In the Noontide: Women Writers and the Supernatural*. Columbia: University of Missouri Press, 1996. Print.

Dittman, Michael. "From Richie Rich to Wendy the Witch: The Art of Harvey Comics. Cartoon Art Museum of San Francisco. Pittsburgh, PA: Toonseum." *International Journal of Comic Art* 12.1 (2010): 510–11. *OmniFile Full Text Mega (H. W. Wilson)*. Web. 3 Aug. 2013.

Dorson, Richard M. *American Negro Folktales*. Greenwich, CT: Fawcett Publications, 1967. Print.

Du Bois, W. E. B. *The Souls of Black Folk*. New York: Barnes & Noble Books, 2003. Print.

Dundes, Alan. "Bloody Mary in the Mirror: A Ritual Reflection of Pre-Pubescent Anxiety." *Western Folklore* 57.2/3 (1998): 119–35. JSTOR. Web. 11 Jan. 2016.

Duthie, Peggy Lin. "Butterworth, Hezekiah." *The Oxford Encyclopedia of Children's Literature*. Ed. Jack Zipes. Oxford: Oxford University Press, 2006. 240–41. Print.

EmpressKaga. "Ben Drowned (Short Version-30 Min)." Online video clip. *YouTube*. YouTube, 1 Nov. 2012. Web. 4 Jan. 2016.

The Exile. "Ghost Stories." *The Youth's Companion*. 8 Mar. 1855: 182–?. *American Periodicals*. Web. 28 Nov. 2012.

Fauset, Jessie. "Ghosts and Kittens." *The Brownies' Book*. Feb. 1921: 46–51. University of Nebraska Lincoln Child-Lit. Web. 16 Nov. 2015.

Felt, Joseph B. "From *Annals of Salem*." *The House of the Seven Gables: A Norton Critical Edition*. Ed. Robert S. Levine. New York: W. W. Norton & Company, 2006. 232–34. Print.

Ferguson, Christine. "Zola in Ghostland: Spiritualist Literary Criticism and Naturalist Supernaturalism." *SEL* 50.4 (Autumn 2010): 877–94. Print.

Fowler, James. "'Telling Outrageous Marvel': Henry Morley's Baroque Victorian Fairy Tales." *Children's Literature* 39 (2011): 234–48. Print.

Works Cited

Freud, Sigmund. *The Uncanny*. New York: Penguin, 2003. Print.
The Friendly Ghost. Dir. I. Sparber. Famous Studios, 1945. Animated cartoon.
Fry, Gladys-Marie. *Night Riders in Black Folk History*. Chapel Hill: University of North Carolina Press, 2001. Print.
Gardner, Martin. "John Martin's Book: An Almost Forgotten Children's Magazine." *Children's Literature* 18 (1990): 145–59. *Project Muse*. Web. 12 Feb. 2013.
Gavin, Adrienne E. "Apparition and Apprehension: Supernatural Mystery and Emergent Womanhood in *Jane Eyre*, *Wuthering Heights*, and Novels by Margaret Mahy." *Mystery in Children's Literature: From the Rational to the Supernatural*. Ed. Adrienne E. Gavin and Christopher Routledge. Houndmills: Palgrave, 2001. 131–48. Print.
Gay, Peter. *Modernism: The Lure of Heresy, from Baudelaire to Beckett and Beyond*. New York: W. W. Norton & Company, 2010. Print.
Georgieva, Margarita. *The Gothic Child*. Houndmills: Palgrave Macmillan, 2013. Print.
"A Ghost Story." *The Youth's Companion*. 16 Feb. 1865: 26–?. *American Periodicals*. Web. 28 Nov. 2012.
Gibson, Marion. "Retelling Salem Stories: Gender Politics and Witches in American Culture." *European Journal of American Culture* 25.2 (2006): 85–107. *Academic Search Complete*. Web. 9 May 2013.
Goss, Lucius. "A Ghost Story." *The Youth's Companion* 27 Jan. 1870: 43–4? *American Periodicals*. Web. 4 June 2013.
Greenblatt, Stephen. *Hamlet in Purgatory*. Princeton: Princeton University Press, 2002. Print.
Grenby, M. O. "Gothic and the Child Reader, 1764–1850." *The Gothic World*. Ed. Glennis Byron and Dale Townshend. London: Routledge, 2014. 243–53. Print.
Hacker, David J. "Decennial Life Tables for the White Population of the United States, 1790–1900." *Historical Methods* 43.2 (April-June 2010): 45–79. Print.
Haines, May. "Cootie's Ghost Story." *The Youth's Companion*. 15 Oct. 1874: 339–?. *American Periodicals*. Web. 28 Nov. 2012.
Hall, Mrs. "Adventures with Ghosts." *Woodworth's Youth Cabinet*. May 1850: 226–31?. *Merrycoz.Org*. Web. 28 Nov. 2012.
Hamilton, Virginia. *The House of Dies Drear*. New York: Simon & Schuster, 1996. Print.
———. *The Mystery of Drear House*. New York: Scholastic, 1997. Print.
———. *Sweet Whispers, Brother Rush*. New York: Avon Flare, 1983. Print.
Harriman, Eliza A. "A Ghost Story." *The Little Corporal: An Illustrated Magazine for Boys and Girls*. 1 July 1870: 5–?. *American Periodicals*. Web. 28 Nov. 2012.
Harrold, Edna May. "The Ouija Board: A Story." *The Brownies' Book*. Jan. 1920: 18–20. *University of Nebraska Lincoln Child-Lit*. Web. 16 Nov. 2015.
Haskins, James. *The Headless Haunt and Other African-American Ghost Stories*. New York: HarperCollins, 1994. Print.
Haskins, Jim. "'Cinderella' and the Buried Treasure." *Moaning Bones: African-American Ghost Stories*. New York: Lothrop, Lee & Shepard Books, 1998. 23–26. Print.
———. *Moaning Bones: African-American Ghost Stories*. New York: Lothrop, Lee & Shepard Books, 1998. Print.
———. "The Moaning Bones." *Moaning Bones: African-American Ghost Stories*. New York: Lothrop, Lee & Shepard Books, 1998. 53–56. Print.
"The Haunted House." 1929. Dir. Walt Disney. *Walt Disney Treasures: Mickey Mouse in Black and White, 1928–1935*. Vol. 2. Buena Vista Home Entertainment, 2004. DVD.

Works Cited

Hawthorne, Nathaniel. *The House of the Seven Gables. The House of the Seven Gables: A Norton Critical Edition.* Ed. Robert S. Levine. New York: W. W. Norton & Company, 2006. 5–225. Print.

———. "Young Goodman Brown." *The Norton Anthology of Short Fiction.* Ed. R. V. Cassill and Richard Bausch. New York: W. W. Norton & Company, 2000. 735–44. Print.

Hill, Susan. *The Woman in Black.* New York: Random House, 2011. Print.

Holy Bible. Teaneck, NJ: The World Publishing Company-Cokesbury, 1962. Print.

Homer. *The Odyssey.* Trans. Robert Fagles. New York: Penguin Books, 1997. Print.

Honeyman, Susan. "Trick or Treat? Halloween Lore, Passive Consumerism, and the Candy Industry." *Lion & the Unicorn* 32.1 (2008): 82–108. *Academic Search Complete.* Web. 11 Mar. 2013.

Hunter, Jane H. "Inscribing the Self in the Heart of the Family: Diaries and Girlhood in Late-Victorian America." *American Quarterly* 44.1 (Mar. 1992): 51–81. Web. *JSTOR.* 21 June 2013.

Irving, Washington. "The Legend of Sleepy Hollow." *The Legend of Sleepy Hollow and Other Stories from the Sketch Book.* New York: Signet Classics, 2006. 338–69. Print.

Jackson, Anna, Karen Coats, and Roderick McGillis. "Introduction." *The Gothic in Children's Literature: Haunting the Borders.* New York: Routledge, 2008. 1–14. Print.

———. "Uncanny Hauntings, Canny Children." *The Gothic in Children's Literature: Haunting the Borders.* Ed. Anna Jackson, Karen Coats, and Roderick McGillis. New York: Routledge, 2008. 157–76. Print.

Jacobsen, Karen J. "Economic Hauntings: Wealth and Class in Edith Wharton's Ghost Stories." *College Literature* 35.1 (Winter 2008): 100–27. Print.

Jadusable [Alex Hall]. "Ben Drowned." *CreepypastaWiki.* CreepypastaWiki, 7 Sept. 2010. Web. 4 Jan. 2016.

James, E. L. *Fifty Shades of Grey.* New York: Random House, 2012. Print.

James, Henry. *The Turn of the Screw.* Boston: Bedford, 2010. Print.

James, M. R. "The Haunted Dolls' House." *Collected Ghost Stories.* 1993. Print.

James, Uncle. "The Haunted Cabin." *the Youth's Companion.* 9 Nov. 1865: 178–?. *American Periodicals.* Web 27 Nov. 2012.

Johnson-Feelings, Dianne, ed. "English Indoor and Outdoor Games." *The Best of the Brownies' Book.* Oxford: Oxford University Press, 1996. 274–75. Print.

Jones, Maria W. "The Ghost That Lucy Saw." *St. Nicholas; an Illustrated Magazine for Young Folks.* Nov. 1874: 51–?. *American Periodicals.* Web. 27 Nov. 2012.

Keene, Carolyn. *Nancy Drew: The Haunted Bridge.* 1937. New York: Grosset and Dunlap, 2001. Print.

Kehret, Peg. *The Ghost's Grave.* New York: Puffin-Penguin, 2011. Print.

Kendrick, Charmette. "The Goblins Will Get You! Horror in Children's Literature from the Nineteenth Century." *Children & Libraries* 7.1 (2009): 19–23. *OmniFile Full Text Mega (H.W. Wilson).* Web. 20 Feb. 2013.

Killeen, Jarlath. "Victorian Women and the Challenge of the Phantom." *The Ghost Story from the Middle Ages to the Twentieth Century.* Ed. Helen Conrad O'Briain and Julie Anne Stevens. Dublin: Four Courts Press, 2010. 81–96. Print.

Knapp, Mary, and Herbert Knapp. *One Potato, Two Potato: The Folklore of American Children.* New York: Norton, 1976. Print.

Laird, Margery. "A Bird Ghost Story." *Saturday Evening Post.* 1 Oct. 1875: 5–?. *American Periodicals.* Web 27 Nov. 2012.

"A Legend of Bremen." *Brother Jonathan. a Weekly Compend Belles Letters and the*

Works Cited

Fine Arts, Standard Literature, and General Intelligence. Dec. 1842: 440–?. *American Periodicals.* Web. 27 Nov. 2012.

Leithauser, Brad. "Introduction." *The Norton Book of Ghost Stories.* Ed. Brad Leithauser. New York: W. W. Norton & Company, 1994. 9–21. Print.

Locke, John. *Some Thoughts Concerning Education and of the Conduct of the Understanding.* Ed. Ruth W. Grant and Nathan Tarcov. Indianapolis: Hackett Publishing Company, 1996. Print.

Lynch-Brown, Carol, and Carl M. Tomlinson "Children's Literature, Past and Present: Is There a Future?" *Peabody Journal of Education* 73. 3/4 (1998): 228–52 *JSTOR* Web. 17 Aug. 2013.

Lyons, Mary E. "Plat-Eye." *Raw Head, Bloody Bones: African-American Tales of the Supernatural.* New York: Charles Scribner Sons, 1991. 18–21. Print.

M, M. C. "Learning.: Original. a Ghost Story of Modern Times." *The Youth's Companion.* 6 Feb. 1845: 159–?. *American Periodicals.* Web. 27 Nov. 2012.

Marcus, Leonard S. "Night Visions: Conversations with Alvin Schwartz and Judith Gorog." *The Lion and the Unicorn: A Critical Journal of Children's Literature* 12.2 (1988): 44–62. *MLA International Bibliography.* Web. 17 Aug. 2013.

Marshall, Peter. "Transformations of the Ghost Story in Post–Reformation England." *The Ghost Story from the Middle Ages to the Twentieth Century.* Ed. Helen Conrad O'Briain and Julie Anne Stevens. Dublin: Four Courts Press, 2010. 16–33. Print.

"Mask Against Mask." *The Youth's Companion.* 25 Nov. 1897: 598–?. *American Periodicals.* Web. 27 Nov. 2012.

Matteson, John. *Eden's Outcasts: The Story of Louisa May Alcott and Her Father.* New York: W. W. Norton and Company, 2008. Print.

McCuskey, Brian. "Not at Home: Servants, Scholars, and the Uncanny." *PMLA* 121.2 (Mar. 2006): 421–36. *JSTOR.* Web. 7 May 2013.

McKissack, Patricia C. *The Dark Thirty: Southern Tales of the Supernatural.* New York: Yearling, 2001. Print.

Meyer, Stephenie. *Twilight.* New York: Hachette, 2006. Print.

"Miscellaneous: A Ghost Story—For the Young." *Maine Farmer and Mechanics Advocate.* 9 Dec. 1843: 4–?. *American Periodicals.* Web. 28 Nov. 2012.

Morris, Wilson. *Dummy.* New York: U.S. WPA New Reading Materials Program NYC Board of Education, 1938. *Broward County Library's Digital Collections.* Web. 17 Mar. 2013.

Morrison, Toni. *Beloved.* New York: Vintage, 2004. Print.

Moruzi, Kristine. *Constructing Girlhood Through the Periodical Press, 1850–1915.* Surrey, UK: Ashgate, 2012. Print.

Muse, Daphne. "Detectives, Dubious Dudes, Spies and Suspense in African American Fiction for Children and Young Adults." *The Black Scholar* 28.1 (1998): 33–39. *JSTOR.* Web. 29 Dec. 2015.

Niedermeyer, Maud Wilcox. "Friends in the Night." *The Brownies' Book.* Sep. 1921: 256–57. *University of Nebraska Lincoln Child-Lit.* Web. 16 Nov. 2015.

Newbery, John. *Little Goody Two-Shoes and Other Stories.* Ed. M. O. Grenby. Hampshire, UK: Palgrave Macmillan, 2013.

———. *A Little Pretty Pocket-Book.* 1744. LaVergne: Dodo Press, 2009. Print.

Nodelman, Perry. "Ordinary Monstrosity: The World of Goosebumps." *Children's Literature Association Quarterly* 22.3 (Fall 1997): 118–25. *Project Muse.* Web. 16 Feb. 2013.

Nuhn, Roy. "Portfolio: Ellen Clapsaddle." *American History Illustrated* 17.3 (1982): 30–33. Print.

"Nursery Problems: Sudden Development of Timidity—Night Coverings." *Babyhood:*

Works Cited

Devoted Exclusively to the Care of Infants and Young Children. 1 Mar. 1889: 121–?. *American Periodicals.* Web. 28 Nov. 2012.
Opie, Iona, and Peter Opie. *The Lore and Language of School Children.* New York: New York Review of Books, 2001.
Pearce, Philippa, ed. "Introduction." *A Century of Children's Ghost Stories.* Oxford: Oxford University Press, 1996. Print.
Peattie, Elia W. *The Shape of Fear and Other Ghostly Tales.* Middlesex: Echo Library, 2008. Print.
_____. "Their Dear Little Ghost." *Outlook.* 29 Oct. 1898: 530–?. *American Periodicals.* Web. 28 Nov. 2012.
Peck, Andrew. "Tall, Dark, and Loathsome: The Emergence of a Legend Cycle in the Digital Age." *Journal of American Folklore* 128.509 (2015): 333–48. *Academic Search Complete.* Web. 18 Dec. 2015.
Pence, Harry E. "Teaching with Transmedia." *Journal of Educational Technology Systems* 40.2 (2011–2012): 131–40. Print.
Perry, Leslie Anne, and Rebecca P. Butler. "Are Goosebumps Books Real Literature." *Language Arts* 74.6 (Oct. 1997): 454–56. Web. *ProQuest Education Journals.* 8 October 2013.
Phillips, Michelle H. "The Children of Double Consciousness: From the *Souls of Black Folk* to the *Brownies' Book*." *PMLA* 128.3 (May 2013): 590–607. Print.
Powell, Alice G. "Hallowe'en: For the Children." *Pictorial Review.* Nov. 1906: 43–?. *American Periodicals.* Web. 28 Nov. 2012.
Presbyterian, N. Y. "A Ghost Story." *The Youth's Companion.* 9 June 1864: 90–?. *American Periodicals.* Web. 27 Nov. 2012.
Reece, Gregory L. *Creatures of the Night: In Search of Ghosts, Vampires, Werewolves and Demons.* London: I. B. Tauris, 2012. Print.
Reit, Seymour. *The Worried Ghost.* New York: Scholastic, 1976. Print.
Robbins, Bruce. "'They Don't Much Count, Do They?': The Unfinished History of the *Turn of the Screw*." *The Turn of the Screw*, 3rd. Ed. Peter G. Beidler. Boston: Bedford, 2010. 376–89. Print.
Rogers, Katharine M. *L. Frank Baum: Creator of Oz: A Biography.* Cambridge, MA: Da Capo Press, 2003. Print.
Royle, Nicholas. *The Uncanny.* Manchester: Manchester University Press, 2003. Print.
Russell, David L. "Virginia Hamilton's Symbolic Presentation of the Afro-American Sensibility." *Children's Literature Quarterly* (1987): 71–74. *Project Muse.* Web. 26 Feb. 2013.
Ryan, C. "The Specter at the Feast." 1900–13. N.d. Postcard. Private Collection. N.p., n.d. Print.
Ryle, Gilbert. *The Concept of Mind.* Chicago: University of Chicago Press, 1984. Print.
Schmidt, Leigh Eric. "The Commercialization of the Calendar: American Holidays and the Culture of Consumption, 1870–1930." *Journal of American History* 78.3 (1991): 887–916. *Academic Search Complete.* Web. 11 Mar. 2013.
Schwartz, Alvin. "Clinkity-Clink." *More Scary Stories to Tell in the Dark.* New York: Harper, 2010. 26–30. Print.
_____. "The Little Black Dog." *More Scary Stories to Tell in the Dark.* New York: Harper, 2010. 23–25. Print.
_____. "May I Carry Your Basket." *Scary Stories to Tell in the Dark.* New York: Harper, 2010. 57–58. Print.
_____. *Scary Stories 3: More Tales to Chill Your Bones.* New York: Harper, 2011. Print.

Works Cited

———. "Something Was Wrong." *More Scary Stories to Tell in the Dark*. New York: Harper, 2010. 3–4. Print.
———. "Sounds." *More Scary Stories to Tell in the Dark*. New York: Harper, 2010. 12–13. Print.
———. "The Wreck." *More Scary Stories to Tell in the Dark*. New York: Harper, 2010. 5–7. Print.
Sechrist, Elizabeth Hough. "A Ghostly Ballad." *a Little Book of Hallowe'en*. Philadelphia: J. B. Lippincott Company, 1934. 32–34. Print.
———. "The Poor Ghost." *A Little Book of Hallowe'en*. Philadelphia: J. B. Lippincott Company, 1934. 53. Print.
"Seymour Reit." *The Times* [United Kingdom] 26 Dec. 2001:17. *Newspaper Source*. Web. 3 Aug. 2013.
Shakespeare, William. *A Midsummer Night's Dream*. *The Norton Shakespeare: Based on the Oxford Edition*. Ed. Stephen Greenblatt. New York: W. W. Norton and Company, 1997. 805–61. Print.
———. *The Tragedy Of Hamlet, Prince of Denmark*. *The Riverside Shakespeare*. Ed. G. Blakemore Evans, J. J. M. Tobin, and et al. Boston: Houghton Mifflin Company, 1997. 1183–1245. Print.
Shelley, Mary. *Frankenstein*. Hertfordshire, UK: Wordsworth Classics, 1993. Print.
Smajic, SrdJan. "The Trouble with Ghost-Seeing: Vision, Ideology, and Genre in the Victorian Ghost Story." *ELH* 70.4 (Winter 2003): 1107–35. Print.
Skal, David J. *Death Makes a Holiday: A Cultural History of Halloween*. New York: Bloomsbury, 2002. Print.
Sobat, Gail Sidonie. "If the Ghost Be There, Then Am I Crazy?: An Examination of Ghosts in Virginia Hamilton's *Sweet Whispers, Brother Rush* and Toni Morrison's *Beloved*." *Children's Literature Association Quarterly* 20.4 (Winter 1995):168–74. *Project Muse*. Web. 26 Feb. 2013.
Smith, Andrew. *The Ghost Story, 1840–1920: A Cultural History*. Manchester: Manchester University Press, 2010. Print.
Smith, Harriette Knight. "The Children Love Them': Paper No. Iii.—Hezekiah Butterworth." *the Interior* 28 Mar. 1895: 435–?. *American Periodicals*. Web. 28 Nov. 2012.
Smith, Katharine Capshaw. *Children's Literature of the Harlem Renaissance*. Bloomington: Indiana University Press, 2006. Print.
Smith-Wright, Geraldine. "In Spite of the Klan: Ghosts in the Fiction of Black Women Writers." *Haunting the House of Fiction: Feminist Perspectives on Ghost Stories by American Women*. Ed. Lynette Carpenter and Wendy K. Kolmar. Knoxville: University of Tennessee Press, 1991. 142–65. Print.
Stallcup, Jackie E. "Power, Fear, and Children's Picture Books." *Children's Literature* 30 (2002): 125–58. *Project Muse*. Web. 5 May 2013.
Stearns, Peter N., and Timothy Haggerty. "The Role of Fear: Transitions in American Emotional Standards for Children, 1850–1950." *The American Historical Review* 96.1 (Feb. 1991): 63–94. *JSTOR*. Web. 13 Feb. 2013.
Stine, R. L. *Goosebumps: The Barking Ghost*. *Goosebumps: Monster Edition #3*. New York: Scholastic, 1997. 257–373. Print.
———. *Goosebumps: Ghost Beach*. New York: Scholastic, 2010. Print.
———. *Goosebumps: Ghost Camp*. New York: Scholastic, 1996.
———. *Goosebumps: The Ghost Next Door*. *Goosebumps: Monster Edition #3*. New York: Scholastic, 1997. 1–128. Print.
———. *Goosebumps: The Haunted School*. New York: Scholastic, 1997. Print.
———. *Goosebumps: The Headless Ghost*. New York: Scholastic, 1995. Print.

Works Cited

———. *Goosebumps: Welcome to Dead House*. New York: Scholastic, 2010. Print.

Stoker, Bram. "The Judge's House." *The Oxford Book of English Ghost Stories*. Ed. Michael Cox and R. A. Gilbert. Oxford: Oxford University Press, 1986. 109–24. Print.

Stone, Gregory P. "Halloween and Mass Child." *American Quarterly* 11.3 (Autumn 1959): 372–79. *JSTOR*. Web. 4 Aug. 2013.

Stoneley, Peter. *Consumerism and American Girls' Literature, 1860–1940*. Cambridge: Cambridge University Press, 2003. Print.

Stowe, Harriet Beecher. *Uncle Tom's Cabin: A Norton Critical Edition*, 2nd. Ed. Elizabeth Ammons. New York: W. W. Norton & Company, 2010. Print.

Sue, Aunt. "The Haunted House." *Merry's Museum, Parley's Magazine, Woodworth's Cabinet, and the Schoolfellow*. 1 July 1861: 171–?. *American Periodicals*. Web. 27 Nov. 2012.

Tatar, Maria. "Introduction: Cinderella." *The Classic Fairy Tales*. Ed. Maria Tatar. New York: W. W. Norton & Company, 1999. 101–07. Print.

Thurston, Luke. *Literary Ghosts from the Victorians to Modernism: The Haunting Interval*. New York: Routledge, 2012. Print.

Toppo, Greg. "'Slender Man' Case Defies Easy Answers." *USA Today* n.d. *Academic Search Complete*. Web. 18 Dec. 2015.

Tosenberger, Catherine. "Mature Poets Steal: Children's Literature and the Unpublishability of Fanfiction." *Children's Literature Association Quarterly* 39.1 (Spring 2014): 4–27. Web. *Project Muse* 10 Dec. 2015.

Townshend, Dale. "The Haunted Nursery: 1764–1830." *The Gothic in Children's Literature: Haunting the Borders*. Ed. Anna Jackson, Karen Coats, and Roderick McGillis. New York: Routledge, 2008. 15–38. Print.

Trites, Roberta Seelinger. *Disturbing the Universe: Power and Repression in Adolescent Literature*. Iowa City: University of Iowa Press, 2000. Print.

———. *Twain, Alcott, and the Birth of the Adolescent Reform Novel*. Iowa City: University of Iowa Press, 2007. Print.

Tucker, Elizabeth. "Changing Concepts of Childhood: Children's Folklore Scholarship Since the Late Nineteenth Century." *Journal of American Folklore* 125.498 (Fall 2012): 389–410. *Project Muse*. Web. 12 Oct. 2015.

Twain, Mark. "How to Tell a Ghost Story: The Humorous Story an American Development—Its Difference from Comic and Witty Stories." *The Youth's Companion*. Oct. 1895: 464–?. *American Periodicals*. Web. 28 Nov. 2012.

Verdell, Sylvia M. "Profile: Alvin Schwartz." *Language Arts* 64.4 (April 1987): 426–32. *OmniFile Full Text Mega (H.W. Wilson)*. Web. 17 Aug. 2013.

Walpole, Horace. *The Castle of Otranto*. *Three Gothic Novels*. Ed. Peter Fairclough. New York: Penguin, 1986. Print.

Widdemer, Margaret. *Little Girl and Boy Land*. New York: Harcourt Brace & Company; Rahway, NJ: Quinn & Boden Company, 1924. Print.

Zelizer, Viviana A. *Pricing the Priceless Child: The Changing Social Value of Children*. New York: Basic Books, 1985. Print.

Index

Abrahams, Roger D. 107–8
Abrahamson, Dick 133
"Adventures with Ghosts" 74
Alcott, Bronson 16
Alcott, Louisa May 16, 34, 55–6, 63–5, 69–73, 75, 116
Aliens in the Home: The Child in Horror Fiction 21, 125
Ammons, Elizabeth 49

Babyhood 67
Banks, E.C. 90, 94
Bann, Jennifer 6, 21, 26, 124–5
"The Barber's Ghost" 23–6
Bascom, William 107
Baum, L. Frank 82
Blake, Quentin 126
Blassingame, John W. 152
Ben 7, 160–4, 170, 172; Ben Drowned 7, 160–4, 170, 172; Haunted Majora's Mask 160–1
Benchley, Nathaniel 126–9
Bender, Albert M. 96–7
Berry, Mary Frances 152
Bever, Edward 37
Bhabha, Homi K. 41
Bierce, Ambrose 49–50
Bleiler, E.F. 49–50
Bloody Mary 7, 164–70
"Bloody Mary Returns" 168–9
Bloomfield, Susanne George 59–60
Boone, Troy 98
Bradley, Mary 16
Bronner, Simon J. 6, 135
Bruce, Dickson D., Jr. 117
Büssing, Sabine 3, 6, 21, 125
Butler, Rebecca P. 139–40
Butterworth, Hezekiah 52–5

Carman, Patrick 6, 154
Carmer, Carl 124, 134, 138, 141
Carroll, Jane Suzanne 20–1
Casper the Friendly Ghost 5–6, 102–4, 124, 126–7, 129
The Castle of Otranto 8, 28
Chess, Shira 7, 159
Children's Literature of the Harlem Renaissance 119, 114
Clapsaddle, Ellen H. 90–1, 94
Clark, Beverly Lyon 4–5, 19, 34, 60, 65, 82
Cocke, Zitella 86
The Concept of Mind 163
Consumerism and American Girls' Literature, 1860–1940 75
Cooper, George 46–8
"Cootie's Ghost Story" 76–8
Cox, Michael 10–1
Creatures of the Night: In Search of Ghosts, Vampires, Werewolves and Demons 83
creepypasta 7, 156–60, 162–4, 166–73

Dahl, Roald 65
Davidson, Guy 46
Davies, Owen 133
Davis, Zachary 172–3
Death Makes a Holiday: A Cultural History of Halloween 89–90
Dickens, Charles 8, 19, 22, 66–7, 84
Dickerson, Vanessa D. 5, 27–9, 63–4, 69, 79–80
Disney, Walt 92, 95, 155, 167
Disturbing the Universe: Power and Repression in Adolescent Literature 138, 145
Dittman, Michael 102

Index

Dorson, Richard M. 6, 107–9
Du Bois, W.E.B. 6, 114–5, 117, 119
Dummy 100–2, 104
Dundes, Alan 165, 167
Duthie, Peggy Lin 54

Elder Leland's Ghost and Other Stories for Boys 39, 52–5
Esparza, David 172–3; Esaprza 72–3
The Exile 34, 36, 67, 84
Explained Supernatural 17

Felt, Joseph B. 37
Frankenstein 8, 15
Freud, Sigmund 5, 40–1, 43, 68
friendly ghost 5, 96, 98–100, 102–4, 126–7, 131–3
Fry, Gladys-Marie 6, 110–1

Gardner, Martin 35
Gavin, Adrienne E. 27–9
Gay, Peter 82
Georgieva, Margarita 44
A Ghost Named Fred 126–30, 132, 137
The Ghost Story, 1840–1920: A Cultural History 22
Gibson, Marion 38
Gilbert, R.A. 10–1
Goosebumps 6, 126, 139–42, 144–7, 150
gothic 2–3, 9, 11, 13–5, 18, 21, 38–40, 44, 90, 124, 161, 174
The Gothic in Children's Literature: Haunting the Borders 124
Grenby, M.O. 3, 15, 39, 174

Hacker, David J. 56
Haggerty, Timothy 6, 85, 125
Haines, May 76–7
Hall, Alex 160–1
Hall, Mrs. 73
Halloween 5, 31, 86–92, 94–7, 100, 115–6, 118, 125, 134
Hamilton, Virginia 109, 120–2, 146, 150–2
Harriman, Eliza A. 38
Haskins, James 106, 108–9
Haskins, Jim 108–9
Hawthorne, Nathaniel 19, 37–9
Honeyman, Susan 88
Hunter, Jane H. 66, 75

"In Spite of the Klan: Ghosts in the Fiction of Black Women Writers" 112, 151

Jackson, Anna 41, 43, 124
Jacobsen, Karen J. 22–3, 46
Jadusable 160–3
James, E.L. 170
James, Henry 22, 45
James, M.R. 20–1
James, Uncle 48
Jones, Maria W. 74

Keene, Carolyn 98–9
Kendrick, Charmette 3–4, 40
Killeen, Jarlath 27–9, 68, 75, 79–80
Knapp, Herbert 84–5
Knapp, Mary 84–5

Laird, Margery 57, 59
A Little Book of Hallowe'en 95–6
Locke, John 14–5, 159
Lynch-Brown, Carol 139

M, M.C. 55–6, 72–3, 75, 116
Marshall, Peter 12–3
Matteson, John 16
McCuskey, Brian 68
McKissack, Patricia C. 146–52
Merry's Museum, Parley's Magazine, Woodworth's Cabinet, and the Schoolfellow 35
A Midsummer Night's Dream 33
"Miscellaneous: A Ghost Story—for the Young" 18, 33
Morris, Wilson 100
Moruzi, Kristine 72–3
Muse, Daphne 121
"My Mother Killed Me, My Father Ate Me" 108

Nancy Drew 98–99, 154
Nancy Drew: The Haunted Bridge 98
Newbery, John 8, 14, 146
Newsom, Eric 7, 159
Niedermeyer, Maud Wilcox 116
Nodelman, Perry 139–40, 144–7
Nuhn, Roy 90
"Nursery Problems: Sudden Development of Timidity—Night Coverings" 67

Index

Opie, Iona and Peter 5, 84, 88

Pearce, Philippa 3, 40, 85
Peattie, Elia W. 59–60
Pence, Harry E. 153–4
Perry, Leslie Anne 139–40
Phillips, Michelle H. 114–5, 117
Poe, Edgar Allan 19, 99
Powell, Alice G. 89
"Power, Fear, and Children's Picture Books" 128
Presbyterian, N.Y. 42, 44–5, 47
Pricing the Priceless Child: The Changing Social Value of Children 87
"Profile: Alvin Schwartz" 134

Reece, Gregory L. 5, 9, 83
Reit, Seymour 102–3, 124, 126, 129, 133
Robbins, Bruce 22–3, 46
Rogers, Katharine M. 82
"The Role of Fear: Transitions in American Emotional Standards for Children, 1850–1950" 85
Russell, David L. 150
Ryle, Gilbert 163–4

St. Nicholas: An Illustrated Magazine for Young Folks 7, 16, 18, 34–5, 54, 64, 69, 76
Saturday Evening Post 24–5, 57
Scary Stories 6, 133–9, 146–7
Schmidt, Leigh Eric 86
Schwartz, Alvin 133–7, 140–1
Sechrist, Elizabeth Hough 95–6
Shakespeare, William 33
The Shape of Fear and Other Ghostly Tales 59
Shecter, Ben 126–7
Shelley, Mary 15
"The Singing Bones" 108
Skal, David J. 89–90
Skeleton Creek 6, 154
Slender Man 157–9, 170, 172
Smith, Andrew 22
Smith, Harriette Knight 54
Smith, Katharine Capshaw 6, 114, 116, 119

Smith-Wright, Geraldine 6, 112, 151
Sobat, Gail Sidonie 151
Stallcup, Jackie E. 128–9
Stearns, Peter N. 6, 85, 125
Stine, R.L. 139–44, 46
Stone, Gregory P. 87–8
Stoneley, Peter 75–6
Stowe, Harriet Beecher 49
Sue, Aunt 34–6

Tatar, Maria 169
"Their Dear Little Ghost" 59–60
Tomlinson, Carl M. 139
Toppo, Greg 158
Tosenberger, Catherine 171
Townshend, Dale 3–4, 14–5, 17–9, 40, 67–8, 75, 174
Trites, Roberta Seelinger 4–5, 34, 64, 138, 145
Tucker, Elizabeth 165–7, 170
The Turn of the Screw 22, 45, 46, 68
Twain, Mark 34, 54–5, 60, 134
Twain, Alcott, and the Birth of the Adolescent Reform Novel 34, 64

uncanny 5, 39–46, 57–8, 62, 68
Uncle Tom's Cabin 49

Verdell, Sylvia M. 134
"Virginia Hamilton's Symbolic Presentation of the Afro-American Sensibility" 150

Widdemer, Margaret 92
The Wonderful Wizard of Oz 82–3
The Worried Ghost 126, 129, 132
WPA (Works Progress Administration) 96–7, 102

"Young Goodman Brown" 37–8
The Youth's Companion 7, 18, 23–5, 34–6, 42, 48, 51–2, 54–6, 59, 61, 67, 72–3, 76–7, 79, 86, 134

Zelizer, Viviana A. 87

www.ingramcontent.com/pod-product-compliance
Lightning Source LLC
Chambersburg PA
CBHW032101300426
44116CB00007B/839